THE FUNCTIONS
OF DISCRIMINATION
AND PREJUDICE

THE FUNCTIONS OF DISCRIMINATION AND PREJUDICE

SECOND EDITION

JACK LEVIN
Northeastern University

WILLIAM C. LEVIN
Bridgewater State College

HARPER & ROW, PUBLISHERS, New York
Cambridge, Philadelphia, San Francisco,
London, Mexico City, São Paulo, Sydney

1817

Sponsoring Editor: Alan McClare
Project Editor: Eleanor Castellano
Designer: Michel Craig
Production Manager: Jeanie Berke
Photo Researcher: Myra Schachne
Compositor: University Graphics, Inc.
Printer and Binder: The Murray Printing Company
Art Studio: J & R Technical Services, Inc.
Grateful acknowledgment is made for use of the opening photograph in the following chapters: Chapter 1: Fraenkel, Camera Press, Photo Trends. Chapter 2: Leo de Wys Inc. Chapter 3: (c) Thomson, 1980, Woodfin Camp. Chapter 4: Photo Trends. Chapter 5: Lyon, (c) Magnum. Chapter 6: Freed, (c) Magnum. Chapter 7: (c) Heron, 1980, Woodfin Camp.

The work was originally published under the title *The Functions of Prejudice*.
Copyright © 1975 by Jack Levin.

THE FUNCTIONS OF DISCRIMINATION AND PREJUDICE,
Second Edition

Copyright © 1982 by Harper & Row, Publishers, Inc.

All rights reserved. Printed in the United States of America. No part of this book may be used or reproduced in any manner whatsoever without written permission, except in the case of brief quotations embodied in critical articles and reviews. For information address Harper & Row, Publishers, Inc., 10 East 53d Street, New York, NY 10022.

Library of Congress Cataloging in Publication Data

Levin, Jack, 1941–
　The functions of discrimination and prejudice.

　First ed. published under title: The functions of prejudice.
　Includes bibliographical references and index.
　　1. Discrimination—United States.　2. Prejudices—United States.
3. Minorities—United States.　I. Levin, William C.　II. Title.
HN57.L48　1982　　　303.3'85　　　81-6794
ISBN 0-06-043964-5　　　　　　　　AACR2

To our parents
Max and Flory Levin
and
Jess and Ruth Levin

Acknowledgments

Grateful acknowledgment is made for the use of the following materials:

Elliot Aronson. 1975. "Busing and Racial Tension: the Jigsaw Route to Learning and Liking." *Psychology Today* 8: 43–45, 47–50. Copyright © February 1975, Ziff-Davis Publishing Company.

Bernard Berelson and Patricia Salter. 1946. "Majority and Minority Americans: An Analysis of Magazine Fiction." *Public Opinion Quarterly* (Summer): 168–190. Reprinted by permission of the publishers. Copyright 1946 by the Trustees of Columbia University.

J. David Colfax and Susan Frankel Sternberg. 1972. "The Perpetuation of Racial Stereotypes: Blacks in Mass Circulation Magazine Advertisements." *Public Opinion Quarterly* (Spring): 8–17. Reprinted by permission of the publisher. Copyright 1972 by the Trustees of Columbia University.

Lewis A. Coser. 1972. "The Alien as a Servant of Power: Court Jews and Christian Renegades." *American Sociological Review* (October): 574–581. Reprinted by permission of the American Sociological Association and the author.

S. J. Gould. 1978. "Women's Brains." *Natural History* (October): 44–50. With permission. Copyright The American Museum of Natural History, 1978.

S. J. Gould. 1979. "Wide Hats and Narrow Minds." *Natural History* (February): 34–37. With permission. Copyright The American Museum of Natural History, 1979.

S. J. Gould. 1980. "Jensen's Last Stand." *New York Review of Books* (May): 38–42. Reprinted with permission from *The New York Review of Books*. Copyright © 1980 Nyrev, Inc.

Carl. I. Hovland and Robert R. Sears. 1940. "Minor Studies of Aggression: Correlation of Lynchings with Economic Indices." *Journal of Psychology* (Winter): 301–310. Reprinted by permission of the publisher.

Bernice Neugarten. 1970. "The Old and Young in Modern Societies." *American Behavioral Scientist* 14: 13–24. Copyright © Sage Publications, Beverly Hills, with permission of the publisher.

Diana M. Pearce. 1979. "Gatekeepers and Homeseekers: Institutional Patterns in Racial Steering." *Social Problems* 26, No. 3 (February): 325–342. Reprinted with permission of the Society for the Study of Social Problems and the author.

Ralph L. Rosnow. 1972. "Poultry and Prejudice." *Psychology Today* (March): 53–56. Copyright © March 1972, Ziff-Davis Publishing Company.

Contents

Acknowledgments vii

Preface xiii

1 MAJORITY AND MINORITY 1
The Concept of Minority 1
How Have Minority-Group Situations Been Explained? 14

2 AN ALTERNATIVE TO VICTIM BLAMING: DISCRIMINATION AND PREJUDICE 41
Minority Group Characteristics and Blaming the Victim 41
Exceptionalist Versus Universalistic Programs 44
Discrimination 51
Individual Versus Institutional Discrimination 53
Prejudice 65
The Relationship Between Discrimination and Prejudice 81

3 THE PERSISTENCE OF DISCRIMINATION AND PREJUDICE: THEIR FUNCTIONAL BASIS   91
    The Persistence of Prejudice   92
    The Persistence of Discrimination   95
    Race and Intelligence   103
    Sociobiology   107
    The New Ethnicity   110
    The New Conservatism   112
    Functionalism and the Analysis of Discrimination and Prejudice   114

CHAPTER 4 PERSONALITY FUNCTIONS OF DISCRIMINATION AND PREJUDICE FOR THE MAJORITY GROUP   133
    Displacement of Aggression   134
    Protection of Self-Esteem   140
    Reduction of Uncertainty   149
    Summary   155

CHAPTER 5 SOCIAL FUNCTIONS OF DISCRIMINATION AND PREJUDICE FOR THE MAJORITY GROUP   159
    Acquisition and Maintenance of Economic Advantages   160
    Resolving the Issue of Who "Benefits" from Discrimination   168
    Performance of Unpleasant or Low-Paying Jobs   175
    Maintenance of Power   181
    Summary   184

CHAPTER 6 FUNCTIONS OF DISCRIMINATION AND PREJUDICE FOR THE MINORITY GROUP   189
    Reduction of Competition   190
    Maintenance of Solidarity   192
    Reduction of Uncertainty   196
    Summary   197

CHAPTER 7 DISCRIMINATION AND PREJUDICE IN AMERICAN SOCIETY   201
    Competitiveness and Prejudice in American Society   203
    Zero-Sum Orientation and Prejudice   204

Social Change and Prejudice 207
Prospects for the Reduction of Discrimination and
 Prejudice 213
Summary 225

References 229

Index 250

Preface

The Functions of Discrimination and Prejudice, Second Edition attempts to provide a concise and readable introduction to the study of antiminority discrimination and prejudice. A glance at the Contents of the book will disclose that it represents the perspective of more than a single discipline or school of thought, encompassing theories from sociology, political science, economics, and psychology—from functionalism as well as the conflict point of view.

If this book has some overall message to communicate, it is that majority-minority relations cannot be understood apart from the consequences of discrimination and prejudice. It is therefore necessary to examine *any* of the groups and individuals in a society that gain from the maintenance of the status quo, whether they be persons of power for whom discrimination serves economic or political ends, working-class persons whose sense of self-worth finds protection in the presence of prejudice, or certain elements of minorities whose special advantages would quickly disappear under the impact of full equality of opportunity.

As a major revision, the second edition of this book has provided us with a welcome opportunity to expand and clarify discussions, to update examples, and to correct mistakes. But our most important changes are reflected in the new title. Whereas the first edition focused almost exclusively on the functions of prejudice, we now place great emphasis on the consequences of institutionalized discrimination and on its relationship to prejudice. In this edition, we have also broadened our conception of minority groups, so that it includes the experiences not only of racial and ethnic groups but of women and the elderly as well.

We are indebted to a number of individuals—our friends, students, colleagues, editors, and family members—who contributed in important ways to the development and completion of this book. We are grateful to Norval Glenn, whose review of this work provided both incentive as well as direction at critical times. A debt of gratitude is also due Bob Bohlke, Toni Emrich, Max Hess, Lewis Killian, Ken MacDonald, and Patrick McNamara, who critically reviewed part of an earlier manuscript or a proposal and suggested a number of significant improvements for the final version of this work. Sections of the manuscript also benefited from the comments of John Ost, Max Shulman, and Linda Weinrich. Several insightful recommendations for the book were obtained in conversations with Joan Arches, Richie Arches, Marcia Garrett, Pat Golden, Nina and Herb Greenwald, Louisa Howe, Norman Kaplan, Lila Leibowitz, Sr. Marie Augusta Neal, Bernard Phillips, Dick Robbins, Alex Rysman, Jim Spates, Richard Swedberg, and Gerald Taube. Flea Levin has once again played an essential part at all stages of this work.

The second edition particularly has benefited from the valuable substantive suggestions offered by Evelyn Levin, Nesar Ahmad, Charles Fanning, Max Hess, Curtiss Hoffman, Debbie Kaufman, Michael Kryzanek, Howard London, Phil Silvia, and the Quad Eight. We also gratefully acknowledge the helpful reviews of Joe Feagin, Ralph Grippin, Cheryl Gilkes, and John Perry.

JACK LEVIN and WILLIAM C. LEVIN

Chapter 1
Majority and Minority

People in our society differ in terms of the opportunities they have for acquiring wealth, status, and power. An individual's opportunities for success may depend, in part, on factors such as talent, luck, experience, and training, but they also depend on the group with which he or she is identified. Thus, although you may have all the qualifications to do a certain job or to be admitted to a particular professional school or club, you still might be denied that opportunity because of the group to which you belong.

The Concept of Minority

The tendency to distribute opportunity by ascribed characteristics (such as racial-group membership) rather than by achieved ones (merit) is a serious social problem for a number of reasons. Large numbers of people belong to groups that are systematically denied opportunities. They are prevented from reaching their productive potential, reducing the quality of their lives and also diminishing the productivity of the overall society. They experience painful, and sometimes murderous, levels of deprivation. Society's response is often the costly maintenance of police forces and institutions such as courts to deal with the social control of disruptive responses. Lastly, we Americans still claim to distribute opportunity to all, without regard to race, age, sex, and so on. These beliefs tie us to our earliest beginnings as an idealistic nation and, more than any others, define the very character of our national will. Minority groups like blacks, women and the aged, all too apparently, have experienced lives with which they are justifiably dissatisfied. Their protests against their treatment provide us with a constant reminder of our failure to deliver the national promise of equality of opportunity. As a result, we are, in fact, increasing our awareness of the variety of people who can be considered the minorities of American society. More and more groups seem to be willing, and even eager, to identify themselves as such. The relationship of these minorities to the rest of society will demand our increasing attention, and may actually decrease our ability to deliver on the promise of equality of opportunity.

In the United States the literature of minority–majority relations has been dominated by a concern with race. This is partly because of our history of slavery and the legacy of that past. Despite their relatively large proportion of the population (more than 11 percent) American blacks continue to suffer more severe, even life-threatening, deprivations than any other sizable group of people in America. Native Americans (who, of course, were here long before we ever started calling our country America and therefore could more properly be referred to as natives of the landmass than as either Native Americans or American Indians) have also suffered severe deprivations—as severe as, or even more severe than, those of blacks. But they constitute a smaller percentage of the population and until quite recently have not been conceived of as an important minority group. In fact, we have come to recognize any segment of the population as a potential minority, depending on a variety of factors beyond the extent of the prejudice or discrimination directed against them. Perhaps their proportion of the population has increased or is projected to increase. Perhaps they have begun to organize to the extent that they now are seen as an important constituency by businesspeople or politicians. Perhaps they have begun to be deprived of something to which they had become accustomed. Recently we have begun increasingly to identify women, the physically disabled, the aged, ethnic groups, and even the working and middle classes as potential minorities in American society. Clearly these groups are quite different from one another. They vary in terms of the severity of the prejudice and discrimination directed against them, their cohesion, their willingness to see themselves as minority groups, their contact and closeness to majority-group members, their physical identifiability as members of such groups, their willingness to organize in their own interest, and so on. To what extent, then, can they be considered minority groups, and how can they illustrate the usefulness of the concept of minority?

The concept of minority helps us in our efforts to understand how opportunity is distributed in America. Beyond the influence that talent or hard work may have on our success in life, we also recognize large differences in the success rates between various categories of Americans: between young and old, blacks and whites, males and females. Thus, when all other qualifications are equalized, women have fewer opportunities than men; the aged have fewer opportunities than the young; and blacks have fewer opportunities than whites. The concept of minority attributes such inequality to the unequal distribution of opportunities for success. Some group (or groups) of people must be in a position to distribute opportunity. They must have power, such as control over hiring, promotion, wages, the determination of eligibility for elective or appointive office, definition and determination of criminal liability, contractual responsibility, even the definitions of good looks or behavior. Such a group of people has the ability to control or influence the condition of other people, even against their will. They have social power. Clearly, majority groups will not often have total control. The degree of their ability to distribute opportunity will vary widely. But in comparison with minority groups, whose position in society is assigned them, majority groups are in relative control of their own destinies as well as the destinies of others. We will be concerned here with the experiences and the treatment of minorities—groups whose members have been assigned a subordinate position in society (Sagarin, 1971; Vander Zanden, 1972). The identification of *majority* and *minority* becomes a question of the degree of control that a group of people can exercise over their own destiny. Who qualifies for majority as opposed to minority status? Probably the most widely used definition of "minority" comes from Louis Wirth: "We may define a minority as a group of people who, because of their physical or cultural characteristics, are singled out from the others in the society in which they live for differential and unequal treatment, and who therefore regard themselves as objects of collective discrimination" (Wirth, 1945:347). Minorities, then (1) are recognizably different from the rest of society either physically, or culturally (in their langauge, leisure activities, or other ways of living learned from previous generations), (2) are treated differently from others in the society by majority-group members because of these perceived differences, and (3) have some sort of sense of their differential treatment, which may be interpreted as a consciousness of group membership.

American Blacks

Identifiability American blacks as a minority group are defined by white America as both physically and culturally distinguishable. Discussions of racial groups focus on characteristics such as skin color, hair color and texture, nose shape, lip thickness, head shape, stature, eye color and shape, and so on. Cultural recognizability focuses on language, clothing, leisure activities, food, and religious practices.

Differential Treatment Second, American blacks are clearly treated differently from whites in terms of the opportunities made available to them. The inferior education, medical care, job opportunities, housing, representation, legal services, and so on, made available to black America by white America are documented in a huge literature. One question that this book will confront is why such unequal treatment persists, and what mechanisms contribute to that persistence. In short, when confronted by the fact that the unemployment rate among black teenaged males regularly reaches 50 percent in our cities, the response is no longer, "Prove it," but "How can that be, and what can be done about it?" Part of the unequal treatment that blacks receive can be attributed to the negative stereotypes and feelings about them that are used to justify and perpetuate the discrimination they suffer. There is a significant literature documenting these stereotypes, including depictions of blacks in our mass media.

Group Identity Last, black Americans have strong group identification as a race, although the black concept of self has only recently become positive and aggressive. For many years their group consciousness has been particularly negative, including ambivalence and even self-hatred. Largely as a result of the civil rights struggles of the 1950s and the 1960s, blacks began to develop group cohesiveness out of their awareness of the discrimination against them, which in turn helped them to agitate for greater equality of opportunity. Blacks clearly fit Wirth's definition of a minority group, but what about other groups, such as women, and old people?

The concept of minority is an example of what Max Weber called an ideal type (1947). It is "an exaggeration or caricature of reality that is useful for comparative purposes precisely because it does not totally describe the experiences of any group of people" (Levin and Levin, 1980:66). Actually, most of our definitions work this way. If we were to describe a variety of flower to someone unfamiliar with it, we would describe a perfect example of that flower. The fact that in reality no such perfect example exists does not diminish the usefulness of the definition. When we use the concept of minority group, then, we should expect that minority groups will differ from one another in the degree to which they have the characteristics of Wirth's, or any other definition.

The elderly can be seen as an important minority group in America, one whose size and proportion of the population are growing. In fact, roughly the same proportion of the population is over 65 years of age as is black in America. But are the aged a minority group in the same way blacks are a minority group?

The Elderly

Identifiability First, like black Americans, the elderly are recognizably different from the rest of society, both physically and culturally. We carry around in our heads pictures of what we think an older person looks like. The white hair, wrinkles, stooped posture, slow speech, glasses, and so on, which form the stereotype, are as clear in the American mind as is our picture of any racial group, and this image is apparently planted very early. Seefeldt and others (1977) found in a study of children aged 3–11 that the children already associated images of physical appearance such as wrinkles, short, sprained backs, and arthritis with old age. It is not always possible to tell whether someone is over 65 years of age because the physical characteristics of the stereotype manifest themselves at such widely varying rates (and in some of us never at all). However, the fact that you cannot always tell a person's race has not kept us from using physical appearance as the primary arbiter of racial-group membership. Race is more socially than biologically determined. When judging whether someone should be considered black, we have no particular scale of skin tone, nose or lip thickness, and so on. A person is considered black if he or she is perceived as black in the eyes of the beholder. The same socially defined classification of the aged takes place. In fact, it is even more variable, for the age at which one is considered to be old, or to have the physical appearance associated with old age, has changed during the history of our country along with medical and dietary advances and even with changes in style. According to David Fischer (1977), colonial Americans powdered their hair or wore wigs in order to appear older.

The elderly are also recognizably different in their nonphysical characteristics. According to Rose (1965), the elderly share a number of common interests and concerns and, partly because they are excluded from interaction with the rest of the society, they develop their own subculture. Having experienced their lives together, cohorts of like-aged people often share a view of the world, and even a vocabulary particular to their experiences, that makes them identifiably different. Although not necessarily learned from previous generations, these common interests and ways of behaving make the elderly culturally (or subculturally) distinctive.

Differential Treatment The second component in Wirth's definition of a minority group is the extent to which the elderly are treated differently as a consequence of their perceived difference from the rest of the society. The elderly are the only group of people who on the basis of their group membership, can be denied employment. In fact, it has been legal to discriminate against an individual on the basis of age alone. Recently the age at which this is possible (mandatory retirement) was raised for some occupations from 65 to 70, but one can still be removed from a job without reference to one's competence as an individual after a given age. Largely as a consequence of their removal from employment and consequent dependence on inadequte support programs, a sizable proportion of the population over 65 in this country are below the poverty level. Often they cannot afford to remain in their own homes, even if they own them outright, because they can not afford to pay the taxes. Like other dependent populations living on fixed incomes, many of the aged suffer from inadequate services, such as medical care, for which their need is greatest. The connection between these deprivations and the perception of the elderly by the rest of society is even easier to make than that between the deprivations suffered by blacks and their perceived characteristics; that is, the dependence of the elderly is readily seen as a consequence of the physiological and mental decline perceived by the rest of the society. Our stereotypes about old age justify their removal from the mainstream of life. Since the civil rights movement of the 1950s and 1960s, it has become socially unacceptable in most of America to attribute black deprivations to the nineteenth-century sort of assumptions of black inferiority. As will be shown later in this chapter, modern arguments linking black poverty and black characteristics, such as those reviving the genetic inferiority and the culture of poverty arguments, have become much more subtle. In arguments about this link among the elderly, they remain blunt.

Group Identity The third element of the definition of minority group is the sense of group identity among the elderly. Once again, like black Americans, the elderly have, until recently, displayed a particularly negative group consciousness. Many older people have sought to avoid identification as old, often attempting to look younger than they otherwise might (roughly equivalent to "passing" for membership in another, less stigmatized group) or misidentifying their own age. The preference of many older people for being called "senior citizens," or "mature Americans" (Harris, 1975) is one consequence of the desire to avoid identification as "old," "elderly," or "aged" (Taves and Hansen, 1963). But also like black Americans, the elderly have recently begun to organize and to see themselves as victims of the treatment by the rest of society as much as victims of time. The growth of organizations like the Grey Panthers, which are aimed at the realization of the rights of older people, suggest strongly that the elderly are developing a more positive group identity. Once the aged begin to identify ageism (prejudice against the aged) rather than age as the main source of their difficulties, they are likely to become one more minority group contending for equality of opportunity. According to gerontologist Bernice Neugarten,

As they (the elderly) become more accustomed to the politics of confrontation they see around them, they may also become a more demanding group. There are signs that this is already so, with, for examples, appeals to "senior power" (in some ways analogous to the appeal to "black power"), and with more frequent newspaper accounts of groups of older people picketing and protesting over such local issues as reduced bus fares or better housing projects. [1970:17–18.]

The evidence is that the elderly, because of their physical and cultural characteristics are singled out from the rest of society for unequal treatment and that out of such treatment, develop a particular type of group consciousness and, eventually, a sense of collective discrimination. A similar analysis reveals women to be another important minority group in American society. Briefly, here is some evidence leading to that conclusion.

Women

Identifiability Women are physically recognizable to an even greater extent than other groups of people, including religious, age, ethnic, and even racial groups. In fact, women and men are taught how to enhance such differences by ways of dressing, moving, and other cosmetic differences, such as hairstyling, clothing, and make-up. To the extent that females are taught to emphasize and depend on their attractiveness as a basic way of relating to other peoples' expectations of them, such recognizability becomes a way of life. If you believe that success depends on your attractiveness as a female, then recognizability is what you seek. The tendency for males and females to think this way is normally attributed to the process of socialization, whereby "little girls receive attention and praise for their attractiveness, while boys are admired for their achievements and cleverness" (Weitzman, Eifler, Hokada, and Ross, 1972:1146).

Even given the clear physiological distinction between most males and females, and the tendency for both sexes to enhance such characteristics, the issue of physical identifiability remains difficult. Patterns of behavior not typical of the sex-group membership into which an individual is born (effeminacy among males, masculinity among females), whether or not such behavior is accompanied by homosexuality, variations in hormonal production (estrogen among females and androgen among males), or chromosomal identification in which anomalies occur, contribute to our difficulties in differentiating physiologically between sexes. In fact, in a study of individuals whose sex-group determination was physiologically unclear (e.g., hermaphroditic individuals), Money and Ehrhardt (1972) determined that the sex assigned to the child at birth was a more important determinant of gender role identity than any physical characteristic; that is, sexual identity, like racial-group membership and the status of old age, is socially determined. Women and men, like blacks and older people, are taught ways of thinking and acting that not only make them more recognizable and differentiable from the rest of the population but also influence the way they operate within the larger social order. In terms of success, they are given a different, and not very adequate, set of rules for playing the game, given the ability of majority groups to decide who shall succeed.

Very early in the socialization process our parents and others around us begin to treat us in terms of their own expectations of our behavior. The general expectation that boys be aggressive and tough and girls pretty and mild shows up in parents' treatment of their own children. Rubin, Provenzano, and Luria (1974) asked the parents of 15 male and 15 female babies who had been matched for size at birth to describe their children. Parents of the girl infants described them as significantly smaller, softer, and less attentive. The expectations take hold very early, with children receiving reinforcement and cues for sex-appropriate behavior from toy and clothing selections made by parents and relatives, portrayal of sex-appropriate behavior on television and in children's books, and, of course, from one another. To the extent that women, as a result of this process, act differently from men, or are perceived as acting differently because of differing characteristics such as aggressiveness and competence in business matters, they are culturally (as opposed to physically) recognizable. Interestingly, as with blacks, many of the characteristics and behaviors attributed to women have become, or always were, exaggerations. These stereotypes of how women act or what characteristics they possess have been documented in the growing literature of the sociology of women. For example, in their 1975 study of the evidence on sex differences, Maccoby and Jacklin systematically showed how incorrect were the assumptions that females tend to be more social, less achievement-oriented, lower in self-esteem, more compliant, more nurturant, and less competitive, dominant, and active than males. But once again, what is important in the process of identification is not objective reality but expectations, and those remain in the culture today.

Differential Treatment Stereotypes about women are used to justify the unequal treatment they receive at the hands of males who are in positions that enable them to distribute opportunity. Broverman, Vogel, Broverman, Clarkson, and Rosenkrantz (1972) asked subjects of both sexes to describe the characteristics of men and women. The results are as follows:

Men	Women
Strong	Weak
Independent	Dependent
Worldly	Not Worldly
Aggressive	Passive
Ambitious	Not Ambitious
Logical	Illogical
Blunt	Tactful
Rough	Gentle

It is the belief that women are weak, passive, unambitious, illogical, and generally better at the arts than business or mechanical types of jobs, which makes discriminatory hiring, promotion, and other decisions seem logical. Of course, once such decisions are made, women's opportunities to gain the skills that would destroy the stereotypes are greatly diminished. The self-fulfilling prophecy sets in: "You don't have the temperament for the job so I won't hire you." You then do not get the opportunity to develop or use the skills; so they atrophy, and the original expectations about your characteristics are made to come true. When slaves were prohibited to learn how to read because they were believed to be incapable of learning such skills, all the benefits of reading, all the access to the stored information of centuries was also denied them, and they appeared, in fulfillment of the prophecy, stupid.

As for the discrimination itself, it shows up most starkly in the work world. On the average, women who work full time have, for the last 20 years, only earned approximately 60 percent of what male full-time workers have earned. This ratio has remained fairly constant (U.S. Dept. of Labor, 1976). Cases settled in court have documented the fact that women with the same qualifications and doing the same jobs as men are often paid less, often because an employer believed the male involved "needed the money more in order to support his family." The larger part of the income gap between men and women is due to the types of jobs made available to women rather than to the distribution of rewards for those who enter traditionally male occupations.

Laws prohibiting the entry of women into certain jobs or establishing physical requirements for eligibility for such jobs, admissions procedures that limit the number of females accepted to law and medical degree programs, or more subtle processes, such as the lack of encouragement women receive when they try to enter traditionally male occupations, all these contribute to the funneling of females into certain lower-paying, traditionally female jobs such as nurse, secretary, teacher, social worker, and so on. In a study of how women are treated in graduate school, Freeman (1979) suggests a *null environment hypothesis:* " ... professors don't have to make it a specific point to discourage their female students. Society will do it for them. All they have to do is fail to encourage them" (p. 221). The teachers Freeman interviewed simply did not expect women to be serious students, did not expect them to be competent. So the expectation justified the passive discrimination.

Group Identity Women are becoming increasingly aware of and concerned about their position in society. To be sure, there is a great deal of conflict between men and women over this growing consciousness, and among women as well. Witness the bitter struggle between those opposing and those favoring the Equal Rights Amendment to the Constitution. But such conflicts are part of the process of identification as a minority group. Blacks are divided; older people are divided; and women are divided. After all, no matter how disadvantaged our position, no matter how little we have accumulated for ourselves, it seems a great threat to some to risk what we have in hopes of attaining an uncertain set of opportunities. We are often uncomfortable with change of any sort. But changes are taking place among women. The National Organization of Women (NOW) is increasing in size and activity, and the documentation of inequality is continuing. Courses in the study of women's history and the sociology of women are becoming more and more available, and the language, which is a social construction, not some set of rules set down in the laws of nature, is changing to reflect these forces. Publishers send their authors guidelines for nonsexist language, and words such as "fireman" and "businessman" are being replaced by "firefighter" and "executive."

But these changes are fairly recent, and like blacks and older people, women also have suffered from a sort of negative group consciousness. Just as blacks have expressed prejudice against other blacks and a willingness to avoid identification as black, and just as the elderly have denigrated characteristics associated with old age, so women have shown prejudice against other women. A sample of college females were asked to read a number of professional articles and to rate them for persuasiveness, value, and so on. One-half the subjects read that the articles were by "John T. McKay," whereas the other half read that the exact same articles they were given were by "Joan T. McKay." Independent of the field with which the specific article dealt, the article attributed to the female author was evaluated less favorably (Goldberg, 1968). In sum, to the extent that it is useful to conceive of American blacks as a minority group, because it alerts us to the role of majority groups in distributing opportunity, it is useful also to conceive of women as a minority group. In her 1953 book, *The Second Sex,* Simone de Beauvoir compared the two groups when she wrote of the low wages paid women in Europe and America around the turn of the century:

If employers warmly welcomed women because of the low wages they would accept, this same fact gave rise to opposition from the male workers.... The problem was presented in somewhat the same way as that of the Negro laborer in the United States. The most oppressed minorities of a society seem to their class at first to be enemies, and a more profound comprehension of the situation is needed in order that the interests of blacks and whites, or women workers and men workers, may achieve unity instead of being opposed to each other. [1949:107.]

Similarly, Gunnar Myrdal, the Swedish sociologist and economist, in his classic study of American race relations recognized the parallel between the situation of American blacks and that of women. He concluded that both blacks and women were accorded low status in society; that they were denied rights such as voting, adequate education, and equal pay; and that such differential treatment was justified by their supposedly inferior endowments, such as intelligence and personality weaknesses, all maintained by a paternalistic set of relationships with the dominant group.

In drawing a parallel between the position of, and feeling toward women and Negroes, we are uncovering a fundamental basis of our culture. Although it is changing, atavistic elements sometimes unexpectedly break through in the most emancipated individuals. The similarities in the womens' and the Negroes' problems are not accidental. They were, as we have pointed out, originally determined in a paternalistic order of society. The problems remain even though paternalism is gradually declining as an ideal and is losing its economic basis. In the final analysis, women are still hindered in their competition by the function of procreation; Negroes are laboring under the yoke of the doctrine of unassimability which has remained although slavery is abolished. The second barrier is actually much stronger than the first in America today. But the first is more eternally inexorable. [1944:1078.]

How Have Minority-Group Situations Been Explained?

With the application of Wirth's definition of minority group to a wide variety of people such as women, the aged, and the handicapped, we become more sensitive to the existence of the unequal distribution of opportunity in American society. But merely identifying those who lack the power to define their own social destinies or documenting the degree or type of their deprivations still leaves unanswered our questions about why minorities, or these particular minorities, exist. For part of the answer we should look to the past to discover how the existence of minority groups has been explained. To what have the inferior opportunities and circumstances of blacks, the elderly, and women, for example, been attributed? We have identified three broad ways of thinking that have been used to account for the circumstances of minority groups. In the first, the cause is thought to be a natural, inborn inferiority of minority-group members, whether the traits discussed be physical, psychological, intellectual, emotional, moral, or so on. The second view also focuses on the inferiority of the minority-group members but contends that flaws in the physical, emotional, moral, or intellectual makeup of minority-group members are acquired by their experiences in life. These first two views take what William Ryan has called a "victim-blaming" perspective, which will be described at the end of the section on acquired inferiority. The third view, which is also the dominant view of this book, is that the deprivations experienced by minorities have little to do with their traits but are largely the consequence of the treatment they receive at the hands of majority groups.[1] According to this view, the traits of minority-group members, when not wholly invented, are typically extremely exaggerated. In addition, these traits, although they can develop as a consequence of the treatment minorities receive from majorities, help *justify* the perpetuation of such treatment but should not be seen as a *cause* of the social positions of minority groups.

Natural Inferiority Explanations

Anthropologists repeatedly have noted the tendency of groups of people to evaluate one another in terms of their own beliefs and values. This ethnocentrism, in its most extreme form, can deny the very humanity of other groups, reducing them to or even below the level of any animal that might be subject to the will of the dominating group. For example, the Eskimo word one tribe uses for itself is *Inuit,* meaning "people." They consider the tribe to their south to be other than people. The Inuit consider them to be "dog-faced cannibals," which, of course, they are not. It is much easier to treat an individual cruelly—as a slave, for example—if he or she is not considered to be human, and is therefore not due the same treatment as oneself or one's equals. Enemies in war or violent competition are also dehumanized, given derogatory, insulting nicknames so that they can be treated more cruelly and with less distracting concern for their well-being. During World War II, recruits were taught to call Germans "Krauts" and Japanese "Japs" or "monkeys," and during the Viet Nam War, American soldiers called the Vietnamese "slants," "gooks," "slopes," and so on. It is easier to kill an enemy who is less than human, whether or not their "savage" character is invented for you and then taught during basic training. Throughout history the enslavement or destruction of large groups of people has been accompanied by, and at least partly attributable to, the belief by the dominant group that the victims are somehow different from, and inferior to, themselves.

In the nineteenth century the same sort of ethnocentric thinking was exhibited in the work of its early anthropologists, Lewis H. Morgan and E. B. Tylor. This view distinguished between what were believed to be the levels of cultural evolution assumed to parallel the stages of biological evolution. At the peak of evolution, they placed the civilized peoples, which included, of course, their own cultures. Below that were the barbaric and then the savage levels, with each level populated by beings of lower intellectual ability than that of the level above. Although slightly more elegant in form than the simpler sort of ethnocentrism of groups like the Inuit, the belief that the world could be divided into civilized and lower peoples was useful in the maintenance of control over colonized peoples. If they were less advanced because they were inferior, then their land and labor could justifiably be exploited. In fact, the "civilized" colonial English especially felt it their duty to help those inferior to themselves, not only by developing their resources but also by blessing the inferiors with uplifting contact with their superiors, their white burden.

Race In the eighteenth century America's exploitation of enslaved blacks was justified by the belief that blacks were naturally inferior, born to servitude and ignorance. Beliefs like this enabled Christians to hold slaves while still claiming to follow their religious teachings. If blacks were not humans, were either a different kind of being or were at an earlier stage of evolution than whites, then the normal rules for humane treatment clearly did not apply. It was simply a matter of discovering the "proper" place for blacks in society and treating them accordingly. "Almost the whole of scientific thought in both America and Europe in the decades before Darwin accepted race inferiority, irrespective of whether the races sprang from a single original pair or were created separately" (Haller, 1971:77). In one view, blacks were seen to be greatly inferior in their evolution with little chance of improvement, and in another view, as an entirely different (and inferior) species from whites. Common to these views was the belief that blacks were born inferior and, consequently, were fit only for lives of servitude.

During the nineteenth century, science began to dominate the thinking of the West, as moral and religious authority had dominated the preceding centuries. Justification came more and more from studies conducted by scientists, and in the area of race, physicians and anthropologists provided the bulk of the "proof" of the inferiority of blacks. Their favorite technique was the measurement of cranial capacity as an indication of the intellectual capacity of a person. The weighing of a brain after autopsy or the measurement of the actual volume of the interior of the skull provided only slight improvements in sophistication over the phrenologists' measurements with calipers of the exterior of the skull of the living person.

Race	Authority	Capacity
European	Tiedemann	100.0
Asiatic	Davis	94.3
African	Davis	93.0
American	Tiedemann	95.0
American	Davis	94.7
American	Morton	87.0
Oceanic	Davis	96.9
Chinese	Davis	99.8
Mongol	Morton	94.0
Mongol	Tiedemann	93.0
"Hindoo"	Davis	89.4
Malay	Tiedemann	89.0
American Indian	Morton	91.0
"Esquimaux"	Davis	98.8
Mexican	Morton	88.5
Peruvian	Wyman	81.2
Peruvian	Morton	81.2
Negro	Tiedemann	91.0
Negro	Peacock	88.0
Hottentot	Morton	86.0
Javan	Davis	94.8
Tasmanian	Davis	88.0
Australian	Morton	88.0
Australian	Davis	87.9

Notice that the foregoing list (Haller, 1971:18–19) of descending intellectual capacity (inferred from the average cranial capacity of each category) fits the anthropological theory of cultural evolution and its categories of savagery, barbarism, and civilization. Similar conclusions about the intellectual and cultural potential of various groups were drawn from yet shakier propositions, such as the relationship between facial angle and evolutionary advancement. See Figures 1.1 and 1.2.

Sometimes these researchers were so eager to select data that confirmed their belief in the intellectual superiority of Western whites that they dispensed with even the slightest appearances of scientific rigor. Writing of the work of E. A. Apitzka, "the most prominent practitioner of the trade" (that is, brain-weighers), Stephen Gould illustrated the transparency of such work:

In an outrageous example of data selected to conform with a priori prejudice, he arranged, in order, one of his largest brains from an eminent white male, a bushwoman from Africa, and a gorilla. (He could easily have reversed the first two by choosing a larger black and a smaller white.) Spitzka concluded, . . . "The jump from a Cuvier or a Thackeray to a Zulu or a Bushman is no greater than from the latter to the gorilla or the orang." [1979:37.]

Figure 1.1 Facial angle and evolutionary advancement after Darwin's *Origin of Species*.

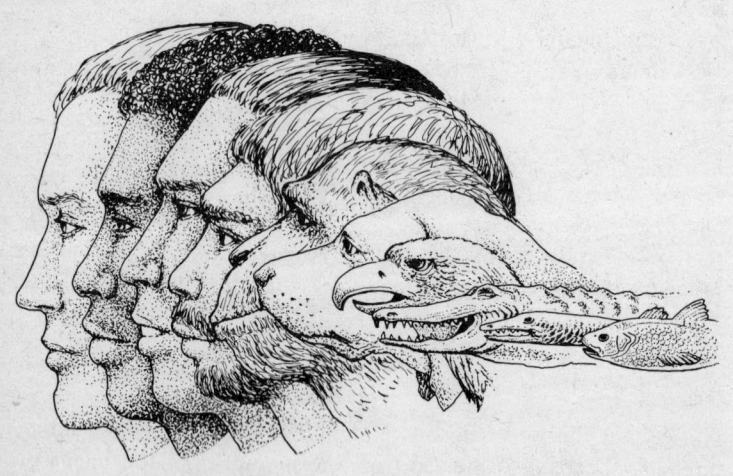

Source: From Ranson Dexter 1874 "The Facial Angle," *Popular Science Monthly*. Courtesy of Indiana University.

What do we know after reading such an assertion? If we live in the mid-nineteenth century and we wish to believe that blacks are inferior, then we have what seem to be objective conclusions drawn by a scientist. Living today we see, instead, subjective conclusions drawn by prejudiced individuals dressed up in lab coats and the trappings of science.

The presumed inferiority of blacks has also been attributed to innate sexual madness caused, according to one view, by the competition between brain and reproductive organ growth during development. Whether the measurements were of brains or genitals, the conclusion was always the same: Blacks are inferior and fit for labor, not education and leadership. In addition, the possibilities for improvement were nil. Attributing these apparent physiological differences to the natural order of the world, these researchers concluded that any attempt to help the unfortunate inferiors would only harm them, for advancement was only possible when facing severe tests of survival, undiminished by the well-

Figure 1.2 Facial angle among humans after Darwin's *Origin of Species*.

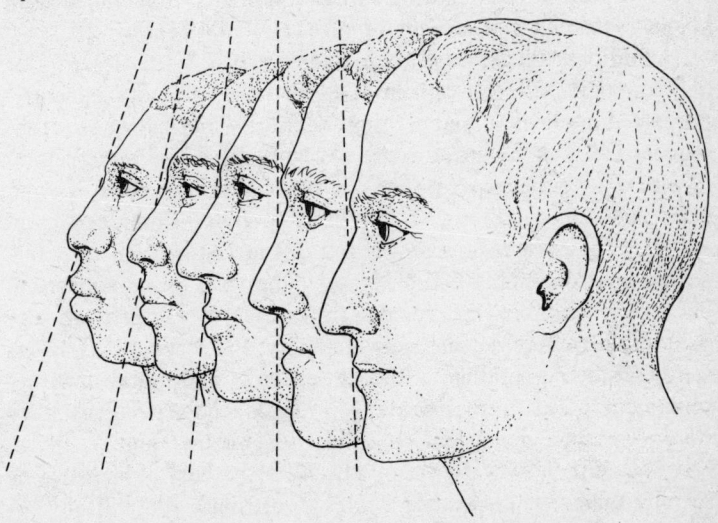

Source: From John J. Jeffries 1869 *Natural History of the Human Races*.

meaning efforts of whites (Haller, 1971). Even after Darwin's work was widely accepted, the possibilities for evolutionary advancement by blacks were denied by the Social Darwinists.

> Spencer's scheme of evolution tolled a note of pessimism for the less civilized peoples of mankind. Progress in intellectual and social development depended upon a natural movement through successive stages from homogeneity to heterogeneity. A savage was unable to live with civilized man as an equal since civilization's complex associations could not be comprehended by his inferior brain whose capacity was geared to a far simpler framework of association. This also meant that, for all practical purposes, evolution concerned only the Caucasian. Whatever progress might come to the savage could accrue only in insignificant stages which in no way approached the accelerated state of the Caucasian's evolution. [Haller, 1971:127.]

With this formidable arsenal of "evidence" as to the natural inferiority of blacks, is it any wonder that people who wished to believe so could assert that slaves were slaves because they were incapable of any task that required them to think, that because they were incapable of learning to read, education was wasted on them, and that without the whites telling them what to do, the black would be lost. One theory even held that freedom caused blacks to devolve and whites to evolve (Haller, 1971).

In addition, blacks have been assumed to be naturally inferior in emotional and moral capacities, partly as a consequence of their purported intellectual and physical inferiority and partly as a consequence of their supposed excess of sexual drive. Characterization of blacks as either animal—on the basis of sexual appetites and behaviors—or childlike—on the basis of moral complexity and capacity for judgment—contributed to the justification of paternalism and manipulation of black Americans. Comparison of blacks with children is reflected in the epithet "boy," with its attendant implication of dependence, simplicity, and servitude. If blacks were considered childlike in their intellectual and moral underdevelopment, it was to the advantage of those who argued that they were, therefore, dependent on others for guidance and "help" in how to lead their lives. By the mid twentieth century, it had become socially unacceptable among whites to attribute the still obvious minority status of American blacks to natural, inborn inferiority.

A somewhat more subtle theory of acquired inferiority, which we will discuss later in this chapter, took the place of the natural inferiority approach. But by the 1970s, the natural inferiority idea was again being discussed in the work of people like Jensen, Herrnstein, Shockley, and E. O. Wilson, among others, more about which we will see later.

Age Unlike theories about race differences, no embarrassment about assuming that the elderly are naturally inferior has yet become widespread. Virtually all the data researchers have produced about the condition of the elderly have focused on how the forces of nature create decline in the elderly and make them physically and mentally inferior to the young. Although the elderly are clearly not born inferior, they are assumed to become inferior as a consequence of the "natural" process of decline, which is synonymous with aging. The research and theories that support this conclusion are endlessly available in the gerontological literature, especially in the psychological evidence.

"Physiologists and biologists virtually universally look upon aging as a period of decline" (Breen, 1960:150). What were once normal, healthy, and competent bodies reportedly become subject to the process called senescence: "a decrease in viability and an increase in vulnerability ... an increasing probability of death with increasing chronological age" (Comfort, 1964:22). Biologists and chemists have documented the processes whereby cells decline in their capacity to reproduce without error, connective tissue hardens and becomes less flexible, the circulatory and nervous systems deteriorate, and diseases increase in frequency and severity as a result. We can read of the increasing frequency with age of the following illnesses: heart disease; hypertension; arthritis; diabetes; nervous breakdown; dental, visual, and hearing problems; ulcer; cancer; stroke; and more. To the natural process of aging are attributed all these conditions that distinguish the elderly from the rest of the population in terms of their ability to operate efficiently in the everyday world as well as all the visible, physical characteristics that make them so instantly recognizable to us and to one another. Their greying and thinning hair, wrinkles, stooped posture, slower movements, glasses, hearing aids (physical appliances that make otherwise invisible physical changes apparent), and shakier voices are the identifying signs of their supposedly inevitable and natural inferiority. We are merely the, as yet, unafflicted population.

The dependence of the elderly, the fact that they do not control their own lives to nearly the extent enjoyed by the younger segments of society, is justified by the belief in their natural inferiority, especially in their physical decline. When we are forcibly removed at 65 or 70 years of age from employment, it is because we are assumed to be incapable of performing on the job the way we once did. Mandatory retirement, at whatever age, is no different from the denial of opportunities to other groups on the basis of characteristics assumed to apply to the entire group to which they belong. Blacks have been denied opportunities in positions other than menial labor in the belief that blacks in general were naturally incapable of learning complex tasks. In the same way, the elderly have been evaluated on the basis of their group membership and have been removed from jobs they have held on the belief that nature has robbed them (or is about to rob them) of their ability to continue to perform. What makes such practices particularly harmful is that individual evaluation seems unnecessary if an entire group is assumed to have inherent inferiorities. In addition, the denial of opportunities reduces the likelihood that the erroneous assumptions about a group's characteristics will be challenged.

Discrimination reduces our opportunities to point to blacks who can, in fact, learn the most complex skills and ideas and apply them equally with whites, or to older people who can, in fact, continue to do the jobs they have held before with no loss of efficiency and, in some cases, with increased skill. In the absence of opportunities to provide evidence contrary to our assumptions about the presumed natural inferiority of a group of people, the appearance of actual inferiority may set in, especially when we are looking for evidence to fulfill our own expectations. The self-fulfilling prophecy, whereby treating a group as inferior causes them to appear inferior, continues to play an important role in the maintenance of minority groups and will be discussed more fully later. For now, it is clear that the elderly are victims of this self-fulfilling prophecy. Believing that they are subject to the natural forces of deterioration, both they and the rest of society accept that the old should stop exercising, working hard, dealing with problems themselves by taking control, taking on new and challenging projects, and so on. These are the very activities that maintain and enlarge our capacities.

The belief in the physical deterioration of the elderly is used to justify their disengagement and isolation from society. One theory about the position of the elderly in society says, "Aged populations must adjust to conditions that are not generally characteristic of other stages of the life cycle, namely, the increased probability of illness and impending death" (Phillips, 1957:212). These "adjustments" are almost always losses in social involvement and control over social memberships. The social-role losses that are attributed to decline include loss of employment, household management, community and organizational leadership, marriage itself (through death of spouse), distant goals and plans, management of funds, control over children (who eventually take over control of their parents), association with the young in general, and maintenance and ownership of ones' own home (due to either decreased ability to afford home ownership or the perceived need to live in age-segregated housing) (Phillips, 1957). The same attribution of role losses to the deterioration with age appears in disengagement theory: "The society and the individual prepare in advance for the ultimate 'disengagement' of incurable, incapacitating disease and death by an inevitable, gradual and mutually satisfying process of disengagement from society" (Rose, 1964:46). Here the process is inevitable because it is presumed to be a result of the impersonal forces of nature. The contention that it is mutually satisfying for the society and for the disengaging older person reminds one of the statements of racists who contended that the inferior position of the black, including his or her slavery, was to the black person's benefit and was even the position in which he or she was happiest. For old people, the parallel story is that the inevitable declines of natural aging make it necessary for the old to contemplate their past lives in making preparations for death. They would, it seems, prefer retirement and disengagement in the same way blacks would prefer not to have to struggle with tasks beyond their abilities.

Beyond the overwhelming focus on the physical decline associated with age, a parallel literature has emphasized the decline in mental adaptive capacity with age. From sensory and perceptual processes (gathering and attaching meaning to stimuli in the environment) to psychomotor performance (the chain of events whereby we decide about and act on events in the environment) to learning, intelligence, memory, creativity, problem solving and thinking, drive levels and personality (the relatively stable combination of all the mental traits that make one individual different from one another), psychologists of aging have employed the same assumption as that made by theorists of the physiology of aging. We have learned to believe that mental adaptive capacities also naturally decline with age. Thus, for the same reasons that we remove people from jobs on the grounds that they will not be able to handle them physically, we also do so because we expect their mental abilities to deteriorate.

Last, we think probably as a sort of cumulative conclusion based on the evidence from the physiological and psychological evidence, that the elderly become morally and emotionally inferior as well, in the sense that blacks have been considered inferior in these ways. The parallel is complete when we acknowledge our belief that old age makes us childlike again. We even use the physical characteristics of old age to further the metaphor, with baldness, toothlessness, wrinkles, and curled posture reminding us of infancy. Old age is seen as a second childhood, especially when we label the elderly as "senile," a catchword for all the symptoms that we take to be characteristic of decline with age. Like children, the aged become dependent and need and prefer to be told what to do.

Sex   As with the elderly, claims that women are naturally inferior to men have only recently become widely challenged and, for those who wish to make such belief public, a source of embarrassment and conflict for them. At least this is becoming the case in North America and in much of the industrialized West. In the Middle East and most Islamic countries, the inferiority of women is institutionalized in the religion and, where the state is officially religious, in law. Even in the United States, the popular debate over the relative status of women is quite new, with the Equal Rights Amendment to the Constitution still not passed as of the writing of this book.

Womens' minority status, like that of blacks and the aged, has been justified by the belief that they are naturally inferior to men:

> Physicians were the first of the new experts. With claims to knowledge encompassing all of human biological existence, they were the first to pass judgement on the social consequences of female anatomy and to prescribe the "natural" life plan for women. They were followed by a horde of more specialized experts, each group claiming that their authority flowed directly from biological science. [Ehrenreich and English, 1978:4.]

Just as blacks' brains were measured, so were womens'. Gould (1978) focused on the efforts of Paul Broca in the mid nineteenth century to attribute to brain size the origins of female intellectual capacity—which, in terms of Broca's assumptions, you can read as "inferiority." Broca's (and others') data consistently showed that womens' brains were smaller than mens' and Gould notes that such observed differences could logically be attributed, at least in part, to the average difference in physical size between men and women:

> But science is an inferential exercise, not a catalog of facts. Numbers, by themselves, specify nothing.... He (Broca) made no attempt to measure the effect of size alone and actually stated that it cannot account for the entire difference because we know, a priori, that women are not as intelligent as men (a premise that the data were supposed to test, not rest upon). [1978:46.]

Broca attributes the womens' smaller-size brain in part to the lower intelligence of women. Amazingly, he then concludes that the smaller size of womens' brains accounts for their lower intelligence.

The parallel between the study of the physiological inferiority of blacks and that of women becomes more than a coincidence when the similarities are made explicit: "Women were denigrated on their own accord, but they also stood as surrogates for other disenfranchised groups.... Consider another from one of Broca's disciples in 1881: 'Men of the black races have a brain scarcely heavier than that of white women'" (Gould, 1978:48). The way to denigrate a black male was to compare his mental capacities to that of a "mere" woman. Given this logic, one shudders to think of the mental insufficiencies likely among black females.

By the 1860s, natural scientists would pinpoint woman's place on the evolutionary ladder with some precision—she was at the level of the Negro. For example, Carl Vogt, a leading European professor of natural history, placed the Negro (male) as follows: " ... the grown-up Negro partakes, as regards his intellectual faculties, of the nature of the child, the female, and the senile white" (Ehrenreich and English, 1978:105). Race, sex, and age have all been included in the same denigrating sentence and all in the tradition of that nineteenth-century "science" that attributed inferior social positions to inferior natural capacities. Those born inferior (namely blacks, females, and children) and those grown inferior (old people) are painted with the same strokes. And like blacks and the elderly, women have been treated as emotionally and morally inferior, especially in the sense that they are compared with simple, naive children. In fact, women continue to be called "girls," whereas males of the same age are referred to as "men."

It is no coincidence that these three groups were treated similarly by the scientists who investigated their capabilities. Gould recognized how a priori thinking is a sign of someone who wishes his or her observations to reinforce a wish more powerful than the belief in scientific objectivity: "To appreciate the social role of Broca and his school, we must recognize that his statements on the brains of women do not reflect an isolated prejudice toward a single disadvantaged group. They must be weighed in the context of a general theory that supported contemporary social distinctions as biologically ordained" (Gould, 1978:48).

As to the possibility that women, like men, could evolve, the theory at the time was that, like blacks, their chances were slim. Darwin believed women to have faculties that " ... are characteristic of the lower races, and therefore of a past and lower state of civilization" (Figes, 1970:114). But others believed the very nature of the female to be flawed, rather than merely less advanced or less capable than man's condition: "In fact, the theories which guided the doctor's practice from the late nineteenth to the early twentieth century held that woman's *normal* state was to be sick. This was not advanced as an empirical observation, but as physiological fact. Medicine had 'discovered' that female functions were inherently pathological" (Ehrenreich and English, 1978:99). Women could, accordingly, not benefit from the experiences that contributed to the improvement of men: "Education which has resulted in developing and strengthening the physical nature of man has been perverted through folly and fashion to render women weaker and weaker" (Monque, 1898). In Darwinian terms, the process of variation and specialization that increased the adaptability of species was thought to exist in men but not in women. As Ehrenreich and English expressed it in summarizing this point of view,

> In the post-Darwinian scientific value system, "specialization" was good ('advanced'); despecialization was bad ("primitive"). Now put this together with the fact that the species as a whole was getting ever more 'specialized' sexually as part of its general evolutionary advance: it followed that men would become ever more differentiated, while women would become progressively de-differentiated, and ever more concentrated on the ancient animal function of reproduction. [1978:107.]

By the twentieth century, the most powerful and lastingly influential statement about the effect of the "natural inferiority" of women on their social opportunities appeared in the work of Sigmund Freud. Starting with the physical facts of female sexual anatomy, Freud built a case arguing that women's lack of a penis dooms them to a life of penis envy, the social consequences of which are legion. He argued that for boys, the fear of castration provides the motivation whereby the Oedipus complex is dealt with. The successful achievement of a superego then results in what we might call a mature personality. However, the female, lacking a penis, also lacks fear of castration. Deprived of the motivation to overcome the oedipal situation, she enters it as a refuge:

> Girls remain in it for an indeterminate length of time; they demolish it late and, even so, incompletely. In these circumstances the formation of the super-ego must suffer; it cannot attain the strength and independence which give it its cultural significance, and feminists are not pleased when we point out to them the effects of this factor upon the average feminine character. [Roszak & Roszak, 1969:25.]

You could bet that feminists would be "not pleased" when informed that their inferior condition in the social world attributes to their lack of a male sexual organ, that they are doomed to a life of envy as the primary facet of the female character, and that as a consequence they are inevitably passive, dependent, domestic, sexually frigid, and incompetent. Far-reaching indeed are Freud's conclusions about the consequences of the physical fact from which he began. For example:

> The fact that women must be regarded as having little sense of justice is no doubt related to the predominance of envy in their mental life; for the demand of justice is a modification of envy and lays down the condition subject to which one can put envy aside. We also regard women as weaker in their social interests and as having less capacity for sublimating their instincts than men. [Roszak and Roszak, 1969:29.]

Imagine all the jobs for which women would therefore be disqualified, such as judge, lawyer, legislator, executive, or, in fact, any position in which objective evaluation of contending rights would have to be made. This is, of course, the entire world of social power. Freud's reasoning reminds one of Paul Broca's convenient use of women's apparently inferior intelligence as both a consequence and a cause of their reportedly smaller brain size. Is Freud's observation that women lack a sense of justice a consequence or a proof of their overwhelming feelings of envy?

The answer is, of course, that like other scientists and other random commentators on the nature of women, Freud wrote more in justification of an assumption than in examination of it. He was raised with the expectations taught a male during Victorian paternalism, and he married a woman who fulfilled those expectations. Had he been less clever in his manipulation of ideas, and less articulate in expressing them, no doubt he would have had no more effect than a common man of his time expounding in the company of contemporaries (never to be quoted) on the proper place of women in the social order of the world. Freud was brilliant, but not so brilliant that he could examine, or understand, the influence of his own socialization on the production of his mind.

Acquired Inferiority Explanations

The belief that blacks and women are naturally inferior was common in the nineteenth and early twentieth centuries but is less common today. (In contrast, the belief that the elderly are naturally inferior is currently popular, more about which will be presented later.) That earlier evidence about race and sex has, with our somewhat more sophisticated understanding of the scientific process, become transparently subjective, even laughable. In addition, as we have become more and more sensitive to the suffering of various minorities, especially to that of black Americans, it has also become increasingly unacceptable to express the old stereotypes about racial inferiority in public. In 1954, the Supreme Court overturned the principle of "separate but equal" as it was expressed in the famous 1896 case of *Plessy* v. *Ferguson*. The desegregation orders of the Brown decision merely marked one important stage in the long struggle to acknowledge the deprivations suffered by blacks in America. By 1964, with the help of John F. Kennedy and Lyndon B. Johnson, the Congress had also joined the spirit of the Supreme Court's attitude toward the injuries of race. Public consciousness was being challenged and changed. The most powerful moral, executive, and legislative bodies of the government had agreed with civil rights advocates that black Americans had grievances that deserved redress and that something would have to be done. But what should be done, and to what effect? Assuming that blacks were not naturally inferior, to what could their difficulties be attributed, other than to heredity, and how could programs designed to improve their conditions be targeted so as to make a difference? To understand how the supposed inferiority of blacks could be blamed on something other than biological forces, we need to look back nearly to the beginning of the twentieth century.

By the 1920s, psychologists like Thorndike and Watson were arguing with increasing popular success that human beings develop their traits as a consequence of learning from their experiences in the environment. Arguing the extreme environmentalist case, Watson made the following famous statement:

Give me a dozen healthy infants, well-formed, and my own specified world to bring them up in and I'll guarantee to take any one at random and train him to become any type of specialist I might select—doctor, lawyer, artist, merchant, chief, and yes, even beggarman and thief, regardless of his talents, penchants, tendencies, abilities, vocations and race of his ancestors. [1926:10.]

Among sociologists the environmental position was marked by a concern with the way in which individuals develop and the way culture is passed from one generation to another by the process called *socialization*. Sociologists Charles Cooley and G. H. Mead argued that individuals can only develop a human character through interaction with other humans. A controversy raged over what contribution is made to human character by environmental versus hereditary forces. The nineteenth-century dominance of natural forces arguments was gone by the mid twentieth century. It turned out to be a mixed blessing.

Now a person's (or a group's) social existence was no longer considered fated by biological forces. If one's impoverished life was no longer the result of genetic inferiority, then improvement might now be possible. However, in place of the natural inferiority argument came the belief that inferiority could be acquired from one's experiences, just as one developed one's adult character by them. That minorities lived poorer lives as a result of their flaws remained a dominant assumption. Only the origins of those flaws had been shifted from biological to environmental sources.

Race In American history, blacks have been the primary targets for oppression and its justification. Native Americans might have qualified for that dubious distinction were it not for the fact that they were pushed aside, ignored, exploited, and even annihilated without the need to resort to complex justifications. They were dismissed as savages, and, because they were never enslaved (their primary asset was land, not labor), no continuing relationship had to be established. They were almost totally isolated (on reservations, for example) from contact with other than the social-control agents (like the cavalry) of the dominant society. The more distant the relationship between adversaries and strangers, the less complex their dehumanizations of one another need be. But blacks were slaves in daily contact with their owners and, after emancipation, with their economic and legal rulers. The bulk of the arguments about the natural inferiority of minority-group members focused on race, and so did the arguments that minority groups acquired their inadequacies.

The best-known and most influential of these ideas has been called the *culture of poverty* or *lower-class* (usually meaning "black") *culture*. These are summary terms for a series of characteristics that poor people are believed to develop and that distinguish them from the wealthier, more middle-class segment of society. The poor are reported in this literature to be different from, and inferior to, other Americans in terms of a number of values, beliefs, and other personal characteristics. These include level of aspiration, concern for the quality of the environment, ability to delay gratification, work ethic, concern for the well-being of their children, commitment to education, and so on. The culture of poverty is, accordingly, a subculture: a set of values, beliefs, and lifestyles that are different from those of the larger culture. It is presumed to develop as a consequence of the particular life circumstances of a group of people and to be adaptive for them; that is, like other cultural systems, the subculture of poverty is seen as an aid to survival for those unfortunates whose social circumstances require the adoption of ways of life less desirable than those of majority-group members (Miller, 1958). What is critical in this view, and must be kept in mind, is that its focus is not on the circumstances to which the poor must adapt (which we will be discussing in some detail in the section on victim blaming) but on the characteristics that the minority-group member develops or acquires and on how very *mal*adaptive such inferior characteristics are for entry into the social world of the majority group.

Oscar Lewis' 1966 article "The Culture of Poverty" stated the underlying proposition of the view as follows: "By the time slum children are six or seven they have usually absorbed the basic attitudes and values of their subculture. Thereafter, they are psychologically unready to take full advantage of changing conditions or improving opportunities that may develop in their lifetime" (Lewis, 1968:88). Like other cultural systems, such attitudes and values are presumed to be transmitted from one generation to another, and to the extent that they are also identified as the reason for the lives led by minorities, a cycle may seem to have been established. Conditions of poverty lead to the development of a distinctive subculture that makes adaptation to the demands of the dominant culture problematic. In turn, the subculture is passed on to the next generation, which dooms them to repeat the conditions of their parents' world.

The following are excerpts from the work of Edward Banfield, who contends that the urban poor are victims of the culture of poverty. In these quotes, notice that the description of the characteristics of the poor are direct opposites of the characteristics of the ideal, typical, middle-class American. They focus on work ethic, future-time orientation, concern for cleanliness and other suburban amenities, desire for predictability and control, and general upward mobility.

The lower-class individual lives from moment to moment. If he has any awareness of a future it is of something fixed, fated, beyond his control: things happen to him, he does not make them happen. Impulse governs his behavior, either because he cannot discipline himself to sacrifice a present for a future satisfaction or because he has no sense of the future. He is therefore radically improvident: whatever he cannot consume immediately he considers valueless. His bodily needs (especially for sex) and his taste for "action" take precedence over everything else—and certainly over any work routine. [1968:61.]

Blacks, then, supposedly have no future-time awareness, no sense of control or sense of the possibility of control over events, no control over impulses, nor ability to suppress those impulses in order to work. Notice especially that the stereotype of excessive sexuality, which in the nineteenth century was attributed to biological sources (with special attention to the measurement of sexual organs), is now attributed to the failure to develop the middle-class values of delayed gratification and the control of ones' animal impulses.

Although he has more leisure than almost anyone, the indifference ("apathy" if one prefers) of the lower-class person is such that he seldom makes even the simplest repairs to the place he lives in. He is not troubled by dirt and dilapidation and he does not mind the inadequacy of public facilities such as schools, parks, hospitals, and libraries; indeed, where such things exist he may destroy them by carelessness or even by vandalism. [1968:72.]

Banfield goes on and on like that, but there is no need to go on about lower-class characteristics except to note that Banfield actually claims that these people come to prefer the slum because it provides the things they love: excitement; action; opportunity for vice and illegal commodities such as drugs, sex, and theft; and protection from the police so that they may engage in their "normal" crimes, like beating their children and getting drunk. No more damning list of attributes could have been compiled by nineteenth-century scientists trying to explain away the slavery or degraded existence of American blacks.

Banfield consistently refers to class rather than to race distinctions. But given the particularly racial nature of the distribution of poverty in American cities (and given the similarity between his descriptions of lower classes and the list of stereotypes of blacks typical of American society), it is clear that this is an argument about the sources of racial deprivation. But the issue becomes even clearer in the work of Daniel Patrick Moynihan. Moynihan's 1965 report "The Negro Family: The Case For National Action" specifically rooted the problems suffered by American blacks in the black family structure. He argued that the family shapes the character of its children and that the black family is characterized by high rates of separation, divorce, illegitimacy, and absence of the father (matriarchy). The children of such families, provided with inadequate role models (the failed father) and typically dependent on relief and other services outside the family, become "so damaged by their family experience that they are unable to profit from educational and employment opportunities" (Ryan, 1971:64). Poorly equipped to take advantage of what scant opportunities exist, the child is presumed to have the seeds of his or her failure already planted in the developing character. The examples of this type of argument, that minority-group members acquire their inadequacies, are numerous. But we can easily summarize them by quoting one of the earliest and certainly one of the most articulate of their critics, William Ryan:

Doesn't the change from brutal ideas about the survival of the fit (and the expiration of the unfit) to kindly concern about characterological defects (brought about by stigmas of social origin) seem like a substantial step forward? Hardly. It is only a substitution of terms. In education, the outmoded and unacceptable concept of racial or class differences in basic inherited intellectual ability simply gives way to the new notion of cultural deprivation: there is very little functional difference between these two ideas. In taking a look at the phenomenon of poverty, the old concept of unfitness or idleness is replaced by the newfangled theory of the culture of poverty. In race relations, plain Negro inferiority—which was good enough for old-fashioned conservatives—is pushed aside by fancy conceits about the crumbling Negro family.... Mental illness is no longer defined as the result of hereditary taint or congenital character flaw; now we have new causal hypotheses regarding the ego-damaging emotional experiences that are supposed to be the inevitable consequence of the deplorable child-rearing practices of the poor. [1971:24–25.]

Apparently, by the twentieth century you did not have to be born inferior to arrive at that condition; there were ways to get there, or at least to be put there by interested others.

Age The theories and research that argued that blacks acquire inferior characteristics were developed during the mid twentieth century, partly out of embarrassment about the obviously biased work of nineteenth-century scientists. In addition, the very theory of inborn character in humans had been severely shaken by the development of an environmentalist school of thought in both psychology and sociology. The nature–nurture debate raged, but with respect to social policy and the creation of law, the environmentalist perspective was, at least temporarily, well ahead. But when the group concerned was the elderly, no such shift occurred. Age had long been considered a consequence of natural forces and continued to be seen as such right through the first half of this century. Therefore, the natural forces argument did not need to be replaced, but it was augmented by a sort of two-step theory about the way the elderly acquire some differentiating characteristics.

The first step of the argument is that natural forces do, indeed, make for physical and mental decline in the aged. The literature dealing with this area is vast. The second part of the argument, the acquired inferiority part, states that as a consequence of the inevitable declines brought on by natural processes (or as a consequence of their differential treatment by society), old people develop some secondary characteristics as well. These learned characteristics include various beliefs, values, and ways of living that distinguish the old from the rest of society. As with the subculture of the poor or the black subculture, such characteristics are often identified as contributing to the difficulties experienced by the elderly.

Two views within social gerontology, role theory (Phillips, 1957) and disengagement theory (Cumming and Henry, 1961), contend that the inevitability of decline in old age (especially focusing on illness and impending death) cause the elderly to focus on preparing for the events which face them. According to role theory, the primary preparation is for the individual to relinquish a large number of his or her previously held social roles, such as worker, homemaker, head of family and community, and independent person. Disengagement theory adds to this formula the contention that such role losses (disengagements) are mutually beneficial to both the individual who is disengaging and to the society that is compelling him or her to disengage. Common to both the role and disengagement theories is the belief that the elderly act differently from the rest of society because they need to adjust to different conditions in their lives.

The psychology of aging has also proposed that as we age, the focus of our energies and behavior change. Kuhlen (1968), for example, suggests that "anxiety and susceptibility to threat increase with the passage of time and that this circumstance tends to be the motivational source for many of the behavioral changes that occur with age" (p. 136). Similarly, Neugarten and others (1964) conclude that the behavior of the older person is likely to change because the personality, rather than motivational patterns, changes with age. They suggest that the internal components of the personality become increasingly important to us in old age, whereas the social-interactional components concerned with role performance, interaction, and social involvement decrease in importance. In each case, we would expect older people to behave differently from younger people in society and also to be treated differently as a consequence.

The closest parallel between blacks and the elderly, however, is between the culture of poverty idea and the theory of the subculture of the aged (e.g., Rose, 1965).[2] According to this view, the aged, excluded from interaction with the rest of the society and forced to face difficulties not encountered by others in society (or by themselves when they were younger), develop a subculture of the aged. They become a group whose beliefs and values are distinct from those of the larger society, a fact which marks them for differential treatment by the young, denying and diminishing their positions in many ways.

The same sort of subculture of the aged is also discussed in Riley's (1971) theory of age stratification (or Riley, Johnson, and Foner, 1972). As part of a larger theory in which the society is seen as stratified by age in much the same way as it is stratified by social class, the elderly are viewed as a stratum whose treatment is based on group or generational membership rather than on an individual basis. Due to this age-graded treatment, each stratum develops its own age-specific subculture as in Rose's conception. In either case, the subculture of the aged leads them to differ from the younger strata of society in terms of concern for the future, emphasis on health, acquisitiveness, attitudes toward marriage and death, and styles of life such as language, hobbies, leisure activities, and so on. These acquired, or cultural, characteristics contribute to the recognizability of the elderly, their exclusion from their mainstream memberships in the social order, and their isolation from the activities that would keep them fully involved, and influential, in society.

Sex As with the elderly, the lot of women has been attributed largely to biological inevitability. Men have been seen as different beings who are more powerful, analytical, dispassionate, competent, and, as such, able to assume certain tasks associated with control. Women, on the other hand, by virtue of their physiology—and especially the fact that they give birth—are seen as qualified only to be wives and mothers. But as early as Aristotle, the elements of a theory of acquired inferiority had been applied to the social condition of women. Aristotle argued that men were suited to the public or political world, with its emphasis on power and its demands on men to fulfill "stern . . . contaminating . . . demoralizing duties" (Elshtain, 1974). In contrast, women were excluded by nature from the political world and were limited to the domestic realm. Accordingly, women could attain only a level of moral goodness lower than that of men since Aristotle saw goodness as a condition of one who rules others and therefore only appropriate to the (man's) world of politics: "... all other persons need only possess moral goodness to the extent required of them (by their particular position)" (Barker, 1962:35).

Jean Elshtain (1974) points out that the modern legacy of this view can be seen in the argument that the domestic lives women lead make them different from men in a variety of ways and that this perspective shows up most surprisingly (and distressingly) in the arguments of the Suffragists during the second half of the nineteenth century. According to Elshtain, Suffragists argued that the votes of women would be more moral and uplifting to the affairs of state than those of men had been. Because they had been protected from the tainting, corrupting affairs of government and power, women were less violent, acquisitive, destructive, and so on, than men. In short, they were morally purer.

But as women's liberationists of the twentieth century have repeatedly noted, the attribution of superior sensitivity and morality to women can be as limiting, as damning in terms of social power and social opportunity, as the attribution of mental or other types of inferiorities (Freeman, 1973). When women are "put on a pedestal" or "in a gilded cage," they are supposedly being protected by men from the contamination of experiences in the world outside the home. Actually they are being protected from opportunity more than from destruction. Women's lovely (to men, that is) limitations are, under the right circumstances, as limiting as the grosser inferiorities attached to other minorities, such as blacks. But clearly, the minority-majority relationship between women and men requires subtle accommodations, given their intimate, day-to-day contact with one another. Blacks or the aged can be more easily segregated from whites or from younger people by housing patterns, for example.

Last, the process of socialization instills in women expectations of behavior appropriate to their role, just as it teaches the role of black or old person. Females are trained by their parents, and later by others, to develop those beliefs, values, and ways of behaving that will fulfill the expectations held for them by the larger society. A huge literature has developed that documents this process, from the very earliest expectation by parents that their female child will be prettier, quieter, and more docile (Rubin, Provenzano, and Luria, 1974), to the channeling of females into traditionally female educational tracks and traditionally female jobs (Schlossberg and Pietrofesa, 1973). Any college textbook on sex roles devotes at least one chapter to sex-role socialization and the reinforcement of those roles by mass media and other depictions of sex roles. One such text (Hoyenga and Hoynega, 1979) summarizes as follows the belief that characteristics associated with the female role in America are acquired by learning:

> Most of the answer to the question of why there are sex differences (at least in humans) must come from the culturally defined stereotypes that are imitated and incorporated by children differentially on the basis of their gender identities, the stereotypes that lead people to reinforce and evaluate behavior differentially based on gender. [Hoyenga and Hoyenga 1979:196.]

NOTES

1. We are suggesting three categories of explanation for accounting for the existence of minority groups in a society. The first contends that minorities exist because they are naturally, by inheritance inferior. The second claims that minority-group members acquire their inferiorities as a result of their experiences in the world, that faulty character is learned the way other traits are learned. The last view argues that the characteristics of minority-group members have nothing directly to do with the deprivations suffered by them but that such experiences are wholly the consequence of the treatment they experience at the hands of others (discrimination) and that prejudice is used to both justify and perpetuate that discrimination which benefits majority-group members. By focusing on three analytical categories, it may seem reasonable to conclude that they are in some way(s) equivalent. We wish to make it clear that they are not in two very important ways. First, they do not have anything like equivalent histories. The first view has been the dominant one for many centuries, probably since the first time that a question about dominance arose. As evidence, think of the consistent tendency of primitive tribes to define themselves as people and other alien groups as subhuman or animallike in the most negative sense. It was not until the beginning of the twentieth century that the concept of acquired characteristics

even became a possible view for the explanation of the deprivations of minority-group members. The third view, we believe, has not yet been taken seriously on a wide scale and so may be thought to have no history we could reliably trace. Second, we obviously do not treat these views as equally valid. We argue that the first two have been merely justifications for the continued discrimination against minorities and that the last is the best explanation as to why minorities have existed and continue to exist. This book is an attempt to show what functions discrimination and prejudice have in society.

2. It should be clearly understood that Rose's purpose in proposing this theory was to attack the forces that created the subculture of the aged, and its consequent effects, rather than to attack the subculture itself. In contrast, Banfield and others seemed more interested in changing the subcultural differences rather than the forces that created them. This issue will be more fully discussed in the section on victim blaming.

Chapter 2
An Alternative to Victim Blaming: Discrimination and Prejudice

Minority-Group Characteristics and Blaming the Victim

Whether it is argued that minority groups come to lead comparatively unpleasant lives because their inadequacies are inherited or learned, one critical assumption exists in both views. Each assumes that the difficulties experienced by minority-group members are due to their own failings. William Ryan (1971) has called this view *blaming the victim*.

Victim blaming is the tendency, when examining a social problem, to attribute that problem to the characteristics of the people who are its victims. In contrast, a non-victim-blaming perspective would focus on the social forces that deny opportunity to the victims of a social problem, while ignoring any apparent differences in them that might be caused by such treatment. But as we shall point out in more detail later, blaming the victim, as opposed to blaming the conditions of society that create victims, is a much neater and, to certain majority groups at least, less costly approach to the control and manipulation of social problems.

The biological inferiority theories clearly have blamed the victim, such as blacks, women, and the elderly for their own problems. Were they not, after all, just naturally inferior? There was a sort of shamelessness about people who excused, and even justified black slavery and poverty, believing blacks to be on an evolutionary scale more like apes than like "civilized" whites (well, white males anyway). In fact, even Ryan seems to give these people, whom he calls conservatives, a sort of begrudging admiration on the grounds that they were at least honest and not sneaky about their racism: "In race relations, plain Negro inferiority—which was good enough for old-fashioned conservatives is pushed aside by fancy conceits about the crumbling Negro family" (Ryan, 1971:24–25). Biological arguments have claimed that women are restricted to domestic lives because they are born to have babies and to provide nurturance for them and their husbands. Others continue to argue that the elderly should not work after a certain age or remain socially involved to the extent that younger people are because the forces of nature are inevitably draining them of their ability, or even desire, to do so. Such theories also blame the victim on biological grounds.

But the kind of victim blaming that drew the attention of William Ryan in the first place, was the type that focused on those supposedly acquired characteristics that we have been describing. According to Ryan, ideas such as the culture of poverty or the decay of the black family have allowed victim blamers to claim humanitarian concern while still rooting social problems in the characteristics of the minority-group members:

We are persuaded to ignore the obvious: the continued blatant discrimination against the Negro, the gross deprivation of contraceptive and adoption services to the poor, the heavy stresses endemic in the life of the poor. And almost all our make-believe liberal programs aimed at correcting our urban problems are off target; they are designed either to change the poor man or to cool him out." [Ryan, 1971:25.]

We blame women's poor performance in business on their *learned* passivity and lack of competitiveness. We attribute the dependence of the elderly to the *learned* beliefs and ways of life that isolate them from the rest of society. We simultaneously ignore the social structure of opportunity and its effects on blacks, the aged, and women. Ryan (1971) describes the system of blaming the victim as follows: "First, identify a social problem. Second, study those affected by the problem and discover in what ways they are different from the rest of us as a consequence of deprivation and injustice. Third, define the differences as the cause of the social problem itself. Finally, of course, assign a government bureaucrat to invent a humanitarian action program to correct the differences" (p. 8). So, blaming the victim is merely a matter of identifying those characteristics, real or imagined, that distinguish some individual from the rest of a population, and then proposing how the problem may result from them. In the example of the culture of poverty, it is primarily the lack of middle-class values that is presumed to keep the poor person from escaping the slums. Inability to delay gratification, lack of respect for the value of education, and lack of ambition presumably cause poverty, not discrimination. If only the proper characteristics could be instilled in the poor, they would obviously become successful and there would be no problem. So programs are designed to teach such values; disincentives to go on welfare are installed; and middle-class characteristics extolled, all in the absence of efforts to diminish the lack of opportunity that is really at the root of the problem. We deal with symptoms of inequality rather than with its sources.

Blaming the victim is a rationalization for those who seek to justify the status quo with respect to majority–minority relations. As noted by Armendáriz, the experiences of Mexican-Americans may be all too characteristic:

1. The representative of a large corporation in Corpus Christi argued that the reason why only eight of his 883 employees are Mexican-Americans has nothing at all to do with discrimination. He claims that he has not been able to locate qualified applicants.
2. A union official testified that the refusal of his trade council to accept applications for training under OEO programs from Mexican-American applicants does not constitute prejudice or discrimination. His

union requires a high school education and a special examination in order to qualify as a house painter.
3. A corporation personnel executive insisted that his Mexican-American employees are unqualified for promotion, yet the white Americans who receive the desired positions are actually less qualified than their Mexican-American counterparts in terms of education as well as other criteria.
4. A school administrator argued that the charge of illegal segregation in Mexican-American schools is due to the concentration of Mexican-Americans in certain school districts. He knows, of course, that a simple alteration in district boundaries would produce integrated schools. [Armendáriz, 1967.]

Exceptionalist Versus Universalistic Programs

Ryan has characterized the programs that blame the victim as *exceptionalist* and those that focus on social forces, such as the distribution of opportunity, as *universalistic:* "The exceptionalist viewpoint is reflected in arrangements that are private, voluntary, remedial, special, local and exclusive.... The problems are unusual, even unique, they are exceptions to the rule" (1971:16–17). Universalistic approaches are "... reflected in arrangements that are public, legislated, promotive or preventive, general, national, and inclusive" (p. 17).

Exceptionalist solutions to problems focus on the symptoms of the problem (the suffering of minorities and their characteristic differences from the rest of society) and ignore the social arrangements that created those conditions and characteristics in the first place:

Consider these two contrasting approaches as they are applied to the problem of smallpox. The medical care approach is exceptionalistic; it is designed to provide remedial treatment to the special category of persons who are afflicted with the disease through a private, voluntary arrangement with a local doctor. The universalistic public health approach is designed to provide preventive inoculation to the total population, ordered by legislation and available through public means if no private arrangements can be made. [Ryan, 1971:17.]

From Ryan's work, a number of comparisons between the two approaches become apparent:

Exceptionalistic	**Universalistic**
Oral surgery	Fluoridation
Abortion	Birth control
Lifeboat or rescue service	Compass or other navigational aid
Welfare and remedial programs designed to make up for unequal opportunities (e.g., remedial education, job training for the "hardcore" unemployed, welfare payments, public housing, and so on)	Legislation against unequal job, education, or other opportunities

Exceptionalist Programs

From Ryan's work it is possible to identify exceptionalist programs at two levels. The first is designed to "cool out" (Ryan, 1971:25) the minority-group member and, in extreme cases, to provide aids to survival. The second type of exceptionalist program is remedial, aimed at "fixing" those flaws in the minority-group member that block his or her successful membership in the majority group. Presumably it would be of little use to be claiming to rehabilitate someone while at the same time failing to try to keep him or her alive and able to work at those menial jobs, which, after all, still need to be done by someone.[1]

Exceptionalist programs that operate as *survival aids* include welfare programs of all kinds on which one can marginally survive; cash payments, provision of public housing, medical care, and so on belong in this category. For the elderly, all these are vital, in addition to home meals (meals on wheels), special transportation services such as senior buses, home nursing care, nursing homes, and medical discounts and medicaid.[2]

William Ryan's focus was primarily on those exceptionalist programs designed to "correct" the flaws of minority-group members that presumably were at the root of their difficulties. When flaws in minority-group members were attributed to natural forces, little could be done. Society merely felt responsible for protecting the unfortunates from the challenges of the everyday world for which they were unprepared. For blacks and women, this included, of course, the provision of manual and domestic tasks to which they were best suited and, for the elderly, the withdrawal of all instrumental tasks and positions of responsibility for which they were no longer suited.

But once the idea of acquired inferiority became widespread, it became possible to rehabilitate the victim, to fix the defects by which he or she was supposedly victimized. If blacks are poor because they are believed to lack an achievement motivation, or cannot delay gratification, then do something to instill such values. Prop up the black family so that it will no longer be "the fundamental weakness of the Negro community" (Moynihan, 1965:51) and will more successfully provide an appropriate male role model for its children. As an example of this approach, Ryan recalls the rash of lead paint poisonings of children which prompted a pharmaceutical manufacturer to launch an educational campaign designed to teach mothers the advisability of keeping children from eating lead paint chips and the irresponsibility of failing to do so. Apparently, the reason lead paint poisoning happened was that the mothers of such children lacked either the knowledge or the concern to prevent it. The universalistic alternative to this obviously exceptionalistic approach requires that the blame for the poisonings be placed where it belonged, with the landlords who painted with lead paint, failed to make repairs when the paint peeled (in spite of the legislation requiring them to do so), and with the agencies that failed to enforce those laws. Malcolm X, the Black Muslim leader, attacked this type of thinking in his metaphor of the black man whose legs were broken by whites, who was then brought to the starting line for a footrace against whites, and criticized for his inability to keep up. Supposedly, the exceptionalistic solution would have been to provide him with improved leg braces or a wheelchair. What would actually have done the job, of course, would have been a program that eliminated the discriminatory treatment in the first place.

Exceptionalistic programs aimed at correcting the "flaws" of old people and women work the same way. For the elderly, such programs include those aimed at socializing the elderly to their new status in society. One program teaches the old person how to adjust to institutional settings in which new "interpersonal skills" are required (Berger and Rose, 1977). The implication is that the cause of problems faced by old people who are institutionalized in nursing homes, for example, is their own inability to resocialize themselves rather than the social structure that requires that they be institutionalized. This sort of criticism applies to a whole range of programs aimed at preparing the aged for disengagement, retirement (including retirement-income planning), and so on. One service for the aged teaches them income management, how to get along on diminished income. It is as though malnutrition among the aged is due to their inability to be thrifty rather than to their inadequate incomes. (A substantial portion of the elderly are below the poverty line.) In addition, all the "keep busy" programs for the elderly are exceptionalistic to the extent that they attribute old people's feelings of uselessness to a growing self-involvement and a preference for sedentary pastimes. The alternative universalistic approach would acknowledge that the isolation and inactivity of the old are due primarily to the denial to the old of opportunities for active engagement in society. This is especially true in the occupational structure. Employers benefit from retirement regulations that allow them to predict the flow of labor demand and supply, control it, and thereby control one more element of labor costs.

For women, exceptionalistic programs aimed at fixing the "flaws" that supposedly contribute to their minority status are also common. One currently popular program provides "assertiveness training" to counteract the passive dependence presumed to be at the root of women's failures in, for example, the business world. The universalistic alternative? End sex discrimination in hiring, promotion, and the granting of raises. In fact, all the attempts to socialize women to the roles they are assigned are as exceptionalistic as the programs aimed at teaching black people or old people to get along in their assigned roles. And just as "keep busy" programs for the elderly, such as voluntary work (e.g., SCORE, service corps of retired executives), are exceptionalistic, so are similar programs aimed at placing women in volunteer-work positions.

Universalistic Approaches—Facing up to Discrimination and Prejudice

The problem with all these exceptionalistic approaches is that if the causes of minority status have nothing directly to do with the characteristics of minority-group members (whether inherited or learned), then exceptionalistic approaches leave the problems totally unsolved. They may be diminished temporarily, the symptoms momentarily held in check, but the underlying causes remain, certain to demand attention again and again. Exceptionalistic approaches are bottomless pits that absorb money and energy endlessly. So why do we bother and why have we not opted for universalistic alternatives?

Our tendency not to attack the roots of our most severe social problems results from our view of social problems and of how they are caused. Like any people, we believe quite strongly that the social order in which we live, our peculiar social arrangements for the accomplishment of our group objectives, provides a good way for going about the job. We generally have faith in our institutions: the structures of relationships and rules for behavior by which we deal with certain universal social issues, such as the distribution of power, procreation, care, socialization and education of the young, the production, consumption, and distribution of goods, and so on. Every society deals with these issues by different institutional arrangements, and each has faith in its own. In American society our institutions of family, or capitalism, or democracy are matters of national pride, just as the parallel institutions of other societies are valued by them. Therefore, it is reasonable that when disruptions to our social order occur, we would wish to believe that such problems are due to "external," nonsystemic forces. To the extent that we believe in and benefit from the social arrangements in which we live, we are reluctant to believe that the same social arrangements that are useful to the creation of our daily well-being are also somehow responsible for the difficulties suffered by some members of that same social order:

It is an expression of our belief in our social order to suggest that criminal behavior is the result of characteristics of the criminal rather than some facet of the legal or political system to which we belong, or to attribute the poverty of an individual to his or her characteristic lack of motivation or skills rather than to the inability of the educational or occupational structure to provide opportunities for wealth. [Levin and Levin, 1980:60.]

Blaming the victim and exceptionalistic approaches allow us to retain our faith in what is broadly referred to as "the system" by assuming that problems are due to special, or unusual deviations from its normalcy.

This approach to social problems can embrace people whose ideologies are often thought of as incompatible. If we define ideology as one's ideas as to the advisability of changing some existing social order, then a conservative is one who wishes the social structure to remain unchanged, and a liberal is one who wishes to retain the basic character of a social structure while making improvements in it. These improvements may range from very slight alterations (tinkering) to rather extensive changes, the limits of which are defined by one's view about the basic structure of the system in question. What conservatives and liberals have in common, then, is that they both believe in the basic structure of their social order (unlike radicals or reactionaries who wish to replace that order entirely). Victim blaming and exceptionalism allow the liberal to express faith in that system, while still pursuing the liberal goal of improvement. Only here, the improvement is in the character of the victim, not in the structure of the system.

Of course, the only time any of this becomes an issue is when something seems to have gone wrong. In the 1940s C. Wright Mills focused on the process whereby social problems are identified and to what forces they tend to be attributed. In his article entitled "The Professional Ideology of Social Pathologists," Mills revealed how social problems textbooks overwhelmingly assumed that social problems such as poverty, alcoholism, crime, and so on were aberrations or deviations from the essentially stable and desirable norms that comprise the dominant social order. The stability and appropriateness of the system was assumed and, therefore, unexamined: "The basis of stability, order, and solidarity is not typically analyzed in these books, but a conception of such a basis is implicitly used and sanctioned, some normative conception of a socially healthy and stable organization is involved in the determination of pathological conditions" (1943:174). When we blame the victims of social problems for their own difficulties we are protecting our belief that the essential order of things is stable and desirable. More important we are also denying the possibility that the same arrangement of human relationships that has benefited, and continues to benefit us and our friends, could simultaneously be causing suffering to others. Acknowledging such a possibility would be very unpleasant to say the least. For those of us who feel some uneasiness about the problems others experience, the possibility that our own comforts, opportunities, and stability was being bought at the expense of others would create great dissonance in us. Victim blaming makes possible the accommodation between our humanitarian concern for the suffering of minority groups (and our desire to feel that we are doing something about it) and our desire to continue to benefit from the social structure in which we live. The main aim of this book is to demonstrate how the structure of American society, and especially certain segments of the society, depend on and benefit from the persistence of discrimination against minorities and the prejudice that justifies and perpetuates it. We do, in fact, enjoy certain benefits at the expense of others, and it should be made clear that we do. We must face up to the functions of discrimination and prejudice.

Our third explanation of the conditions of minorities, which takes the place of natural inferiority and acquired inferiority explanations, should now be that minority groups are created by the discrimination directed against them. Thus the characteristics of minority-group members have nothing directly to do with the creation of minority groups. Concern for them should be seen as evidence of our prejudice, which is, itself, merely an excuse for discrimination, as it has always been. With this perspective we should blame the social forces that surround blacks, women, and the elderly (as well as other minority groups) rather than blame the members of these groups. To understand how discrimination and prejudice function within the larger social structure we will examine these concepts more closely.

Discrimination

Discrimination can be defined as differential or unequal treatment of the members of some group or category on the basis of their group membership rather than on the basis of their individual qualities. One example is the automatic exclusion of a woman from a job because she is presumed to be incompetent by virtue of being female. It is, of course, possible to deny someone a job or promotion without discriminating against them. All that is necessary is that an individual evaluation be made of that person's qualifications for a position, or for advancement, or for any other valued "good." Discrimination is the expression of a system of social relations, not an isolated individual behavior (Antonousky, 1960). Decisions based on group membership unaccompanied by knowledge of the individuals' characteristics or activities inevitably lead to either preferential treatment of people belonging to one's own group (favoritism as a sort of "positive prejudice") or discrimination against people who belong to out-groups (that negative treatment to which we will always refer as discrimination).

Clearly, in order to be able to discriminate against a group, one must not only be able to recognize group differences (in the sense of the more benign meaning of the word "discriminate," as in a "discriminating shopper" or "discriminating palate"), but one must also be in a position to distribute (or deny) rewards or to distribute (or withhold) punishments. These abilities are the measures of one's power. Control over the resources of a society, such as jobs, promotions, access to legal protection or advocacy, the creation of legal barriers or opportunities via the legislative process, or even the control over the process whereby value is attached to activities, beliefs, and so on, is the material of social power. To the extent that a person or a group has superior control over such elements of society, he or she can influence or control the destinies of others, even against their will. They can solidify their control over these goods by limiting the access of others to them and making sure that those who do have access share beliefs about who should benefit and who should not.

Power is not a quality of people but of the structure of relations between people. We have a tendency to speak of powerful people, but really what we should focus on are the situations in which one person, or a group of people, have power at their command. The tendency to see power as a quality of people is due to the frequency with which power stays with certain individuals over time—once they have it in their control they can, and usually do, make sure that it stays with them—and the frequency with which power is passed along to the people chosen by the powerful as their inheritors. What they inherit is a position from which to wield power, not the quality of power itself. Its very transferability suggests that power is not a quality of individual character. Majority–minority relations provide a clear example of the role of power in the establishment of stable relations between groups.

Katznelson (1973) has put minority–majority group relations (especially racial issues) firmly in the context of power:

Power involves the capacity to make and carry out decisions. John Champlin has defined power as "being in a position to get others to do what one wants without having to make unacceptable sacrifices."[3]

Power, then, is relational. It is positional also, in that it depends on an individual or group's structural position in relation to others. Thus, for Gerth and Mills, the political order "consists of those institutions with which men acquire, wield, or influence distributions of power."[4] [1973:21.]

The raw materials of power and their medium of exchange are the assets a group controls:

These assets or resources include money and status, but the most important political assets are positional. Thus, inevitably, there will be conflict between individuals and groups attempting to obtain the institutional positions which confer legitimate rights to make and carry out decisions (the number of such positions being limited, and as such being a scarce resource). [Katznelson, 1973:22.]

When we control legitimate access to the scarce resources of society, we control the very definition of who is to dominate.

In American society we value a variety of types of resources. What sort of job does a person hold? How much does it pay, with what extra benefits and with what level of security? What is the quality of the house one lives in? What level and what quality of education has a person enjoyed? What sort of access to political and legal processes does he or she have? How good are the health and social services to which a person has access. All these "goods" combine to define one's position in the hierarchy of the society. Discrimination systematically limits groups or categories of Americans from equal opportunities to gain any or all of these.

We have a great deal of documentation of the existence of discrimination in America. Numerous government investigations and countless studies by academics and concerned organizations like the NAACP (National Association for the Advancement of Colored People), the National Organization for Women, and the Anti-Defamation League have supplied the evidence that discrimination has existed and continues to exist here.

One good example of a brief summary of discrimination against blacks and women is Feagin and Feagin's *Discrimination American Style* (1978). In it the authors illustrate how discrimination is applied by a variety of institutional mechanisms. For example, in the area of occupations, institutions control recruitment, screen job applicants, promote and "track" employees into controlled internal job markets, manipulate pay and other conditions of employment and use seniority policies to selectively control the effects of layoffs. In housing, institutions control the availability of insurance and money for mortgages and home improvements. For example, they show how banks use the policy of "redlining" to outline on maps the areas of a city which they consider to be inhabited by bad credit risk populations. Since blacks generally live in these areas they can't borrow money to improve their homes, and their neighborhoods tend to remain run down. The control over access to these and other valued resources is almost exclusively in the hands of institutions.

Individual Versus Institutional Discrimination

The distinction between individual and institutional discrimination was made clear in Carmichael and Hamilton's (1967) now famous formulation:

Racism is both overt and covert. It take two, closely related forms: individual whites acting against individual blacks, and acts by the total white community against the black community. We call these individual racism and institutional racism. The first consists of overt acts by individuals, which cause death, injury or the violent destruction of property. This type can be recorded by television cameras; it can frequently be observed in the process of commission. The second type is less overt, far more subtle, less identifiable in terms of *specific* individuals committing the acts. But it is no less destructive of human life. The second type originates in the operation of established and respected forces in the society, and thus receives far less public condemnation than the first type. (1967:4.)

To make the distinction even more concrete, consider the following illustration. "The murder by KKK members and law enforcement officials of three civil rights workers in Mississippi was an act of individual racism. That the sovereign state of Mississippi refused to indict the killers was institutional racism. The individual act by racist bigots went unpunished in Mississippi because of policies, precedents, and practices that are an integral part of that state's legal institutions." (Knowles and Prewitt, 1969:4). Individual discrimination is simply the expression of one person's hatred of another person because of his or her group membership. The discriminator commits overt acts against the target, ranging from murder to less obvious, less extreme forms of discrimination, such as the denial of promotions or raises. In contrast, institutional discrimination allows or causes opportunity to be distributed unequally to various groups in two ways. The first form is the "institutional extension of individual racist beliefs; this consists primarily of using and manipulating duly constituted institutions so as to maintain a racist advantage over others" (Jones, 1972:6). The second way is as a consequence of society's rules and structural arrangements, although those arrangements may appear to have no specific group of people as a target.

As an example of the first form of institutional racism, think of the bigoted election official who wishes to exclude blacks from voting. He merely uses his knowledge that blacks have been denied the opportunity to learn how to read well, then invokes existing literacy requirements against blacks who wish to vote. What purports to be a qualification aimed at screening voters on the impartial grounds of intellectual merit, is used to systematically and intentionally exclude blacks from voting. Residency requirements and poll taxes have had the same effect. For women and the elderly, physical tests for employment as police have been used by bigoted officials in this way (United States Commission on Civil Rights, 1980). Thus, institutional rules become mechanisms for the expression of individual hatreds. If law enforcement officials murder civil rights leaders with no official pretext at all, it is purely individual racism. But if they do so as representatives of the law, on the pretext that some law had been broken, it is an example of this form of institutional racism.

The second form of institutional discrimination, and the more difficult to recognize, stems from more broadly held, apparently group-free, beliefs. One example is the belief that school grades, verbal skills (as they appear in middle-class society), and the results of standardized tests are the best evidence of a person's ability to become a physician or lawyer. As a consequence, because blacks have been systematically excluded from the type of experiences that would develop these characteristics, the use of these criteria for entry into medical or law school is tantamount to the exclusion of blacks from them. One need not say "no blacks need apply" in order to accomplish that same end; one need only take the Graduate Record Exam and college grades seriously.

According to the United States Commission on Civil Rights, such institutional rules may appear to be "color blind" or "gender neutral," but they actually discriminate specifically against minority groups. Their report on these practices lists the following examples:

Height and weight requirements that are unnecessarily geared to the physical proportions of white males and, therefore, exclude females and some minorities from certain jobs.

Seniority rules, when applied to jobs historically held only by white males, make more recently hired minorities and females more subject to layoff—the "last hired, first fired" employee—and less eligible for advancement.

Nepotistic membership policies of some referral unions that exclude those who are not relatives of members who, because of past employment practices, are usually white.

Restrictive employment leave policies, coupled with prohibitions on part-time work or denials of fringe benefits to part-time workers, that make it difficult for the heads of single parent families, most of whom are women, to get and keep jobs and meet the needs of their families.

The use of standardized academic tests or criteria, geared to the cultural and educational norms of the middle-class or white males, that are not relevant indicators of successful job performance.

Preferences shown by many law and medical schools in the admission of children of wealthy and influential alumni, nearly all of whom are white.

Credit policies of banks and lending institutions that prevent the granting of mortgage monies and loans in minority neighborhoods, or prevent the granting of credit to married women and others who have previously been denied the opportunity to build good credit histories in their own names. (1980:11.)

Given the extremely wide range of organizations that are in control of the distribution of valued resources, the job of documenting the forms of institutional discrimination would be vast. There are so many varieties of reward and punishment, so many mechanisms for their application, so many consequences, and so many other dimensions to institutional discrimination that we cannot discuss them all. Here, quite briefly, are some of the dimensions of this form of discrimination.

Distribution of Advantages and Disadvantages

A dominant group can choose to provide advantages to those it favors when hiring; promoting; providing raises, memberships, or opportunities to borrow money or to invest in business ventures; sharing special privileged information; and so on. To the extent that the rewards of a society are in limited supply, preferential treatment of members of one's own group automatically denies opportunities to members of other groups without actually having to do anything else. However, negative or harmful treatment of outgroups can be practiced in a number of ways. They can be paid less for the same work as others, fired first when layoffs become advantageous, policed more closely, arrested and convicted more readily, and sentenced more harshly. In American history the imposition of Jim Crow segregation laws has subjected blacks to extreme humiliation and suffering, and we are now becoming increasingly aware of the sexual harrassment that women have had to experience, especially in the workplace, as the issue is more publicly discussed and litigation pursued. Also, the legalized, forced retirement of the elderly has subjected them to severe decreases in their level of income and, therefore, in their standard of living and level of independence. These are examples of actively harmful treatment of these minority groups, often formalized in law or delivered in institutional settings. In addition, individuals and members of hate groups have otherwise harrassed minority-group members on a daily basis by insults, threats, and even direct attacks, such as assaults against women (for which there has been the separate, and partially legitimized, category of wife-beating) and rape. The elderly continue to suffer a disproportionate amount of crime, which is directed against them especially because of their lack of mobility, dependence on public support, and inability to protect themselves. Blacks have traditionally been the targets of hate groups such as the Ku Klux Klan, which to this day have terrorized blacks and even engaged in organized murder campaigns. Sometimes such behavior (like hiring or firing) is clearly categorizable in terms of advantages and disadvantages. But another issue in this dimension of minority-group treatment is the motives of the groups that distribute such treatment. Perhaps a group of people are institutionalized (as in public housing, hospitals, nursing homes, or even prisons) or in some other way treated negatively primarily as a consequence of their perceived characteristics and "need" for such treatment. It would be unfair to characterize this as the *intentional* distribution of disadvantages because the motive of the majority group might be, for example, either self-protection (as in locking criminals away or removing the elderly from jobs so they do no harm to the efficiency of a business) or exceptionalist humanitarianism (as in rehabilitating or removing the competitive pressures from the lives of the aging). The consequences for the minority-group member, however, are the same, whatever the intentions of the discriminators. When such treatment is the direct outgrowth of hate, however, we should call it what it is—behavior intended to harm or place barriers in the way of minority-group acceptance or mobility.

Action-Inaction, Rule Making and Rule Enforcement

Whether one is discriminating by distribution of advantages or disadvantages, and whether one's intention is benign or malevolent, it is still possible to choose action or inaction as the mechanism of discrimination. So far we have focused on the active distribution of advantages to one's friends and of disadvantages to others. But discrimination is just as effectively delivered by failing to make opportunities available to minorities, or failing to place legitimate barriers before one's friends, or failing to punish them for transgressions (for example, the relatively rare prosecution of white-collar crime). "Nondecision-making, we should note, is as much a form of action as decision-making ..." (Katznelson, 1973:23). This is essentially a matter of keeping some issue off an agenda for action. In this context non-decision-making may be seen as "a means by which demands for change in the existing allocation of benefits and privileges in the community can be suffocated before they are even voiced; or kept covert; or killed before they gain access to the relevant decision-making arena; or, failing all these things, maimed or destroyed in the decision-implementing stage of the policy process" (Bachrach and Baratz, 1970:44). If we fail to take action to halt discrimination or redress the grievances of minorities, we are acting against them, especially to the extent that we purport to have an impartial system of justice.

In a competitive society in which success is often dependent on help from influential friends, in addition to competent effort from the individual, the denial of such encouragement or aid is tantamount to a sentence of failure. It is, in fact, a form of discrimination. Freeman reports how this type of discrimination operates against women in graduate school. Male professors fail to encourage female students while providing help for their male counterparts. "In many ways this environment of subtle discouragement by neglect is more pernicious than a strongly negative one would be.... Everyone needs 'strokes'; and although good strokes are better than bad strokes, bad strokes are better than none" (Freeman 1979:231). Freeman contends that when barriers to success are clear, a woman (or other minority-group member for that matter) has something concrete against which to struggle, something that aids in the marshaling of ones energies: " ... Overt opposition is preferable to motivational malnutrition" (p. 231).

The same sort of problem faces the elderly in America, for whom the lack of goals is an oppressive daily weight that pushes them further and further into isolation and boredom. Burgess (1960) refers to this aspect of the position of the elderly as a "roleless role." Our ability to operate in social situations depends on our having clear and positive expectations for how we are supposed to act. The elderly are provided with no clear positive expectations and so are, like women, at a great disadvantage in competing with majority-group members for opportunities in social structures.

Rule Making–Rule Enforcement Another element of the dimension of action and inaction is the extent to which discrimination (whether positive or negative) is applied by the making or the enforcing of rules. Rule making can be accomplished by judicial, legislative, or executive bodies. The most far-reaching source of rule making is the Supreme Court, whose landmark decisions shape the distribution of opportunity (and the lack of it) for decades or even centuries. In the Dred Scott decision, slaves were deemed to be property that could not be taken from an owner by claims that blacks were humans who were protected by the argument that all men were equal. In the 1896 decision of *Plessy* v. *Ferguson* the court decided that separate but equal facilities for blacks and whites did not violate the equal protection clause of the Fourteenth Amendment of the Constitution. By 1954, when the Supreme Court ordered desegregation of some school systems (with others to be dealt with some years later under an expanded definition of segregation), the shape of the opportunities afforded to blacks had been largely the consequence of the decisions of the court. But when the *Brown* v. *Board of Education of Topeka* decision seemed to threaten to open education to many more blacks, the role of other rule-making bodies became apparent. State legislatures (especially in the South) and school boards acted to thwart the intentions of the court. For the next 10 years in the South (and for 20 in the North), the Brown decision had little effect on school segregation. Decisions like Griffin (1964), Green (1968), Alexander (1969), and Swann (1971) showed the impatience of the court with the slow pace of desegregation. Even the passage of the 1964 Civil Rights Act with its Title VI support for school desegregation was thwarted. The Office for Civil Rights (OCR) in the Department of Health, Education, and Welfare (HEW) in the executive branch of the government was given the responsibility for the enforcement of Title VI. Here, the rule of selective enforcement becomes clear. Unsympathetic with the aims of the legislation, Richard Nixon's administration stood in the way of enforcement efforts by his own department of HEW, encouraging obstruction at the state and local levels (Rogers, 1975). Rules, then, can be written that either create or diminish opportunity for selected groups, and rules can be selectively enforced so as to remove barriers to opportunity or to apply them. See Table 2.1 for a brief illustration of the relationship between the rule-making versus enforcement and the advantage–disadvantage dimensions of discrimination.

Severity of Discrimination

Recorded history is replete with examples of discrimination—instances of actual behavior ranging from the petty indignities of everyday interaction to acts of physical violence and slavery, many of which were perpetrated on a massive scale over the course of centuries. The severity of discrimination can vary from quite mild sorts of disadvantages, such as the inability to advance through an organizational hierarchy as quickly as one would like, to the kind of discrimination that can kill. The life-threatening, or murderous, kinds of discrimination that almost wiped out the native American—and that continue to result in exceptionally high levels of poverty, suicide, alcoholism, and tuberculosis rates among those remaining—make their plight especially urgent. The severity of the deprivations that a minority group suffers depends on the needs and capabilities of the dominant group to distribute advantages and disadvantages. When brutal means of control are possible and, in the opinion of those in control, necessary, then mass herding of populations from one place to another, legislative denial of property or other contractual rights, and other severe forms of discrimination (including genocide in some cases) may result. But less life-threatening forms of discrimination are more common. The denial of the opportunity for a quality education is likely to influence a person's earning and productive potential. It will probably not kill him or her. But even though some forms of discrimination are more directly harmful to individuals than others, they are still extremely important, especially when their cumulative effects are calculated. For example, if the diminution of the productive capacity of women in America, as a consequence of the denial of opportunity to them, were to be multiplied by the number of women in the country, the cumulative effect of such discrimination would be staggering. The

Table 2.1 How the Selective Creation and Enforcement of Rules Can Influence Opportunity

	Enhances Opportunity	Diminishes Opportunity
Rules selectively made	Costs of business deductible but not costs of laborer Tax incentives and loopholes for higher-income individuals and business only	Redlining by banks, which eliminates many blacks from loan potential; Poll taxes Laws disqualifying women from jobs because of physical size or strength Laws permitting mandatory retirement at a given age
Rules selectively enforced	Rules that determine what will be considered qualification for jobs or entry to college, emphasizing the skills gained by middle-class experiences such as those that expensive school systems provide Failure to adequately pursue white-collar crime	Literacy requirements for voting selectively applied Relatively strict (in contrast to white-collar crime) enforcement of laws against typically lower-class crimes (e.g., arrest prostitutes but not customers, focus on cheating by welfare recipients but not by contractors, etc.)

same is true for the combined effect of the denial of opportunity that the elderly experience. As a consequence of mandatory retirement and other social pressures, older Americans often become disengaged from their utilitarian roles and increasingly isolated. So, even beyond the individual severity of discrimination, is the issue of individual versus cumulative group consequences of the denial of opportunity.

Mechanism of Control / Discrimination

Dominant groups or individuals have at their disposal a wide variety of methods for the application of their power over others. Depending on their objectives, feelings of responsibility for the condition of the dominated groups (or their perceived need to hide the fact that they are in control), or the relative costs of using one as opposed to another form of domination, any of the mechanisms of control may be selected. (Refer to Box 2.1.)

Imagine yourself to be in a position of power; that is, you can control or influence the condition of others, even against their will. You can choose to physically force another person to do your bidding, perhaps by putting him or her in chains, jail, uniform (with a gun pointed at him or her as well), or so on. These are, perhaps, rather primitive sounding but, under the right conditions, quite effective. At the other extreme, you might be able to convince the person over whom you have this control that he or she has no other choice than to do your bidding. At that point, the lack of alternatives for the dominated person, the elimination of which alternatives could only be accomplished by a powerful person or group, results in the same benefit for the dominant individual as the actual physical manipulation of the victim—effective again, but perhaps quite costly to accomplish. Probably most effective of all, and also least obvious, would be to convince the minority-group member that to do your bidding would be in his or her own best interests. Perhaps you could even manage to convince that same person that what he or she was doing was actually costly to you but that you either would not interfere or could do nothing about it. The ultimate in sophisticated control is the ability to get others to do your work without having to pay for policing of the dominated, espe-

An Alternative to Victim Blaming: Discrimination and Prejudice

cially likely if he or she is unaware that you are benefiting. How can this be accomplished?

Charles Lindblom provides one possible answer:

> Because it is rewarding to be perceived as a member of the favored class and thus to enjoy its benefits, powerful incentives exist in society to conform to visible characteristics of that class. Among these characteristics are the politico-economic beliefs, attitudes, and volitions of that class and, more particularly, of those members of that class who have the most benefits to offer. They are beliefs in private enterprise, private property, corporate autonomy, and opportunities for great wealth. [Lindblom, 1977:226.]

BOX 2.1

One Typology for the Exercise of Power

It is possible to conceive of a range of mechanisms for the exertion of control over another that fit somewhere between direct physical control on the one hand and control over the beliefs and values of the dominated individual on the other. For example, Bachrach and Baratz (1970) have developed a typology of power that describes the following possibilities:

Coercion I (dominant) get you (subordinate) to do what I want, even though you do not want to do it, by threatening to deprive you of something you want, over which I have control. I might even threaten to harm you physically.

Influence I get you to change your course of actions in line with what I want "without resorting to either a tacit or an overt threat of severe deprivation" (30).

Authority You do what I want because you agree with me that it is a reasonable thing to do, that it is in both of our best interests. This is where the socialization process applies.

Force I get you to do what I want because I make it the only choice you have. Of course, there are a variety of ways for me to accomplish this, ranging from control of the actual availability of alternative courses, to the control of your physical ability to choose other actions.

Manipulation I get you to do what I want, and you never come to realize that I have gotten you to do it.

The primary mechanism for the social control, and motivation of those on whose labor the economic structure depends, is their belief in the possibility that their efforts will be rewarded by upward mobility. They, in fact, have been convinced that just that has happened for those at the top of the hierarchy and that this is also the path for them. That it is probably not true does not diminish their degree of compliance. If minority-group members can be socialized to believe that they belong in their positions of inferiority, then the problems of control diminish greatly. To the extent that women believe that they are best suited to domestic work, they will not agitate to enter the world of paid career work. To the extent that blacks are convinced that they are unsuited to work in the professions, or are naturally lazy, they will not bring suits for equal opportunities in education or the professions. To the extent that the elderly can be socialized to old age, that is, to come to believe that old age is a time of inevitable decline during which they should disengage from their involvements with the occupational and social worlds, they too will fail to compete for the opportunities we value.

If we use Champlin's definition of power as "being in a position to get others to do what one wants without having to make unacceptable sacrifices" (Champlin, 1970:94), then the issue of the cost of any specific mode of control becomes critical. Clearly, it is less costly to the dominant group if control is exerted through the belief (or normative) structure because, having internalized the goals of the dominant culture, subordinate individuals essentially motivate and police themselves. By contrast, the maintenance of external, physical forces—such as police, courts, prisons, systems for the assessment and collection of fines—are very costly to the dominant group. To the extent that these tangible mechanisms are necessary to make threats believable, or to reinforce the beliefs that socialization instills, they are necessary for even a sophisticated system of control. But as the primary line of control, they are both costly and crude.

To some extent, it can be argued that the arrangements that make this form of institutionalized discrimination possible make it necessary for anyone operating within it to actually be a bigot, that is, to be prejudiced. Persistent discrimination by an individual requires that the discriminator be prejudiced. So does the form of institutionalized discrimination in which a prejudiced person uses his or her knowledge of the operation of institutions to express that prejudice. But in order to fully understand how these processes work, it will be necessary to examine the concept of prejudice itself.

Prejudice
Prejudice as an Attitude: The Psychological View

In its original usage, the word "prejudice" referred to a "prejudgment," or an evaluation or decision made before the facts of a case could be properly determined and weighed. This usage was subsequently broadened to include "any unreasonable attitude that is unusually resistant to rational influence" (Rosnow, 1972:53). Thus, an individual who stubbornly committed himself to a position in the face of overwhelming evidence to the contrary could be characterized as prejudiced, whether that position was taken with regard to his children, his politics, his religious convictions, or his friends. Such a broad concept of prejudice may be useful in everyday conversation because it draws our attention to the unfortunate tendency for individuals to jump to conclusions and to make dogmatic judgments, but for our purposes we must assign a more limited meaning.

So that prejudice can be examined within a single, overarching, theoretical framework, we begin by defining it as *interpersonal hostility that is directed against individuals based on their membership in a minority group.* Using this definition of prejudice, we can from the outset exclude the following kinds of phenomena from the purview of our analysis:

1. Prejudices not directed against human beings (e.g., prejudgments about animals, cars, and houses).
2. Preferences in interpersonal relations not based on group membership (e.g., a situation in which two individuals cannot get along because each tries to dominate the relationship).

Our concept of prejudice is meant to focus our attention throughout this analysis squarely on negative feelings or beliefs that are targeted against human beings by virtue of the status they occupy, or are perceived to occupy, as members of a minority group.[5] It is in this more restricted sense that prejudice, especially to the extent that it is related to actual discrimination, has come to be regarded by social scientists as a troublesome and costly phenomenon. The nature of prejudice can be examined in part at the level of individual attitudes. Individuals hold favorable and unfavorable attitudes that serve to orient them toward the myriad persons, objects, and concepts in their lives, such as their parents, friends, nation, and religion. From a psychological perspective, prejudice can be regarded as a negative attitude toward the members of a minority group (Ehrlich, 1972; Kramer, 1949). As such, prejudice is a learned disposition consisting of the following components or dimensions: (1) negative beliefs or stereotypes (cognitive component), (2) negative feelings or emotions (affective component).

Negative Beliefs or Stereotypes In the words of Walter Lippmann (1922:1), stereotypes are "pictures in our heads," beliefs that we hold regarding the members of a category. In this context, we are specifically concerned with beliefs or stereotypes that have become associated with various categories of minority groups. Often such stereotypes are overgeneralized to an extent that no members of the minority can avoid inclusion: All blacks are lazy; all Mexican-Americans are treacherous; all Jews are mercenary; all Puerto Ricans are dirty, all Chinese are sly; all Turks are cruel; all women are emotional; all old people are forgetful and incompetent.

Frequently, however, the prejudiced individual may have to treat contrary evidence—instances that do not fit his or her stereotype—as exceptions to the rule. Bettelheim and Janowitz report the following beliefs about Jewish soldiers as expressed by an especially prejudiced veteran of World War II:

They shirk their duty, they're no combat men. Some will fight, I'll give them that credit, but most of them are out for themselves. If he has a chance to save himself, he'll save himself. A Jew will never give you nothing for nothing either. (But) I've found a couple of good Jews, like in any nationality, but only a few. [1964:139.]

Traits admired or revered in the members of an in-group may be regarded as deplorable when ascribed to out-group members. As Allport observed, Abraham Lincoln was seen as "thrifty, hard-working, eager for knowledge, ambitious, devoted to the rights of the average man, and eminently successful in climbing the ladder of opportunity," whereas Jews are viewed as "tight-fisted, over-ambitious, pushing and radical" (1954:189). In a similar way, anti-Semitic veterans have described effective combat behavior as "courageous" if carried out by non-Jewish soldiers, but "bloodthirsty" if the same behavior had been carried out by Jewish soldiers (Bettelheim and Janowitz, 1964:139). "It is similar with women: an ambitious and assertive man is admired by all. The same traits in a woman are viewed less positively: she is aggressive rather than assertive, and castrating rather than ambitious (Frieze, 1978:280).

Stereotyping frequently contains an element of projection, whereby negative characteristics of the prejudiced individual become associated with the members of a minority. For example, Anglo-Americans have been known to project onto Mexican-Americans the very attributes that they themselves had exemplified in the conquest of Mexicans and their land. Mexicans were regarded as natural-born thieves who indiscriminately stole livestock from white settlers, yet white cattle barons were noted for stealing livestock from powerless border Mexicans. Mexicans were also widely regarded as treacherous and cruel (attributable in part to their "Indian blood"); yet the Texas Rangers, lynch mobs, the U.S. Army, white sheriffs, and drunken cowhands often murdered innocent Mexicans without fear of punishment (Jacobs and Landau, 1971).

What are the stereotypes about minority groups that traditionally have been held by members of American society? In a pioneering study of ethnic stereotypes, Katz and Braly (1933) sought to provide a partial answer by investigating the characteristics ascribed by 100 Princeton undergraduates to various racial and ethnic groups. Their findings indicated a high level—sometimes reaching 75 percent—of agreement among the Princeton students that:

Jews are "shrewd," "mercenary," and "industrious."
Blacks are "superstitious," "lazy," and "happy-go-lucky."
Turks are "cruel," "very religious," and "treacherous."
Chinese are "superstitious," "sly," and "conservative."
Italians are "artistic," "impulsive," and "passionate."
Irish are "pugnacious," "quick tempered," and "witty."

But Bettelheim and Janowitz, in their study of 150 World War II veterans, similarly found much consensus that Jews "have the money," "run the country," "use underhanded business methods," and are "clannish," whereas blacks "depreciate property" are "dirty," and "lazy" (1964:141–142).

Widely shared stereotypes about America's ethnic groups have found their way into the mass communication messages of our society (see Box 2.2). As early as 1946, Berelson and Salter analyzed the characters in popular magazine fiction to find stereotypical portrayals for virtually every minority and foreign group in their fictional population. The following are only a few examples of the stereotyped treatment found in this sample of stories:

The Italian Gangster. Louie di Paolo, an amiable racketeer with a debt of loyalty to an heiress, furnishes her with money and a kidnapping so that she can get her own way with a young man. Louie is "a sinister-looking individual with a white scar over one eye . . . known as Blackie, Two Rod, and Smart 'Em Up in various police precincts, and among the underworld citizenry. . . ." Says he: "'Beer was my racket. I made my pile and been layin' low ever since. If you want twenty-five G's, all I got to do is stick up my own safe-deposit box.'" He drives "a coupe with bulletproof glass and a specially built steel body, ready for anything."

The Sly and Shrewd Jew. Jew Jake, manager of a troop of barnstorming stunt flyers, shows greater concern for money than for the safety of his employees. He has an "ungainly and corpulent figure," and he rubs his hands "in a familiar and excited gesture." In answer to his question, "'Maybe you'd like to make five bucks easy?'" the hero says: "'Jake, you would not put out five bucks for anything less than a suicide.'" Another character says: "'You ought to know the way Jake is. He'd like it better if I did not pull it (the parachute cord) at all. It would give the customers a thrill.'"

The Emotional Irish. Ellen, an Irish cook is overwhelmed by her first sight of the new baby: "Ellen—who, being a Celt, was easily moved—flew out of the kitchen, saw a fraction of David's face, and burst into a flood of tears."

The Primitive and "Backward" Pole. A Polish-American girl thinks of escape from her national community: "I began to despise our way of life. . . . The American men did not value a wife who could work all day on her knees at his side, taking only a day or two off to bear a child.

BOX 2.2

Mass Media Advertisements that Portray Anti-Mexican Stereotypes

Advertiser	Content of Ad	The Message
Granny Goose	Fat Mexican has guns, ammunition.	Mexicans are overweight and carry weapons.
Frito-Lay	"Frito-Bandito"	Mexicans are sneaky thieves.
Liggett & Meyers	"Paco" never "feenishes" anything, not even revolution.	Mexicans are too lazy to improve themselves.
A. J. Reynolds	Mexican bandit.	Mexicans are thieves.
Camel Cigarettes	"Typical" Mexican village, all asleep or bored.	Mexicans are do-nothings and irresponsible people.
General Motors	White man holds Mexicans at gunpoint.	Mexicans should be arrested by superior white men.
Lark	Mexican house painter is covered with paint.	Mexicans are sloppy workers.
Philco-Ford	Mexican is sleeping by a TV set.	Mexicans are always sleeping.
Frigidaire	Mexican banditos are interested in a freezer.	Mexicans are thieves who want Anglo artifacts.
Arrid	While Mexican sprays underarm, voice says, "If it works for him, it will work for you."	Mexicans stink more.

Source: Adapted from Thomas M. Martinez. 1969 "Advertising and Racism: The Case of the Mexican-American." *El Grito* (Summer):27.

They love the weakness, not the strength in their women; love the job of looking after and supporting them." [1946:180.]

Likewise, stereotyped descriptions of minority Americans have been found in television programs (Smythe, 1954), magazine pictures (Shuey, 1953), textbooks (Cole and Wiese, 1954), motion pictures (McManus and Kronenberger, 1946), newspapers (Simpson and Yinger, 1972), and comic strips (Spielgelman, Terwilliger, and Fearing, 1953).

In 1975 a survey of Americans' attitudes toward "most people over 65" reported that they were seen as not very open-minded and adaptable, not very sexually active, not very useful members of their community, not very bright and alert, and not very good at getting things done (Harris, 1975). In 1977 researchers conducting a study comparing jokes dealing with the elderly with jokes about children discovered that whereas more than 70 percent of the jokes about the children were positive, more than 66 percent of those dealing with the aged were negative (Richman, 1977). The negative stereotypes about the elderly can be seen in concentrated form in Butler's following summary:

An older person thinks and moves slowly. He does not think as he used to or as creatively. He is bound to himself and can no longer change or grow. He can learn neither well nor swiftly and, even if he could, he would not wish to. Tied to his personal traditions and growing conservatism, he dislikes innovations and is not disposed to new ideas. Not only can he not move forward, he often moves backward. He enters a second childhood, caught up in increasing egocentricity and demanding more from his environment than he is willing to give to it. Sometimes he becomes an intensification of himself, a caricature of a lifelong personality. He becomes irritable and cantankerous, yet shallow and enfeebled. He lives in his past; he is behind the times. He is aimless and wandering of mind, reminiscing and garrulous. Indeed, he is a study in decline, the picture of mental and physical failure. He has lost and cannot replace friends, spouse, job, status, power, influence, income. He is often stricken by diseases which, in turn, restrict his movement, his enjoyment of food, the pleasures of well-being. He has lost his desire and capacity for sex. His body shrinks, and so too does the flow of blood to his brain. His mind does not utilize oxygen and sugar at the same rate as formerly. Feeble, uninteresting, he awaits his death, a burden to society, to his family, and to himself. [1975:6.]

In one study of the attribution of traits to either male or female roles, Broverman (1972) found that respondents who represented various ages, educational levels, and sexes agreed strongly about which characteristics on a list were appropriately male or female. Females were described as being emotional, subjective, easily influenced, submissive, excitable in a minor crisis, passive, illogical, home-oriented, sneaky, and with feelings that get easily hurt. In addition, they were believed to be not at all independent, not at all competetive or skilled in business, and not at all self-confident. Males, in contrast, were believed to have the opposite, more positively evaluated characteristics consistently through the list (Broverman, Vogel, Broverman, Clarkson, and Rosenkrantz, 1972).

Negative Feelings In his analysis of race relations in the United States James Comer recounts the story of a white adolescent girl who was scolded by her father for having put a coin in her mouth: "He yelled, 'Get that money out of your mouth—it might have been in a nigger's hand!' His message: blacks are untouchables, contaminating and not to be taken in or inserted" (1972:135). Comer's story illustrates that stereotypes regarding a minority group may be accompanied by negative feelings or emotions—hatred, fear, revulsion, contempt, or envy—evoked by the symbolic or actual presence of out-group members.

The idea of patronizing a washroom, of eating at the same restaurant, or of shaking hands with a Jew or black may excite horror or disgust within some individuals. Black movement into a previously all-white neighborhood may produce fear and anxiety among many whites. The social standing of a prominent Jewish businessman or doctor may elicit envy among some Gentiles. [Vander Zanden, 1972:21.]

When prejudice involves the emotional and the irrational, then it may become a more or less persistent characteristic of an individual, one that is deeply imbedded in his personality. In order to emphasize the enduring nature of prejudice, a social psychologist found the occasion to recall his early childhood experience in a poultry shop in a Jewish section of East Baltimore:

How well I remember the dark little figure in the back room, the dread shochet, the ritual butcher; bent over his cutting board he resembled a brooding nursemaid at the bedside of her charge—except that he had a sinister blade in his right hand, and with his left hand was pinning a chicken to the board by the base of its throat, holding it steady for the one swift, effortless stroke. In an instant it was done. Blood spurted from the neck, the decapitated torso throbbed and trembled, the wings flapped wildly. And as the spasms subsided, a wave of nausea swept over me. To this day, I am unable to eat chicken. I find its flavor unpleasant, its odor worse, and its claim on the status of delicacy rather tenuous. [Rosnow, 1972:53.]

Negative feelings associated with minority groups may develop early in life and persist into adulthood, long after an individual has rid him or herself of prejudicial stereotypes or beliefs. In the words of Sartre (1965), an individual's prejudice may become his or her "passion." We will have more to say about the development of prejudice in children when we later view prejudice from a sociological perspective.

The emotional component of prejudice is also evident in the negative feelings aroused in some people by the very presence of older people but may not be as easy to recognize because they take a more paternalistic, pitying, or protective character. For example, during visits to nursing homes our students frequently report feeling sorry for the patients and, sometimes, disgusted by their physical appearance or condition. Whatever the character of their emotional response to seeing the lives of old people in nursing homes, the students are usually not eager to stay for long.

The emotional component of prejudice toward women is still more difficult to recognize and understand, for it is easily confused with more positive and desirable emotions. We are speaking, of course, of the feelings of sexual arousal that men feel for (or in the presence of) women. When such feelings are a consequence of the belief that women exist primarily for the sexual satisfaction of men and that (to use a word that has been popular in the women's movement) dehumanizes women, the emotions in question should appropriately be considered part of the prejudice against women. Dehumanization is a process of treating a person not as an individual but as a member of a larger category of less-than-human beings. In the sense of minority groups this is a matter of ignoring those characteristics of women that make them whole persons rather than sexual objects. To acknowledge that what under these conditions should be called a negative, harmful emotion (perhaps lust is the best term) should not preclude the existence of the positive attraction that people have for one another. The first type of response involves contempt and even hatred, whereas the second, most certainly, does not.

Prejudice as an Element of Culture: The Sociological View

We contend that prejudice develops in order to justify discrimination in the minds of discriminators. For example, in the South, slavery was perceived to be beneficial to whites, both to operating plantations at minimum costs and to imitating some of that sense of European aristocracy, which they so envied (Genovese, 1961). But slaveholding ran counter to the Christian ideals that were also a part of the American ethic generally and of southern life particularly. The result was a variety of prejudice against blacks that removed them from the normal realm of Christian concern by contending that blacks were a different kind of being lacking souls and, therefore, not subject to the same treatment as whites. Or, alternatively, another component of that prejudice that justified slavery argued that blacks were different products of evolution, best suited for the labors and "protection" that slavery provided (Vander Zanden, 1963), (Haller, 1971). The conditions for the exploitation of blacks occurred first, and the justification later.

When prejudices develop, they tend to become part of the structure of beliefs that shape the culture of a people. They are taught in homes, schools, and churches and on street corners. In the South they became an important part of a subculture in which norms for the treatment of blacks and beliefs and feelings about them were particularly negative. Prejudice was a normal part of the southern way of thinking (Dollard, 1937). As such, prejudice tended not only to justify discrimination but to perpetuate it as well. Normative systems as they exist within cultural patterns are extremely stable. They are learned involuntarily from previous generations; they are shared broadly within the culture; they may persist even after the conditions that gave rise to them are gone; and they are extremely resistent to change.

Prejudice, then, to the extent that it becomes a part of our culture, can be thought of as a mechanism for the maintenance of discrimination, both as a justifier and, by analogy, as a sort of flywheel. The flywheel is a physical object of large mass which, once set in motion, tends to keep moving. A potter's wheel, for instance, has a large round stone wheel, which the potter kicks into motion. Once it is going, the potter can allow the wheel to keep spinning, and the flywheel will maintain its momentum. The analogy with prejudice is, we feel, apt, for prejudice becomes a part of the culture and persists like other facets of the culture. Thus, even when an individual is in no position to discriminate against a minority group, perhaps because he or she has no opportunities to distribute, that person may still have been taught prejudice. To what extent, then, is prejudice a part of the culture?

Prejudiced attitudes may be widely shared among the members of a society. Americans separated by virtue of differences in region, ethnicity, or socioeconomic status nevertheless express surprisingly similar beliefs, feelings, and action tendencies regarding the members of minority groups. These are expressed in terms of patterns of "social distance," whereby out-group members are excluded from having personal relations with members of the dominant group. Since Bogardus developed his Social Distance Scale in 1925, numerous investigators have asked such groups as native white businessmen, schoolteachers, Jews, blacks, and white female college students to which level of the following scale they were willing to admit the members of various ethnic groups:

1. to close kinship by marriage
2. to my club as personal chums
3. to my street as neighbors
4. to employment in my occupation
5. to citizenship in my country
6. as visitors only to my country
7. would exclude from my country

Studies of social distance have yielded astonishingly consistent findings across groups: an unwillingness among Americans of diverse ethnic backgrounds and socioeconomic positions to have close social relations with blacks, Japanese, Chinese, Hindus, and

An Alternative to Victim Blaming: Discrimination and Prejudice

Turks, and a widespread preference for individuals of English, German, and Spanish descent (Derbyshire and Brody, 1964). Compare the social distance preferences that Bogardus obtained from samples of white businesspeople and teachers, black Americans, and Jews (Simpson and Yinger, 1972):

110 Native White Businessmen and Schoolteachers	202 Black Americans	178 Native-Born Jews
1. English	1. Negro	1. Jewish
2. French	2. French	2. English
3. German	3. Spanish	3. French
4. Spanish	4. English	4. German
5. Italian	5. Mexican	5. Spanish
6. Jewish	6. Hindu	6. Italian
7. Greek	7. Japanese	7. Mexican
8. Mexican	8. German	8. Japanese
9. Chinese	9. Italian	9. Turkish
10. Japanese	10. Chinese	10. Greek
11. Negro	11. Jewish	11. Chinese
12. Hindu	12. Greek	12. Hindu
13. Turkish	13. Turkish	13. Negro

Strong patterns of social distance have been uncovered by students of mass communication. For instance, Berelson and Salter's (1946) study of popular short stories revealed that "American" characters—white Protestants with no distinguishable ancestry of foreign origin—were rarely depicted as loving and marrying minority and foreign characters. Where marriage and love occurred in fiction, it was typically the American boy who courted and married the American girl. Barcus and Levin (1966) similarly reported finding more intimate social relations between fictional characters of like ethnic background than between characters differing in this respect. Moreover, the preference for intragroup relations was found in both black as well as white magazine fiction. Prejudice often becomes an enduring characteristic of a society, being transmitted by its members from generation to generation and receiving strong support in the form of custom or the enforcement of legal codes. To take an extreme example, Indian students continue to carry caste stereotypes similar to those that have existed for many generations despite radical changes in India's traditional caste relations (Sinha and Sinha, 1967).

Far from being deviant or abnormal, prejudice often becomes the normal and expected state of affairs in a society. From a sociological point of view, therefore, we can regard prejudice as an element of the culture—the normative order—of the society in which it exists (Westie, 1964).

When prejudice is cultural, we learn it through socialization, just as we learn other conceptions of "what ought to be"—conceptions such as motherhood, patriotism, love of church, and economic achievement. Prejudice transmitted by agents of socialization—including parents, peers, and teachers—represents an expression of firmly established and widely held ideals regarding the character of social relationships. Thus, the acceptance of prejudice may begin early in life. Comer relates the story of the wife of a black physician in Mississippi who was followed down the street by a 2-year-old white toddler dressed only in a diaper who pointed at her yelling "nigger, nigger" (1972:135).

By age three, most children seem to be aware of ethnic differences. Moreover, there seems to be a strong preference for "whiteness" on the part of both black and white preschool children. For example, when asked to choose between a white and a brown doll identical in every other respect, black and white preschoolers express strong preferences for the white doll, which they perceive as being "the doll they want to play with best," "the doll that is good," and "the doll that is a nice color." By contrast, the brown doll tends to be viewed as "the doll they don't want to play with," "the doll that is bad," and "the doll that is not a nice color" (Clark and Clark, 1947; Greenwald and Oppenheim, 1968; Morland, 1958). As shown by Morland (1969), these findings cannot be a result of a universal preference for "whiteness," since Chinese children in Hong Kong prefer and identify with dolls representing their own race rather than Caucasians. It is a tragic fact that minority group members often come to believe in and actually adopt the prejudice directed against them by majority group members. (See Box 2.3.)

BOX 2.3

An Example of Minority Group Self-Hatred

As a cultural phenomenon, prejudice frequently finds widespread approval. The writer of the following passages—an Islander of part-Hawaiian ancestry—illustrates that the acceptance by members of a minority of the prejudice directed against them can lead to severe forms of self-hatred:

> I think I waste a lot of my time on my own kind, I mean the Hawaiians. They are not enlightened, not developing, not progressive people.... All they do is to eat and sleep and play the guitar.
>
> I'm a Hawaiian myself and I hate to say this, but I don't care much for them ... they are not ambitious people. Their only ambition is to play music. They don't care for anything else. Then you see a Hawaiian does not come to work after a pay-day. Pay-day today and the next day no work. I don't know what they do with their money, but I think they drink a lot.
>
> They are so dirty. They eat just like pigs with their hands. Gee, there's one Hawaiian boy who sits right next to me ... and his feet are full of dirt and mud. Gee! dirty, can't stand it! And over here (pointing to his neck) full of dirt. When I see him like that, I turn my back to him.
>
> I hate Hawaiians, oh, I hate Hawaiians! If you treat 'em good they come back and treat you bad. If you do good to them, they do bad to you. They talk about you and tell all kinds of things about you. That's true, I feel this way. If you say something they tell people something you never said. That's how they make trouble.
>
> I hate Hawaiian! Oh, Hawaiian kind of low. I wish I didn't have any Hawaiian blood. I regret I have Hawaiian blood.

Source: Margaret M. Lam 1936 "Racial Myth and Family Tradition-Worship Among Part-Hawaiians." *Social Forces* (March):156.

Prejudice as Normative

As an element of culture, prejudice against certain minorities throughout the history of American society has been translated into ideal norms regarding the proper behavior of minorities in their dealings with members of the dominant group. From the 1600s, rules governing the enslavement of black Americans permitted separating the children of slaves from their parents and forbade legal marriages between slaves. In the antebellum South, black Americans could not own books, inherit money, learn to read or write, or vote. Even in nonslavery states before 1865, antiblack norms were imposed and rigorously enforced by whites. Northern blacks could not vote, enter hotels or restaurants (except in the role of servants), and were segregated from whites with respect to formal education, trains, steamboats, church seating, and theaters (Burkey, 1971).

Antiblack norms thrived for more than a century following the Civil War, despite the abolition of slavery and the establishment of a short period of reconstruction. In most regions of the United States, blacks were restricted to entering the most undesirable occupations and continued to be segregated from whites in terms of formal education, membership in unions, public accommodations, and housing. Moreover, especially in the South, blacks were subjected to a complex system of petty indignities. Such restrictions included prohibitions against interracial dating, against social visits by blacks to the homes of whites, against sexual relations between black men and white women, and even against blacks interrupting conversations between whites. Intergroup norms required, for example, that physicians serve their white patients before their black patients, that blacks remove their hats when in the presence of whites, that black domestics enter the homes of whites by the back door, and that black automobile drivers yield the right of way to their white counterparts (Burkey, 1971).

Norms for women have been markedly similar to those for blacks, including prohibition of voting rights and expectations that women defer to men in social situations, treat their own careers as less important than their husbands', provide domestic services for men, and generally attend to the comforts of the male provider. (For a recent reiteration of these norms, see Marabel Morgan's

Total Woman, 1975. This prescription for what the author feels is the best way for women to be fulfilled calls for females to serve the desires of men. It is controversial because it reiterates a set of norms such as submission of women to the will of men, that have been under attack for some years, especially by the women's liberation movement.)

There are also sets of norms that apply to various age groups. Young people, for example, are expected to be adventurous, aggressive, acquisitive, and active. Norms for old people, however, are just the opposite. According to Rosow (1974), norms for the elderly are particularly weak and negative and cluster about an undesirable dependency. They consist primarily of the inappropriateness of acting like a young person. So, rather than believe that older people should be engaging in one sort of activity or another, we have norms for the elderly that merely prohibit them from activities we consider appropriate only for the young: "Isn't it time you stopped riding around on motorcycles?" or "Haven't you had enough of going to work every day?" are typical of normative statements with no positive content. Retirement itself is an example of a norm for the elderly which is essentially empty of active content. We retire *from* work, not *to* any other specific activity.

Playing the Role Because the norms for the elderly are so weak and negative, they provide a particularly poor basis for the development of a role for the older person to play. The role is that set of expected behaviors that are deemed appropriate for a person in a given status. Given the character of our norms for the elderly, it is no surprise that Burgess (1960) has called this a "roleless role." Old people are expected, then, not to work, not to be active, not to be involved, not to engage in sex, not to plan for the future, not to exercise control, and so on.

In contrast, the role of women, especially before it was attacked by the women's movement as degrading, was clear and specific. Women were expected to be passive, submissive, gentle, dependent, family oriented, emotional, sentimental, idealistic, and intuitive (Eitzen, 1980).

Negative stereotypes and feelings about a minority group that become widely shared and enduring elements of a culture often assume the force of prescribed rules that other out-group members are expected to play. The complex network of formal and informal norms regarding the relationships between black and white Americans has generated what Pettigrew (1964) has called the social role of "Negro," a label prescribing that black Americans "play the game" by "wearing their masks" and acting out the role of the inferior in dealings with whites. Under the American form of slavery, for example, blacks were expected to be unconditionally obedient to their masters and to express respect for all whites (Blassingame, 1972). Slaves often "played the role assigned to them, acted the clown, and curried the favor of their masters in order to win the maximum rewards within the system" (Silberman, 1964:79).

Many of the stereotypes traditionally associated with black Americans actually became their role prescriptions. Blacks were supposed to be "lazy" and "happy-go-lucky." If they should have refused to play this role, blacks were usually evaluated by whites as "not knowing their place" and, as a result, were ridiculed, discouraged, ignored, or severely punished (Redding, 1950). So goes the Herblock cartoon, "You don't understand boy. You're supposed to just shuffle along." Those who removed their masks and dared to not shuffle risked the consequences of their actions. Yet those who played the role of "Negro" also paid dearly, as illustrated in the work of Paul Laurence Dunbar, a black poet who lived at the turn of this century. He wrote:

We smile, but O great Christ, our cries
To thee from tortured souls arise.
We sing, but oh, the clay is vile
Beneath our feet, and long the mile;
But let the world dream otherwise,
We wear the mask. [1940:14.]

We emphasize the distinction between expected and prescribed role, for it may help to explain why the nature of discrimination has differed depending on the minority group against whom it has been directed. As we have seen, many stereotypes about black Americans have represented both expected as well as prescribed behavior (for example, blacks are expected to be and ought to be "lazy" and "happy-go-lucky"). If they played the game and fulfilled their stereotype, blacks were usually permitted by the dominant group to survive and perpetuate themselves as a group, though thereby robbed of their dignity and self-esteem. By contrast, many stereotypes about Jews have involved expected but proscribed behavior. (For example, Jews are expected to, but ought not to, "have the money," "run the country," and be "shrewd.") As a result, though Jews could maintain their cultural heritage, many Jews were not permitted to remain within a society, especially if they played the game and fulfilled their stereotypes.

The Relationship Between Discrimination and Prejudice

We are interested in prejudice only to the extent that it is related to actual discrimination. This is especially true in a country such as America, which has asserted that people are free to think what they like as long as they do not infringe on the guaranteed rights of others. We legislate rights and opportunities, not beliefs. However, we have come to recognize the close relationship between what people believe and the behavior they exhibit. If we are to guarantee opportunity, in part by outlawing discriminatory practices, then the role of prejudice in all this might be critical.

It should be emphasized that there is a strong tendency for attitudes and behaviors to be consistent with one another, or congruent. A positive behavior toward an object or idea is normally accompanied by a positive attitude toward it. Discriminators are usually also bigots, and nondiscriminators are not. Two problems, however, are of interest to us here:

1. Can dissonant situations occur in which a person acts in a way that differs from his or her attitudes?
2. Can behaviors persist in the absence of reinforcing attitudes because the structure of some social system compels such behaviors?

The first issue is brought up, for example, in a typology developed by Merton (1949), and the second is the issue of individual versus institutional discrimination. We shall deal with each briefly in order to introduce our conception of the relationship between discrimination and prejudice.

In Merton's typology the possible relationships between prejudice and discrimination are developed as in Table 2.2. In the two consonant cells (1 and 4), the relationship between the attitude and the behavior make perfect sense to us. They seem reasonable and so are not that interesting to discuss. But the dissonant conditions (2 and 3) are fascinating. How is it possible to not hate blacks, for example, but to discriminate against them anyway, or to hate them but to decide not to do anything about it? Merton tells us that in both dissonant situations, the key is the social-situational pressure brought to bear on the individual. The fair-weather liberal may, if he or she owns a business in a region populated by active bigots, lose a great deal of trade if discrimination is not practiced. This person's lack of prejudice is less important than his or her business success, and so he or she discriminates in order to suit the pressures of the community. Similarly, a person who would like to discriminate may refrain from doing so either because the community is populated by nondiscriminators (all-weather liberals in Merton's terminology) or because situational pressure is brought to bear by laws against discrimination. It is better, in this case, to swallow one's prejudices than to go to jail.

These dissonant categories are fascinating partly because they

Table 2.2 Merton's Model for the Relationship Between Discrimination and Prejudice

		Is the Person Prejudiced?	
		Yes	No
Is the person a discriminator?	Yes	1. Active Bigot *Congruency* between attitude and behavior (both negative)	2. Fair-Weather Liberal *Dissonance* between attitude and behavior (positive attitude and negative behavior)
	No	3. Timid Bigot *Dissonance* between attitude and behavior (negative attitude and positive behavior)	4. All-Weather Liberal *Congruency* between attitude and behavior (both positive)

illustrate the power of social pressures to compel us to act in accordance with them. But the main reason that they have such appeal to us is that they are exceptions to the rule. They are, we believe, special cases, the frequency or stability of which is not known. As to the stability of such cases, Merton presents us with a "snapshot" view, that is, a picture of what the relationship between discrimination and prejudice may be at one moment. As we will argue in the next section, such dissonant situations are very unstable. As to the frequency of such cases, by itself, the 2×2 table that illustrates the four categories (Table 2.2) might make it look as if there are roughly equal frequencies of each type because the four cells are of equal size. However, in another description of the relationship between prejudice and discrimination, Simpson and Yinger deal with this problem:

No one expression of the relationship between prejudice and discrimination is adequate:

1. There can be prejudice without discrimination.
2. There can be discrimination without prejudice.
3. Discrimination can be among the causes of prejudice.
4. Prejudice can be among the causes of discrimination.
5. Probably most frequently they are mutually reinforcing. [1972:29.]

Notice that Simpson and Yinger emphasize that prejudice and discrimination should be thought of as mutually reinforcing and, therefore, congruent.

Another instance of dissonance can be seen in the concept of institutional discrimination. As we have noted, individual discrimination is the expression of a person's hate against a group of people in visible, overt acts of discrimination. Institutional discrimination, however, causes opportunity to be distributed unfairly as a consequence of the structural arrangements of a society, which may, at least on the surface, have nothing to do directly with the relationships between dominant and minority groups in the society. For example, society's belief in the value of a middle-class education can systematically deny opportunities to blacks without anyone's ever expressing a preference for one race over another. These nongroup-specific arrangements of the institutions of society are seen, then, as capable of perpetuating race-, age-, and sex-related advantages without anyone seeming to hold specifically prejudicial attitudes. As in Merton's typology, this is another instance of dissonance, this time originating at the level of the social structure rather than at the level of the individual.

We believe that the frequency with which such discrimination without prejudice exists is exaggerated. First of all, it is merely a semantic distinction to distinguish class bias from race, sex, or age prejudice. These minorities, as we have shown, are clearly denied opportunities to develop the qualifications for further opportunities (such as professional education) that dominant groups reserve for themselves. The members of the dominant group, by choosing self-selecting criteria for opportunity (such as Scholastic Aptitude Test scores), are expressing their particularly tailored biases for their own advantage, are also, inevitably, expressing a systematic set of negative prejudices. In a world in which desired goods and opportunities are in limited supply (or in which the supply is intentionally limited) "positive prejudices" are only by the barest of margins distinguishable from outright negative group prejudices.

In addition, even discriminatory institutional arrangements require that someone extend advantages to certain people while at the same time denying them to others. This brings the problem down to the level of the individual again and to the issue of individual consonance (with which we will deal next). In her study of how blacks are systematically discriminated against in the housing market, Pearce (1979) sent matched black couples and white couples to real estate agents. It was found that agents either failed to show the blacks homes at all or showed them inferior homes in terms of price or location. Pearce asks whether this type of treatment should properly be called institutional racism, especially because

These are not isolated instances of individual racism. . . . These data do document discrimination that took place during personal interviews, whereas racism is often seen as "no fault" discrimination. That is, the unequal outcomes are portrayed as the accidental by-products of actions taken for purposes other than racial exclusion. Certainly one cannot attribute intention solely on the basis of the sort of data we obtained on the real estate agents' actions (and inactions); but their actions are far from random and it is highly unlikely that they are done blindly or unwittingly.

I would argue, therefore, that a clearer answer to the question of whether the manifest differences in treatment afforded black and white homeseekers is institutional racism requires reconceptualization of institutional racism. As a start, I think we must first reject the image of an automaton heedlessly and helplessly grinding out differential treatment. [Pearce, 1979:339.]

In institutional arrangements that discriminate, there must be operators, or agents, who deliver the discrimination. These people, even if they are only the "business end" of a complex structure for the distribution of opportunity, are subject to the same pressures by which discrimination and prejudice tend to be consonant with one another. To that extent, even institutional discrimination is reinforced by prejudice. The logic by which such a consonant relationship between prejudice and discrimination exists is the subject of the next section.

Prejudice as a Justification or Excuse for Discrimination

The problem of why, or how, prejudice (the attitude) and discrimination (the behavior) tend toward consistency with one another can be clarified by recognizing that attitudes are often constructed in order to make sense of events. When we try to explain what we have done to others, or to ourselves, we are put into the position of having to justify our behavior in terms that make it reasonable. What is reasonable depends, of course, on what is acceptable at any time to a group of people or to ourselves. But within the boundaries of what pass for acceptable beliefs and values, we must justify our actions. Two well-known psychological theories focus on this process; Bem's *self-perception theory* and Festinger's *theory of cognitive dissonance.*

According to Daryl Bem (1970), when we are asked what we believe or think about something, we often do not know because we have not considered the question. We do not have to have attitudes in order to act. But when asked what we think about something, we evaluate ourselves exactly as others evaluate us. Others look at what we have done in order to *infer* our attitudes: "He goes to horror movies, so he must like them." Asked what you think about a certain food, for example, you will go through the same process but in this case with your own beliefs: "I must like artichokes, I eat them all the time." Our self-perception, then, is constructed from the evidence of our own behavior. As a consequence, attitudes are necessarily consistent with behaviors. If we normally think that we know our own attitudes, then the process of inferring them from our behavior may be hidden: " ... We may think that we are always reading our internal states directly, but we 'cheat' and peek outside to look at the same clues that others look at when they want to know our internal states. Furthermore, we are usually unaware that we do so" (Bem, 1970:50). In one study that illustrated this principle, experimental subjects took a drug that induced physiological reactions associated with strong emotional conditions. Half the subjects were then placed in a social situation with a person who established a very playful and lighthearted atmosphere in the room, while the other half of the subjects were placed in a room with the same person who, this time, complained, grumbled, and established a tense and unpleasant atmosphere. "Those who had been with the angry confederate described their own mood as one of anger; those who had been with the happy confederate felt slightly 'euphoric' and happy" (Bem, 1970:51). No such differences in the evaluation of their own emotional condition was reported by subjects who had received a placebo (neutral) injection, no matter what type of behavior the confederate exhibited with them. In other words, people who were injected with the actual drug (adrenalin) knew they were experiencing emotional states, but they had to rely on outside cues (the behavior of the confederate) in order to decide what kind of emotional experience they had gone through.

Leon Festinger's theory of cognitive dissonance (Festinger, 1957) like Bem's theory, explains how attitudes and behavior tend to become consonant. According to Festinger, if a person is induced to act in a way that is inconsistent with whatever beliefs he or she may already have, the individual will experience the unpleasant condition of dissonance. As a result, the individual will alter his or her beliefs to bring them into balance with the behavior in question. For example, think of any time you have decided to buy something and then narrowed down your choices to only two possibilities. You finally choose one and, inevitably, you have rejected a choice with some good qualities and accepted one with some bad qualities. (Otherwise they would not have been so close in your final evaluation.) You then go about the process of altering your evaluation of them to reduce the dissonance the choice produced. You amplify the good qualities and diminish the seriousness of the bad qualities of the object you selected, and you amplify the bad qualities and diminish the good qualities of the one you rejected. Once again, as with Bem, attitudes follow behaviors.

In the best-known experimental evidence for this theory, subjects were asked to write essays arguing a position with which they disagreed. Some were paid very little to write the essays, whereas others were paid a good deal more. After the essays had been written, the subjects who had been paid more to write the essays continued to disagree with the position they had been asked to support. By contrast, those who had been paid very little changed their minds in favor of the position they had formerly opposed. For those who had written the essay for more money, the dissonance between this behavior (writing) and their attitudes (disagreement with what they were writing) was justified by the money they had received: "I did it for the money." But for those who had been paid very little to write the essay, the money was inadequate to justify this behavior, and so they could only justify their behavior by changing their beliefs: "I wouldn't have done it for so little money, so I guess I must agree with what I wrote."

We believe that in just this way prejudice is an attitude that is developed and used to justify and to "make sense" of discrimination. We act to diminish the opportunities of others, primarily because we believe it to be in our own best interests to do so. Then, in order to justify the discrimination, we develop prejudices consonant with our actions. Once the prejudices are entrenched in individuals and in the culture, they act to reinforce the correctness of our treatment of minorities and to perpetuate such treatment. (This process is more fully discussed in the section on prejudice as a facet of culture.)

The key to the process whereby prejudice follows discrimination is to identify those conditions under which discrimination is a consequence not of the beliefs of individuals but of the *structure of social circumstances*. This is the way Katznelson (1973) approaches this question: "What are the social economic and political origins of relationships of racial inequality and what social, economic and political factors sustain such relationships? It is a distortion to posit the perceptual, subjective notion of prejudice as the central independent variable in analysing social and political reality" (p. 6). That is, prejudice is not a cause of discrimination but a consequence. As we will show later, prejudice can, because of the nature of the normative structure, contribute to the perpetuation of discrimination. But in terms of our efforts to understand the nature of discrimination, prejudice should be thought of as a secondary contributor and the structural conditions for discrimination as primary. Feagin and Feagin (1978) strongly support this approach when they argue against the traditional assumption that prejudice causes discrimination. They show how discrimination can exist independently of prejudice, carrying a momentum of its own through our institutional structures and practices.

Taking the same sort of position, Schermerhorn (1970) states: "If research has confirmed anything in this area it is that prejudice is the product of *situations;* historical situations, economic situations, political situations; it is not a little demon that emerges in people because they are depraved" (p. 6). For example, prejudices that characterize Mexican-Americans as being "unclean," "drunkards," "criminals," "deceitful," "unpredictable," and "immoral" *serve to justify discrimination and exclusion in the following way:* "If Mexicans are deceitful and immoral, they do not have to be accorded equal status and justice; if they are mysterious and unpredictable, there is no point in treating them as one would a fellow Anglo-American; and if they are hostile and dangerous, it is best that they live apart in colonies of their own"(Simmons, 1961:292).

It is the purpose of this book to illustrate the fact that social-structural situations exist in American society such that some segments of the society benefit from the existence of discrimination; that is, discrimination has certain important system-maintaining functions, especially for the psychological and social-structural well-being of the dominant group. To the extent that such system-maintaining functions of discrimination exist, discrimination will persist. Also, it will continue to generate prejudice in order to justify and perpetuate such treatment of minorities. In the next chapter we will illustrate that prejudice and discrimination remain a serious problem. The final section of the next chapter will explain how functionalism provides us with a way to identify the *structural* conditions under which discrimination flourishes.

NOTES

1. Exceptionalist survival aids and programs that lessen the severity of the deprivations experienced by minorities more than just make us feel better about their difficulties. They also insure that minority-group members, denied access to better jobs, are available to do society's least pleasant work. In addition, the maintenance of marginally unemployed or underemployed populations depresses wages, provides a negative comparison group by which societal norms for work are emphasized, and generally, via the welfare structure, acts as a primary social control mechanism for the maintenance of social order. All these consequences will be more fully discussed later.
2. For women, exceptionalist programs designed to aid in their survival or to ameliorate their suffering as minority-group members are less common than they are for blacks or the elderly. This is because women, generally living with or married to males, therefore live approximately as well as the majority group that holds the social power. The interdependence of male and female in everyday life is much greater than that of black and white or old and young. But when the intimate ties between women and men are severed, when women are on their own, these types of exceptionalist programs do come into play. Divorced women often have been dependent on a husband for support and are generally unable to find work that supports herself and her children. Programs exist that will provide payments to those women not able to provide for their children (AFDC) or for themselves (alimony). Widows often must take advantage of survivor's benefits, and, when the relationship between a husband and wife reaches an extreme state, there are shelters available where a battered woman can go for protection from her own husband—the ultimate survival aid. So, as long as a woman is living with a man, her survival and the quality of her life is normally assured to the extent that he perceives his own well-being as dependent on hers and provides willingly, even eagerly, for her. But when on their own, women are often perceived as needing help to get along.

3. John Champlin, "On the Study of Power," *Politics and Society,* November 1970, p. 94.
4. Hans Gerth and C. Wright Mills, *Character and Social Structure* (New York: Harcourt Brace Jovanovich, 1954), pp. 192–193.
5. The commonly held definition of an attitude system includes, beside the feelings and beliefs components that we have stressed, what has been called an *action-tendency component*. This is the disposition on the part of the person holding an attitude to act in accordance with that attitude, would such an opportunity arise. However, as will be seen in our discussion of the relationship between prejudice (an attitude) and discrimination (a behavior), the discussion of an action tendency as a component of an attitude structure is unnecessary. This is especially true given our belief in the primacy of behavior in the structuring of attitudes.

Chapter 3
The Persistence of Discrimination and Prejudice: Their Functional Basis

American society during the late 1960s seemed to have experienced a downward trend in regard to prejudiced attitudes against such minorities as blacks and Jews. Traditional stereotypes, negative feelings, and discriminatory practices apparently had to some degree eroded with the passage of time and, more importantly, with the passage of appropriate legislation as well as activism on the part of minorities. There is some evidence that younger generations of Americans have indeed demonstrated greater tolerance and more careful thinking about ethnic groups than have their older counterparts in former generations (Karlings, Coffman, and Walters, 1969; Taylor et al., 1978).

The Persistence of Prejudice

As determined by large-scale surveys of white racial attitudes from 1942 to 1968, for example, there was a sizable increase in the proportion of white northerners as well as Southerners willing to support the integration of public schools. Over the same period of time, the proportion of white Americans who regarded the intelligence of blacks as equal to that of whites rose considerably in both the North and the South (Bellisfield, 1972–1973; Hyman and Sheatsley, 1956, 1964). Data from a series of surveys of the American population in 1964, 1968, and 1970 suggest that white and black attitudes did not move farther apart on questions regarding principle and policy but, in fact, may have moved somewhat closer together (Campbell, 1970).

Condran (1979) reports that "from 1963 to 1972 there is unambiguous evidence of generally liberalizing attitudes in our society" (p. 474), and Grabb (1980) finds that whites have, since the 1960s, increased their tolerance for racial integration. But Condran's data also report that between 1972 and 1977 the liberalizing process slowed down greatly in some areas, halted entirely in others, and, in attitudes toward integrating housing and general black assertiveness (called intrusion), these attitudes had actually begun to reverse toward intolerance. In fact, the evidence is all too compelling that prejudice still has a tenacious hold on many members of American society, persisting at an alarming level, especially against such groups as blacks, Puerto Ricans, Mexican-Americans, American Indians, Jews, women, and the eldery. For example, Karlins, Coffman, and Walters (1969) compared the stereotypes held by Princeton undergraduates in 1967 with those found in the earlier study by Katz and Braly (1933) and in a 1951 replication by Gilbert. The findings of Karlins, Coffman, and Walters failed to support the contention that minority stereotypes have been fading. Instead, traditional stereotypes that may have declined in their frequency of usage seemed to have been replaced by other stereotypes, in many cases resembling the original ones. For example, the old view of blacks as being "superstitious" and "lazy" gave way to the view that they were "musical," "happy-go-lucky," "lazy," and "ostentatious." In a similar way, rather than being stereotyped as "pugnacious" as in previous studies, the Irish were seen as primarily "quick-tempered" and "extremely nationalistic."

The substitution of new stereotypes for traditional ones may have become incorporated into the mass-media images of minority groups. For example, a 1953 study by Shuey of popular magazine advertisements concluded that blacks were being stereotypically portrayed as servants, porters, and waiters. A similar analysis of magazine advertisements appearing between 1965 and 1970 determined that advertising still perpetuated racial stereotypes, though in more subtle ways:

Indeed, if the advertising image were to be believed, the black is a record star, an entertainer, a celebrity; if not one of these, he is a child, a woman, or a foreigner. As a male, he is in need of public or private charity, and he seldom if ever enjoys the occupational status of the whites with whom he is depicted. Missing from these ads are black families and black males, at work and at leisure—in short, the black American, rather than the black stereotype. [Colfax and Sternberg, 1972:17.]

Though changes have occurred, there is reason to believe that many of our long-standing traditional stereotypes have been maintained intact (see Box 3.1). Selznick and Steinberg (1969), in their interviews with a representative cross section of the national population in 1964, found that 54 percent of their respondents thought "Jews always like to be at the head of things"; 52 percent agreed that "Jews stick together too much;" and 42 percent felt that "Jews are more willing than others to use shady practices to get what they want" (p. 6). Moreover, Petroni (1972) found frequent usage of minority-group stereotypes among white, midwestern high school students who were highly critical of the prejudices of their parents and yet who failed to recognize they had prejudices of their own.

With reference to stereotypes associated with blacks, Brink and Harris (1964) reported that a substantial proportion of a nationwide cross section of white Americans taken in 1963—in some cases reaching almost 70 percent agreement—was willing to agree that blacks

laugh a lot
tend to have less ambition

BOX 3.1

Sexism and Ageism: Experimental Evidence

Most of the research that has studied the attitudes we have toward various minority groups is survey research. But sometimes we recognize that our level of prejudice is being measured, and, feeling that it is socially undesirable to express prejudice, we answer in a more socially acceptable way than we actually feel. There are two studies that have employed an experimental approach to examine attitudes toward women and toward the elderly. They were designed to overcome the effect of the transparency of some survey measures of prejudice.

Solomon (1979) measured the attendance of psychiatrists at various lectures during an academic conference. Attendance by male psychiatrists was significantly lower if a woman had been listed as the presenter of the talk than if a man had been listed. This result emerged regardless of the area of expertise of the speaker. No such difference in attendance rates was recorded among the female psychiatrists.

Levin and Levin (1981) asked undergraduate students whether they would be willing to attend a lecture and informal coffee hour with a guest lecturer who was supposed to visit the campus. The age and the socioeconomic status of the lecturer was varied by describing him on six different versions of his résumé as either young (25 years), middle-aged (50 years), or old (75 years), and as earning either $5,900 per year (low SES) or $59,000 (high SES). When the visiting lecturer was described as high socioeconomic status, his age made no difference in the students' willingness to attend the coffee hour. But when he was described as poorer, students were significantly *less* willing to attend when he was also described as old than when he was described as either young or middle-aged.

In spite of our increasing sensitivity to the problems of these minority groups, when we are unaware that such attitudes are being measured, our underlying prejudices can still show up.

smell different
have looser morals
keep untidy homes
want to live off the handout
have less native intelligence

breed crime
are inferior to whites
care less for the family.

In a 1966 survey, Brink and Harris (1967) again conducted a nationwide study of white Americans, finding a softening in some of their negativism regarding blacks but still reporting about 50 percent who agreed that blacks "laugh a lot," "smell different," "have looser morals," and "want to live off the handout." Campbell's 1968 survey determined that of the whites living in the 15 cities studied.

6% say Negroes are pushing too fast for what they want;
56% believe that Negro disadvantages in jobs, education, and housing are due mainly to Negroes themselves rather than to discrimination;
51% oppose laws to prevent racial discrimination in housing;
33% say that if they had small children, they would rather they have only white friends; and
24% of those old enough to vote say they would not vote for a qualified Negro of their own party preference who was running for mayor. [Campbell, 1970:4-5.]

More recently, Culley and Bennett (1976) studied the images of blacks and women in advertising and found that despite strong pressure on the mass media in the early 1970s to reduce the stereotyped images of blacks and women they had been presenting, by 1974 no improvement had taken place. In general, they found that women and blacks were underrepresented in more respected and prestigious roles and overrepresented in subservient and demeaning ones. Women were typically pictured in the home or in some other domestic or service role. The images of blacks were less clearly negative or subservient than those of women, but blacks were greatly underrepresented in general. They simply did not appear in proportion to their percentage in the population.

The Persistence of Discrimination

Thus, the findings of even recent surveys of American attitudes strongly suggest that hostile stereotypes and feelings regarding various minorities are being perpetuated in American life. Moreover, white Americans have consistently resisted the possible integration of significant numbers of blacks (Knapp and Alston, 1972–1973). Reflecting on the data from a 1968 national survey of American adults, Levy (1972) reports a "polarization in racial attitudes" and concludes that "the prognosis for race relations in the nation is not hopeful" (p. 233). In his insightful but pessimistic account of the "Negro revolution," Killian similarly warns "there is no way out" of the racial crisis that confronts us. Citing the destructive nature of American racism as a basis, he grimly predicts that white Americans "are not likely to make the sacrifices needed to change the fact that America is still a white man's society" (1968: xv).

As though to confirm the gloomy findings of attitude surveys and impressionistic accounts, there is convincing evidence that discriminatory practices and attendant inequities have retained their support in the fabric of American life. Most obviously, perhaps, there is widespread discrimination based on race. As noted in the Report of the U.S. Advisory Commission on Civil Disorders (1968), great numbers of nonwhite Americans continued to be denied the benefits of economic progress. Discrimination occurs in employment and education and is a fact of life in housing and the courts.

The Commission on the Cities in the 1970s, in its visits to major American cities in 1971, found a worsening of the "shameful conditions of life in the cities" with respect to crime, disease, heroin addiction, and welfare rolls. According to findings of the commission, though nonwhite Americans made progress during the 1960s, they continued to lag discouragingly behind whites in important areas such as median income, education, unemployment, life expectancy, and infant mortality (see Box 3.2). What is more, American institutions—its corporations, courts, legislatures, schools, police officers, mayors, and banks—were increasingly being viewed as unresponsive to human needs and rapidly losing the confidence of the American people. Projecting on the basis of the 1970 census and more current trends, the commission concluded that "most cities by 1980 will be preponderantly black and brown, and totally bankrupt." Obviously they were painfully accurate in their predictions.

BOX 3.2

Is Race Declining in Importance?

Part of the debate about whether the position of blacks in American society has improved has focused on the work of William Wilson. In his book *The Declining Significance of Race* (1978), Wilson argues that "race relations in the United States have undergone fundamental changes in recent years, so much so that now the life chances of individual blacks have more to do with their economic class position than with their day-to-day encounters with whites" (p. 160). That is, discriminations specifically aimed at blacks *because they were black* have been replaced by class discriminations that influence the opportunities of blacks only because they happen to be poor. Supposedly the opportunities of poor people of other races are influenced in the same way. Wilson is not claiming that blacks are therefore equal to other races in terms of opportunity but merely that the obstacles to success are not race-specific in the way that they once were.

In contrast, Charles Willie (1978) contends that the significance of race is actually increasing and that the distribution of opportunity is very much a consequence of decisions made by dominant power groups on the basis of race. Willie especially cites evidence of the economic, educational, and housing differences between the races in making his case, but he also claims that Wilson has exaggerated the gains made by blacks during the preceding decades.

In a sense, whether the discriminations experienced by blacks are a consequence of their race or their economic position makes little difference. The result is pretty much the same. The consequence of such a distinction is primarily political. What tactics become possible, or effective, when one view is chosen over the other? For example, if racism is the culprit, does the solidarity of blacks become more possible and can blacks therefore more effectively press for equality? On the other hand, if we believe that racism has declined significantly and that blacks are caught up in class discrimination in which their race is very marginal, does the unification of the various subgroups that comprise the larger underclass become more, or less, possible? The facts of black poverty and lack of opportunity are very real whatever their source. The consequences of deciding this question are most important when we ask what can be done to improve minority-group opportunities.

A look at some of the statistics on income and employment rates by race, age, and sex readily confirms these unpleasant facts about the status of minority groups during the 1960s and shows that they have continued into the 1970s as well.

The data in Table 3.1 make the income situation of black families in America all too clear. Although blacks have increased their median earnings over the last 30 years, they continue to lag far behind whites. Blacks earned only slightly more than half what whites earned until the early 1970s, but even then, when improvement came, it was only to the level of about 65 percent of white earnings in the best year. In addition, even that ratio began to decline as of the end of the decade to 60 percent. In terms of actual dollars earned, although blacks have been increasing their incomes relative to their own poor history of income, the gap between white and black income in absolute dollars has consistently *increased*. White earners continue to improve at a faster rate than blacks. Part of this is due to the fact that because whites tend to have the higher-level jobs in the economy, both in terms of income and security, blacks cannot keep up with inflation or weather economic

Table 3.1 Money Income of Families: Median Income in Constant (1977) Dollars

Year	Race White	Race Black	Dollar Difference	Ratio of Black to White Income
1950	8,672	4,704	3,968	.54
1955	10,439	5,757	4,682	.55
1960	11,940	6,610	5,330	.55
1965	13,927	7,670	6,257	.55
1970	15,975	10,169	5,806	.63
1974	16,476	10,541	5,935	.63
1975	16,065	10,495	5,570	.65
1976	16,539	10,455	6,084	.63
1977	16,740	10,142	6,598	.60

Source: U.S. Bureau of Labor Statistics, 1979, *Handbook of Labor Statistics, 1978.* Washington, D.C.: GPO, p. 448.

recessions or depressions nearly as well. But the dominant fact is that black unemployment is consistently greater than white. See Table 3.2 for some rates of unemployment experienced by both groups from 1948 to 1977.

The rate of unemployment for blacks in America is consistently higher than that for whites, and, although it fluctuates some, it has remained at roughly *twice* that for whites for the last 25 years (see Figure 3.1). The rate, is, in fact, an underrepresentation of black unemployment because it is calculated only for those actively searching for jobs at the time of the calculation. Blacks, because they are concentrated in jobs at the lower end of the pay scale—jobs that are much less stable and only marginally capable of keeping them solvent—are much more likely to give up looking for work and to become dependent on social welfare programs. Thus, the actual figure for unemployed blacks is certainly much higher. Even more dramatically, the unemployment rate for black male teenagers regularly reaches 40 percent and sometimes, especially during the summer, more than 50 percent. In addition, the percentage of blacks who are below the poverty level has consistently been at least *three times* that of the percentage of whites who are below the poverty level. The figure for blacks has recently been around 30 percent, down from highs of over 50 percent in the 1950s. Is it any wonder that urban problems continue to plague both black Americans and urban areas in general?

The figures for income and employment among women differ somewhat from those for blacks but are startlingly similar in one important area. As with blacks' income with respect to whites', females have consistently earned approximately 60 percent of what men have earned. For example, the median annual income for women who worked full time in 1977 was $8,618, whereas that of men for the same year was $14,626. Part of this wage differential is due to actual wage discrimination, in which cases a male is paid more for doing the same work as a woman does, even when they have the same qualifications. However, the bulk of the wage differential is due to the fact that women are disproportionately found in lower-status, lower-paid jobs. As of 1977, for example, about 70 percent of the women who held jobs were employed in clerical,

Table 3.2 Unemployment Rates of Persons 16 Years and Over by Race

Year	White	Black and Other	Ratio of Black to White Unemployment Rate
1948	3.5	5.9	1.68
1949	5.6	8.9	1.58
1950	4.9	9.0	1.83
1951	3.1	5.3	1.70
1952	2.8	5.4	1.92
1953	2.7	4.5	1.66
1954	5.0	9.9	1.98
1955	3.9	8.7	2.23
1956	3.6	8.3	2.30
1957	3.8	7.9	2.07
1958	6.1	12.6	2.06
1959	4.8	10.7	2.22
1960	4.9	10.2	2.08
1961	6.0	12.4	2.06
1962	4.9	10.9	2.22
1963	5.0	10.8	2.16
1964	4.6	9.6	2.08
1965	4.1	8.1	1.97
1966	3.3	7.3	2.21
1967	3.4	7.4	2.19
1968	3.2	6.7	2.09
1969	3.1	6.4	2.06
1970	4.5	8.2	1.82
1971	5.4	9.9	1.83
1972	5.0	10.0	2.00
1973	4.3	8.9	2.06
1974	5.0	9.9	1.98
1975	7.8	13.9	1.78
1976	7.0	13.1	1.87
1977	6.2	13.1	2.11

Source: U.S. Bureau of Labor Statistics, 1979, *Handbook of Labor Statistics, 1979.* Washington, D.C.: GPO, p. 175.

sales, and service positions and were paid the lower salaries associated with them. At the same time, less than 5 percent of the people employed in medicine and law were women, with even fewer employed in the highest-paying, most prestigious surgical positions. Women are still similarly underrepresented in executive boardrooms of private industry. Although it is true that in the last decade women have improved their representation in many job areas, it has often seemed like significant improvement only in comparison with past female employment. Going from 1 percent of an occupation to 2 percent can be paraded about as a 100 percent improvement. But comparison with male employment tells the real story. As of 1978 women were, for example, less than 3 percent of all engineers and less than 10 percent of all judges and lawyers but more than 92 percent of all registered nurses, dietitians, and therapists; more than 96 percent of prekindergarten and kindergarten teachers but less than 1 percent of all stock and bond sales agents; more than 71 percent of all retail salesclerks, more than 91 percent of keypunch operators, 97 percent of receptionists, 99 percent of secretaries but only 1 percent of carpenters and less than 1 percent of electricians or automobile mechanics. The list can go on, but what is clear is that occupations are still overwhelmingly sex-stereotyped (U.S. Department of Commerce, 1979).

Figure 3.1 Unemployment rates: 1948 to 1975 (annual averages).

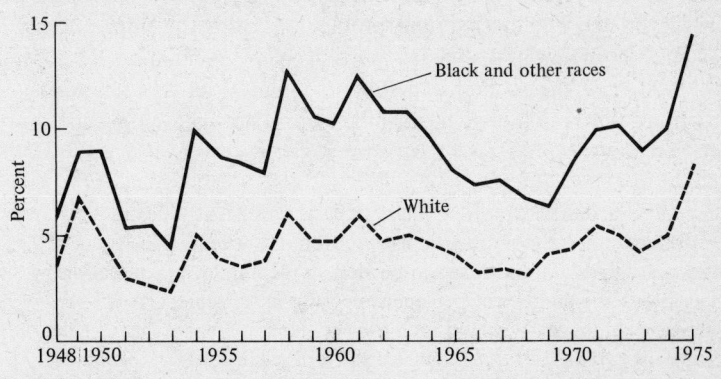

Source: U.S. Department of Commerce, Bureau of the Census, 1978 *Social and Economic Status of the Black Population Reports,* Special Studies Series P-23, No. 80. Washington, D.C.: GPO, p. 59

Among the elderly the problems are somewhat different but still serious. About one of every seven Americans over the age of 65 was below the poverty level in 1977, and among older people living as unrelated individuals, their poverty rate was approximately twice that figure. But the most pressing problem among the elderly is not even the current rate of poverty but their dependence on fixed sources of income such as Social Security:

> Families without earnings income and families whose major source of income was Social Security, either as their only income source or in conjunction with Supplemental Security Income, had a high incidence of poverty. About 31 percent of families with Social Security income only, and about 49 percent of those with Social Security and Supplemental Security incomes, were below the poverty level in 1977. [U.S. Dept. of Commerce, Bureau of the Census, 1978:33.]

Clearly, Social Security in America does not by itself provide adequate income for the elderly. It was never intended to, but that is no consolation to the individuals over 65 years of age who have depended on such fixed and inadequate sources of income in the last few years. In 1977 approximately 26 percent of older Americans living in families and 40 percent of those living as unrelated individuals were reported as dependent on some sort of fixed income solely (U.S. Dept. of Commerce, Bureau of the Census, 1977:124–6). The most serious problem faced by the elderly is that as their numbers and their proportion in the population increase, the ability of the economy to support a variety of dependent populations, the aged included, shrinks. Here is how gerontologist Robert Atchley summarizes the dilemma:

> Since 1965, American economic policy has consistently favored lowered retirement ages and more adequate retirement benefits. . . . Aging of the population will increase the burden on the employed population by increasing the number of persons supported in retirement. Any increases in longevity would increase the burden even further. At the same time, reduced fertility since 1957 will mean fewer employed people. Add to this the prospect that declining nonhuman energy resources may curtail the economy's capacity to produce an economic surplus as large as we are used to. [1980:291.]

To these facts we must add the fact of inflation. The problems for older people who try to live on fixed incomes inevitably will be worse in the coming decades. Social Security was originally intended, in large part, to make it possible for older workers to disengage from their occupations in order to make space for younger workers (Schulz, 1976). Now, as sentiment for the payment of support to dependent populations decreases, the elderly are likely to be compelled to stay on the job for more years or to reenter the job market to relieve the strain on Social Security and other retirement plans. It will be to the advantage of the elderly to have some influence over the terms on which such intended occupational engagement is based. There is a huge difference between remaining on a job in which the worker has accumulated seniority and a high salary over the years and reentering the job market after some temporary retirement, only to have to settle for minimum wages and little or no job security, as often happens today.

Race and Intelligence

Another sign that the facts of discrimination and prejudice are still a part of American life is the reappearance of a debate in the intellectual community once thought to have been put to rest. In Chapter 1 we discussed a theory of minority-group status that we called the *natural inferiority explanation*. We also suggested that the belief that some groups of people are destined by their genetic makeup to lead lives of inferior quality had dominated the thinking on the subject for centuries, only to be replaced quite recently by a theory that such inferior characteristics are learned rather than genetic. By the beginning of the 1970s, however, the natural inferiority argument had reappeared, this time armed with the methodological and statistical sophistication of biogenetics.

In 1969, Arthur Jensen, an educational psychologist, published an article in the *Harvard Educational Review* entitled "How Much Can We Boost IQ and Scholastic Achievement?" In it he argued that intelligence, as measured by IQ tests, is approximately 80 percent a consequence of genetic inheritance; that is, he claimed that the experiences we have in our lives have little effect on our ability to learn as measured by IQ. As a consequence, Jensen argued, special efforts to provide educational help for groups of people who have low IQ scores is a waste of time and money. Also, Jensen argued that the demonstrated difference in white and black IQ scores—blacks have been shown to score about 15 points lower on the average than whites—means that blacks are genetically inferior to whites.

By itself, such an argument would be of little importance. But the fact that it was published in such a respected journal by a respected academician and the fact that it was later supported, directly and indirectly, by other scientists, some of whom were quite well known, made the idea extremely important. In a survey of members of the American Psychological Association, Friedricks (1973) found that 28 percent tended to agree, or agreed outright, with Jensen's 1960 genetic thesis (p. 432). Among the better-known people who responded publicly to the idea were Richard Herrnstein, (1971) and Hans Eysenck, (1971). They agreed with Jensen's apparently carefully documented case for the genetic basis of intelligence, although they differed about what should be done as a consequence. A most extreme position in the debate was taken by William Shockley, who proposed in speeches that genetically "inferior" individuals (based on IQ) be prevented from having children. He devised a program of incentives whereby people with IQ scores below the national average of 100 "be paid $1,000 for each IQ point they are below 100 as incentive to be sterilized" (Berry and Tischler, 1978:77). Shockley also favored the establishment of a sperm bank, so that the genetic makeup of superior individuals be available for the creation of other "superior" beings. He, of course, having won a Nobel prize in engineering, volunteered to contribute. He never did publish in print any work of note on the IQ debate. But as a result of his public statements and scientific standing, it was very much written about.

The point of this discussion is that arguments claiming that social position and potential are expressions of the natural order of things did not die in the nineteenth century, nor are they solely the province of obviously incompetent minds. Generally, these men have been very well respected academicians. But just as nineteenth-century thinkers had allowed their wishes to shape their findings,

Jensen and others were merely playing out their own prejudices on a "scientific" stage. The parallel with the nineteenth-century experience is startling.

To begin with, Jensen's arguments had rested, in large part, on data published by the English psychologist Sir Cyril Burt, who was knighted for his accomplishments. But, by 1974 (Kamin, 1974), strong suspicions had developed about the honesty of Burt's work. Burt had studied the IQ scores of identical twins who had been raised apart from one another. One suspect element of his work was the fact that in three separate studies, each with different sample sizes, Burt reported that the IQ scores of twins were correlated with one another *to the exact same degree* ($r = .771$); that is, he claimed that even when raised in different homes of different social classes, the IQ scores of genetically identical twins remained substantially the same. Thus, Burt "proved" that intelligence is inherited. The problem was that he had very probably invented the data. By 1978, the evidence that Burt had essentially created studies to conform to his beliefs was overwhelming (Dorfman, 1978).

Although there is no reason to believe that Jensen knew in 1969 that Burt's data had been fabricated (although the discovery since has not caused Jensen to withdraw his theory), it is nevertheless true that Jensen has also (perhaps less consciously than Burt) shaped his data to suit his prejudices. In his review of Jensen's 1980 book *Bias in Mental Testing,* Stephen Gould exposes the flaws in Jensen's reasoning. The statistical flaws are extremely difficult to ferret out. Even a reader with some statistical training needs Gould's expert guidance to follow the subtle, but killingly fallacious, assumptions in Jensen's work. For example, Jensen argues that IQ tests are without bias. What he means is that they are without statistical bias, not without the bias by which we mean the extent to which IQ tests reflect cultural, as opposed to innate, sources of intelligence. Statistical bias is absent to the extent that knowledge of scores on one test (IQ, for example) allow us to predict other related scores or characteristics, independent of one's group membership. IQ scores allow us to do that. But we still cannot determine the extent to which IQ scores result from environmental experience, even in statistically unbiased IQ tests. And although Jensen admits that one cannot calculate the degree to which experience influences IQ, he persists in contending that intelligence is genetic.

Gould points out an even more damning flaw:

> Jensen, for example, enthusiastically reports a correlation coefficient of brain size and IQ of about 0.3. He doesn't doubt that this correlation records natural selection operating for greater intelligence through larger brains. . . .
>
> Yet at the bottom of the very same page, he records a correlation of equal strength (average of 0.25) between IQ and body stature. This, he doesn't doubt, "almost certainly involves no causal or functional relationship." Jensen is so attached to his preferred scheme of argument that the obvious interpretation of these facts has not occurred to him—that the weak correlation of IQ and height reflects environmental (largely nutritional) advantages favorable to both and that the correlation of IQ and brain size is a noncausal consequence of it, since big people have bigger body parts, including brains, arms and legs (except that none has ever thought of computing a correlation of leg length with brain size). Choice of question is, indeed, a function of expectation. [1980:43.]

Notice that here Jensen is engaging in precisely the type of reasoning that the brainweighers like Paul Broca used during the middle of the nineteenth century to bolster their argument that larger brain size was related to intelligence and that white male Europeans were superior in both respects. The only difference is that in the nineteenth century, they blatantly selected the brains and skulls they measured to support their beliefs. Jensen did not have to fake his data (although Burt did); all he had to do was misinterpret it.

It is important to emphasize here the potential consequences of accepting the genetic argument. During the early part of this century, psychologists found that immigrants coming from Poland, Russia, Greece, Turkey, and Italy tended to score lower on intelligence tests than did immigrants coming from northwestern Europe: "Psychologists of the time did a host of studies to demonstrate that what they called Mediterranean–Latin–Slavic people, having done much worse on intelligence tests than 'Nordics,' had to be genetically stupid and that if they were admitted to this country in large numbers, they would lower the national level of intelligence" (Kamin, 1973:22). This finding and its interpretation became a basis for the restrictive immigration laws of the 1920s.

Addressing himself to the issue of group differences in intellectual capacity among immigrants to the United States, a Princeton University psychologist argued in 1923:

> Immigration should not only be restrictive but highly selective. And the revision of the immigration and naturalization laws will only afford a slight relief from our present difficulty. The really important steps are those looking toward the prevention of the continued propagation of defective strains in the present population. If all immigration were stopped now, the decline of American intelligence would still be inevitable. This is the problem which must be met, and our manner of meeting it will determine the future course of our national life. [Brigham, 1923:210.]

In a like manner, Sweeny wrote in *North American Review* that the time had come to awaken to the need for protection from the influx of the "worthless" eastern and southern European immigrants who scored lower on intelligence tests than their counterparts from western and northern Europe. He argued that the "stream of intelligence" was being "polluted" by "this emptying of undesirables into this country . . ." (1922:600).

Arguments like Richard Herrnstein's (1971), that socioeconomic status is a result of inherited differences in intelligence, might lead to the justification of rule by IQ elites. Any theory of genetic sources of social or economic position seems necessarily conservative. It would, like Social Darwinism, have the effect of saying that those who dominate do so as a consequence of their innate qualification to do so. Any such theory, therefore, might also reduce our willingness to do anything to improve the opportunities for minorities, based on the logic that nothing can be done to alter our genetic fates.

Sociobiology

Probably the most widely debated version of this pervasive controversy over the origins of social inequality was sparked by the publication in 1975 of Edward Wilson's massive book *Sociobiology: The New Synthesis*. Wilson, an internationally respected student of insect behavior, wrote this exhaustive study of the biological bases of animal behavior and then applied the theory to the social behavior of humans. He argued that genetics strongly influences how we adapt to our environment, the shape of our social behavior, and our overall potential. More specifically, sociobiology has contended that genetic structure exists for specific traits in human behavior, including spite, aggression, conformity, homosexuality, domination of men over women, social class, and altruism. For example, one element of the sociobiological position holds that altruism, that is, helping others at one's own expense, seems to be contrary to natural selection. Thus, its evolution as an undeniable human social characteristic has to be explained if genetic structure can be at the root of human social behavior. The sociobiological solution is that by helping others to survive, we are, to the extent that we share genetic information with the helper, helping our own genetic information to survive. The "selfish gene" is the gene that wishes to be passed on. Our primary "orders," accordingly, are to engage in behaviors that increase the likelihood that our own genetic information will be passed on. When we save a relative from drowning, we are really helping that genetic information which we share to survive. The application of this idea to the structure and closeness of the family as a social system is apparent. The controversy surrounding this idea focuses on two different, though highly related, areas. The first is the merit of the argument itself, and the second is the use to which the ideas have been, and are likely to be, put.

The Merits of Sociobiological Thought

Even among its detractors, there is little but praise for the treatment Wilson gives the role of heredity in the structuring of social behavior among animals other than humans. It is when these principals are extended to human social order that violent objections are raised. (Wilson has been shouted down at scientific conferences; has been called a racist, sexist, elitist; and has even been subjected to physical abuse when he has tried to speak. At one meeting of the American Sociological Association, which we attended, Wilson's talk was the only packed room we saw—in the largest ballroom in the hotel—and the banners that proclaimed him a racist and sexist were held by chanting students and opponents who shouted with anger at every remark with which they disagreed.)

At the heart of this debate is the speculation that human social behavior is strongly influenced by genetic imperatives, like the "selfish gene." Opponents of sociobiology have contended that human behavior is shaped by forces entirely different from those that shape the social (and nonsocial) behavior of other animals. Specifically, they claim that human social behavior is symbolic in nature. Instinctual (inborn) or stimulus-response (implanted or conditioned) patterns of behavior are automatic. The response to a stimulus is the consequence of inborn patterns in the first system and learned patterns in the second, but in either case, such responses are entirely predictable. Change the weather, and geese migrate. Ring a bell, and Pavlov's dog salivates. No variations. In contrast, humans interact at the symbolic, or meaningful, level. Stimuli are evaluated or interpreted before they are either acted on or not acted on. Not only can we decide whether to act, we can decide how to act depending on our evaluation of the meaning of a stimulus. Say "sit" to a conditioned dog, and it will. Say "sit" to a human, and he or she may then ask, "where?" or even say, "No, thank you." This symbolic level of interaction, in the belief of most critics of sociobiology, is unique to humans. It has been used to explain the fact of cultural variations; the very same behavior can mean entirely different, even opposite, things in different cultures. We believe that the many and varied substantive attacks on sociobiology have hinged on these differing assumptions about the nature of human social behavior.

The Uses of Sociobiology

The most aggressive objections to sociobiology stem more from its uses, actual and potential, than from the merits of the argument. The instant one claims that there is a biological basis to human behavior and potential, the use to which the statement will be put is predictable. Especially when the source of the claim is a scientist of some (or, in this case, great) respectability, people with other than purely scientific interests are bound to latch onto the idea to promote their own, more base purposes. Even if an original investigator thinks other people are misusing his or her work, the fact remains that scientists do not retain control over their theories. Wilson has said he is distressed to be grouped with blatant bigots when they have invoked sociobiological arguments to promote racist and/or sexist schemes for a restructuring of opportunity in their own interests. But the fact remains that once the idea is out, its uses cannot be controlled. Sociobiology is extremely vulnerable to being used by eugenicists as scientific "proof" of the superiority of one group of people to another. (Too often this means the superiority of eugenicists themselves.)

This is, once again, precisely the use to which the "science" of the nineteenth century was put by those who wished to justify their dominant positions in society. Here is how the parallel with sociobiology is described by a group formed specifically to attack the theory:

DNA has replaced gross anatomical features as the supposed determinant of human nature. Now we are told that the genes of blacks or members of the working class, rather than the shapes of their skulls, doom them to an inferior status in a species in which the status hierarchy is itself an inevitable result of the "human genotype." [Sociobiology Study Group, 1979:3.]

Whatever one thinks of the merits of the sociobiological theory, the fact that it is likely to do harm to the opportunities available to minority-group members makes it hated by many. To the extent that we believe that human potential is related to genetic character, we seem also to reduce our belief in the possibilities for social change and improvement. Why offer special educational programs if their recipients do not have "what it takes" to benefit from them? Why support affirmative action if those who have landed in positions of inferiority did so as a consequence of their innate potential? Why redistribute opportunity to any group that has, by its social position, shown itself to be capable of only what it has so far accomplished? These are the questions raised by proponents of sociobiology, and they explain something of the violence of others' hatred for the theory.

The New Ethnicity

As of the writing of this book, opposition to school integration has remained strong in America's cities. In Boston, for example, desegregation orders from the federal court were greeted with powerful opposition from citizens' groups and political officeholders who promised to relieve their constituents of the burden of busing to achieve desegregation. When no such relief was forthcoming from the courts or via the legislative process, white residents responded by removing their children from public school systems in mass movements called *white flight*. This has been especially true in schools with higher proportions of black students and in schools close to white neighborhoods to which the whites could move (Levine and Meyer, 1977).

In Boston, for example, opposition to court-ordered busing put white ethnic groups and blacks into direct conflict with one another. Irish Catholic Bostonians, many just one generation removed from their own most painful experiences as minority-group members, demanded control over their neighborhood schools. They put pressure on their elected officials to represent their desires in the search for relief from the requirements of school desegregation. Blacks, for their part, confronted white, working-class ethnics as majority-group members and showed no apparent feelings of a common set of experiences as minority-group members. The Boston busing case is just one example of how a debate arose about the impact of the rising ethnic consciousness in America.

Following the focus on the black civil rights struggle during the 1960s, several groups began to develop a new consciousness of their place in American society. Besides women and Spanish-speaking people, various white ethnic groups such as Irish-, Italian-, and Polish-Americans expressed a rediscovered pride in their preimmigration heritages and a newer awareness of their pasts as victims of postimmigration discrimination. Glazer and Moynihan's *Beyond the Melting Pot* (1963) and Novak's *The Rise of the Unmeltable Ethnics* (1971) questioned the inevitability and the advisability of assimilation, a previously unquestioned norm of American culture. What is the meaning of the new ethnicity? Is it, as Andrew Greeley (1978) argues, another example of the "throbbing" and "vital" pluralism which has, by its diversity, strengthened and enriched America? Or is Andrew Patterson (1977) correct in characterizing it as ethnic chauvinism? Patterson contends that ethnic pluralism divides the society, makes it easier for dominant forces to deny minorities their rights, and prevents minorities from joining together to fight for what they want. Greeley responds that ethnic identity is opposed mainly out of "nativist bigotry," that set of prejudices and quotas against the newer immigrants who have followed them to America. The issue of ethnic identity is not only still important, it is increasing in importance. As of 1980 the Chicago school system was under pressure to desegregate. Chicago is a city with a very large white ethnic population, and the conflict between white ethnics and blacks threatens to be extremely serious.

Perhaps even more important to the rise of ethnicity has been the inflation and recession of the 1970s. Minority groups have had a difficult enough time making claims on the wealth of our economy when it was growing. But as the economy has entered difficult times, the American consumer and taxpayer has been increasingly squeezed. As a consequence, many more people have begun to see themselves as relatively disadvantaged. Each group has also become willing to lay special claim on our shrinking resources. There is an increasing potential for conflicts between traditionally recognized minority groups, such as blacks, and groups that have only recently begun to see themselves as victims of discrimination, such as women, the elderly, and a variety of white ethnics.

The New Conservatism

Just as Ronald Reagan was elected to the presidency, both houses of Congress passed legislation that would *bar the Justice Department* from taking actions that would require school districts to use busing to desegregate their dual school systems. And just before he took office, the new president-elect announced that he would support such legislation. The new conservative tone the nation adopted toward the end of the 1970s and at the beginning of the new decade seemed to threaten that, just as the position of minorities in America had not materially improved during the inflationary years just past, the likelihood of such improvement during the next few years was dim indeed. In fact, it also appeared that even legislative and status improvements made by minorities during the 1960s were also threatened. The new conservative majority that swept into the Congress with Reagan took over committee chairmanships (they were all men, so the term is apt) and began to announce its legislative intentions. Senator Strom Thurmond, soon to become chairman of the Judiciary Committee, stated that he planned to act to repeal the 1965 Voting Rights Act. At the same time Senator Orrin Hatch, Chairman of the Public Works Committee, announced his intention to introduce legislation that would outlaw affirmative action programs.

The types of programs that had been developed, primarily during the 1960s, to try to improve conditions for minority-group members, such as legal aid programs, affirmative action, civil rights and desegregation legislation, all these had been attacked during the late 1970s. Although claiming to support the need of such minorities to experience expanded opportunity, Reagan has opposed efforts such as court-ordered plans for school desegregation and the Equal Rights Amendment. It remains to be seen whether whatever the more conservative nation has in mind for its most disadvantaged minorities will diminish the deprivations they have experienced.

BOX 3.3

The Persistence of Anti-Semitism

An important part of the political victory of conservative candidates for national office during the 1980 elections were fundamentalist religious organizations. They acted in coordinated campaigns to put conservatives into office and to defeat selected liberals. One example, the largest such organization, was the group called the "moral majority." Their position was a combination of religious fundamentalist dogma and political, ideological, and military conservatism. Near the end of the campaign a furor arose over a comment attributed to a Baptist preacher and a leader of the Moral Majority, to the effect that God did not hear the prayers of Jews. In a televised interview he explained that he had been misunderstood, but the issue of anti-Semitism was not erased in all parts of society. The following article appeared in the *Boston Globe* on November 15, 1980, and illustrates both the petty indignities that Jews have in the past, and may in the future, to suffer and the more serious prejudices (such as the belief that Jews cannot reach heaven) that have been used to make Jews outcasts in many societies.

Baptist Offers Jews an Apology
Associated Press

Del City, Okla.—The president of the Southern Baptist Convention, insisting he was only "teasing," apologized yesterday for his remark in a broadcast sermon that "Jews got funny-looking noses."

"I sincerely apologize to anyone who was offended by my teasing," said Bailey Smith, the Oklahoma preacher who leads the nation's largest Protestant denomination.

Smith said the remark about noses, made Sept. 14 at the end of a sermon on God's special people and special places, was "an aside."

Two weeks before the remark, Smith had sparked controversy when he told a 15,000-member audience at the National Affairs Briefing in Dallas that "God almighty does not hear the prayer of a Jew" because Jews do not accept Jesus as the Messiah.

The Dallas Morning News obtained a transcript of the sermon, which was broadcast on an Oklahoma radio station from the First Baptist Church in Del City. It quoted Smith as saying from the pulpit:

"There are some people with whom God works more intimately than others. Why, you say? I don't know. Why did he choose the Jews? I don't know why he chose the Jews.

"I think they got funny-looking noses, myself. I don't know why he chose the Jews. That's God's business. Amen."

Functionalism and the Analysis of Discrimination and Prejudice

By way of introduction to the final section of this chapter, it would be useful to summarize our argument to this point. Minority groups are characterized by recognizability, unequal treatment on the basis of their characteristics, and some sense of being treated differently, either in the form of positive or negative group identity. Examples of such groups are American blacks, women, and the elderly. Those who in the past have tried to explain why such minority groups exist have tended to rely on two dominant theories. The *natural inferiority approach* claimed that minority groups are composed of individuals who are inherently inferior and suited only for the life of inferiors in society. Although this approach was strongest during the nineteenth century, there is evidence that it is still with us in the work of Jensen, Shockley, the sociobiologists, and others. The second view, called the *acquired inferiority approach,* contends that minority groups are composed of individuals who are inferior as a consequence of their experiences rather than as a consequence of genetic inheritance. Both acquired and natural inferiority approaches can be characterized as *victim blaming;* that is, they root the problems of minority groups in the characteristics of the victims, rather than in the social forces that distribute opportunity *to* them.

An alternative to these approaches is to blame the social distribution of opportunity for the creation of minority groups. In order to make it possible to develop a *system-blaming,* rather than a *victim-blaming* theory, it is necessary to understand the role of discrimination and prejudice and the relationship between them. Prejudice develops in order to justify discrimination, and, once prejudice has become a part of the culture, it tends to become very stable. It acts to perpetuate discrimination.

The beginning of this chapter has been devoted to illustrating the fact that despite the popular belief that prejudice and discrimination have been greatly diminished, they are still very much with us and may, in fact, be increasing. It is the primary goal of this book to propose, as an alternative to the victim-blaming approaches, a system-blaming theory that can help us explain why, in the face of our almost universal hatred of their existence, prejudice and discrimination persist. We contend that discrimination and prejudice persist because they have some extremely important system-maintaining, or positive functions, especially for the most powerful segments of our society. They benefit many people who are in a position to contribute to their persistence. In order to illustrate that there are structural conditions in American society that make it advantageous to many segments of society to act (or fail to act) in order to contribute to the persistence of prejudice and discrimination, we will need to present a general model for the analysis of social forces. Just how do certain actions or ideas benefit selected segments of society, and how can they be maintained even when they harm the well-being of other segments? These are the very important questions dealt with in this section on functionalism.

Functionalism

When we say that prejudice and discrimination have some positive functions, it may sound as if we are saying that prejudice and discrimination are good or desirable. We are not. Perhaps prejudice and discrimination have not been analyzed in functional terms because we often misunderstand the nature of the functionalist view. The major difficulty arises from the failure to distinguish between that which is good in a moral sense and that which is functonal. To make the difference clear, we will begin with a discussion of functionalism.

Functionalism is a way of thinking about how things are arranged and how they work within complex systems. Functionalism assumes that objects, actions, and ideas are arranged in systems, each of which has a number of parts. Each part is assumed to have consequences for the system of which it is an element and even for systems to which it does not obviously belong. We make functionalist judgments and statements all the time in our everyday conversations.

For example, we think of the human organism as a system with many parts. If we wanted to explain to someone what one of those constituent parts was we would most likely explain it in terms of what it does, that is, how it operates within the more complex structure of which it is just one element. What is the human heart? It is what it does for the human organism; it is a pump. Rather than describe the heart in terms of its size, shape, color, texture, sound, temperature, and so on, we identify its importance in terms of its consequences for the system of which it is a part. The leg of a chair is normally viewed in terms of its consequences for the stability of the chair, although, admittedly, a chair is not a very complex system. A spark plug or carburetor is explained in terms of its consequences for the operation of an engine or car. Notice that the level of the system to which a constituent part is related may be chosen at a lower or higher point. The spark plug is part of several systems—ignition, engine, automobile—each of which may be thought of as a constituent part of the next more complex system up the scale.

Functional relationships between parts and the systems they influence are so central to the way we understand the world that it is not possible to operate normally without thinking functionally. When we answer a child's question "What's that?", it is in functional terms. "That is for eating," or more often, "That isn't food, take it out of your mouth." One of the most basic assumptions we make, then, and one of the basic assumptions of the functionalist perspective, is that the world is composed of systems with interrelated parts, each system operating at some level of stability or equilibrium. The complexity of the systems may vary widely as may the degree of the stability of that system. At the very least, to be called a system, it must be capable of not dissolving or dissipating spontaneously. To some degree systems remain recognizably intact from one moment or year to the next and may even be capable of adjusting to changes around them. In analyzing systems, then, we often speak of their stability or adjustment. A table, then, has a stability of not changing its shape from one time to the next, and the heating system of a home has the ability to adapt to the temperatures in the home, a slightly different type of equilibrium.

So far, the examples of systems we have used are from the physical world. Rather than study engines or buildings or even the human organism, social scientists have focused on human psychological and social systems. Our personal mental well-being (or mental adaptive capacity) and our social structures can be thought of as systems in relative balance. Each has constituent parts with consequences for the operation of such systems.

Function and Dysfunction

These questions in the social sciences raise a very important issue in functionalism. Notice that the examples of objects from systems in the physical world were all *helpful* to the systems to which they belonged. The heart aids the human organism toward stability, and the same is true for the leg of the chair, the spark plug, and so on. Each, then, is *positively functional*. Following Merton's (1957) usage, a *function* (or positive function) is a consequence that *aids in the adaptation or adjustment of a system.* However, Merton also identified the concept of *dysfunction,* a consequence that *diminishes or detracts from the adaptation or adjustment of a system.*[1] It is possible, then, to see how an event, such as failing an exam, could *diminish* the stability or adaptation of the personality. Perhaps it reduces one's confidence. As a consequence of failure, are we less able to operate at the personality level? At the social level, do increases in the price of oil increase or decrease the stability of our economic structure—an important part of the social system in America? What are the functions of a variety of ideas or actions likely to be for another important social structure, the family? Increasing opportunities for women in the labor market, availability of birth control throughout the population, day-care programs, increasing leisure time, inflation, passage of the Equal Rights Amendment, each of these is likely to have consequences for the American family structure in its current form. To analyze this issue in functionalist terms, we have to remain within the guidelines of the functionalist approach. In terms of the family as a social structure in its present form (whatever opinion one has of the usefulness of that structure), would a given action, idea, or object contribute to its stability as it is, or would it diminish that stability? If we analyze the consequences of such events for the traditional family, with its division of labor, then it becomes clear that these named events are likely to be *dysfunctional* for such a family. Those objects, actions, or ideas that would tend to perpetuate and strengthen the family *as it is* would have to be considered functional, whereas those that tended to contribute to the weakening of the family in its present form would be considered dysfunctional. But what if you think the traditional family structure *needs* to be changed. Are events that would lead to such changes still to be considered *dys*functional for the *family* structure? So in the way that we are using functionalism, it must be thought of as a sort of "snapshot" type of analysis, that is, the consequences of an action, idea, or object for a system *as it is at a given time* limit our thinking and make the analysis possible. What were the consequences of Richard Nixon's resignation for the stability of the government at the time he resigned? In the model for functionalism that we are using, the resignation would have had to be termed dysfunctional, for it caused changes in the way government operated, decreases in our certainty about what would happen, and questions about the appropriateness of the way we choose and evaluate the work of elected officials. Most of the analysis of the consequences of the resignation, however, focused on the long-term stability that may have resulted. If, after the initial difficulties of the impeachment and resignation a changed governmental structure had evolved, one even more stable, more capable of dealing with such problems in the future, then we probably would feel justified in saying that the resignation had positive, system-stabilizing consequences. But notice that in terms of functional analysis we are now talking about a different system, one that evolved, in theory, out of the instability of the previous system. By limiting our analysis of the functions of some event for the systems as they were at the time of the event, we sacrifice the longer view in the interest of speaking the same functionalist language. It is only a convention but an important one if our argument is to be understood. The "snapshot" character of this functionalist model is illustrated in Figure 3.2.

Functional Versus Moral Evaluations

Now it is possible to clarify the difficulty we encounter when we confuse functional with moral evaluations. To conclude that something is functional for a system is not to conclude that it is therefore good in a moral sense. That judgment depends on how one feels about the system for which it is functional. For example, there is no disagreement with the assertion that the human heart is functional for the operation of the body as a system. In a functional sense, then, the heart is positively functional for the human organism, independent of our judgment of the goodness of the specific human being. Therefore Adolf Hitler's heart was functional in a system sense, although evil in a moral sense, for it contributed to the existence of a person we believe to have been evil. We commonly make judgments about the desirability of a variety of behaviors, events, objects, and the systems to which they belong, but if we are to understand their persistence, it is necessary to isolate our evaluation of them from their functional consequences for the systems of the world. Let's return to the example of the consequence of day-care programs and increased availability of work for women outside the home for the family structure. If we conclude that the consequence of these events is to diminish the stability of the traditional American family, then clearly these events are dysfunctional for the family. Two sorts of evaluations of that conclusion are still, however, possible. Half the people in the country seem to be saying, "Good, the sooner these changes come about, the better," whereas the other half says, "Stop the funding of day-care centers and don't support programs or legislation that would increase opportunities for women to work outside the home, because these would destroy the traditional family structure." At

Figure 3.2 Illustration of the "snapshot" character of functionalism.

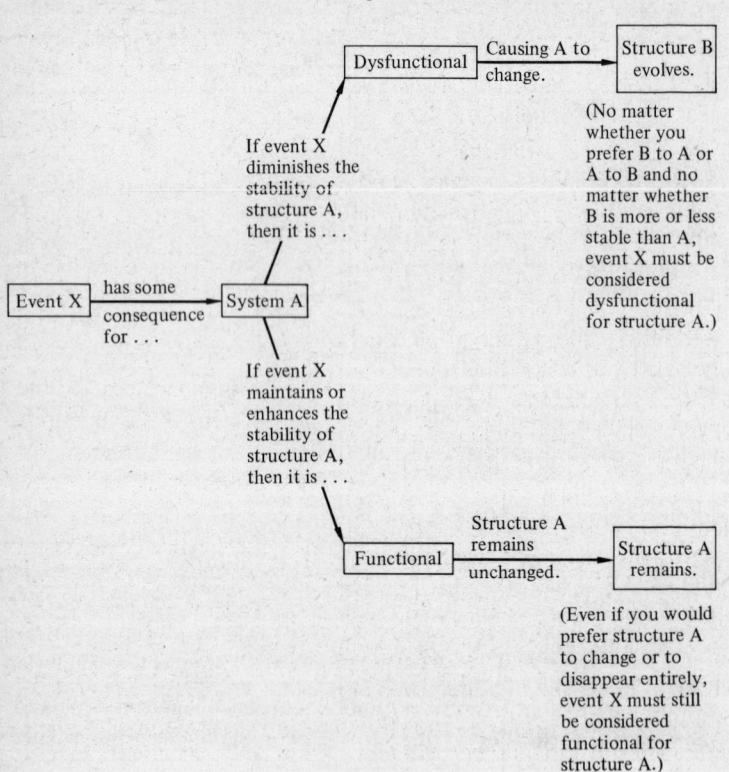

Event X has some consequence for... System A

If event X diminishes the stability of structure A, then it is... Dysfunctional — Causing A to change. → Structure B evolves.

(No matter whether you prefer B to A or A to B and no matter whether B is more or less stable than A, event X must be considered dysfunctional for structure A.)

If event X maintains or enhances the stability of structure A, then it is... Functional — Structure A remains unchanged. → Structure A remains.

(Even if you would prefer structure A to change or to disappear entirely, event X must still be considered functional for structure A.)

times during our discussion it will seem difficult to answer what have been treated traditionally as moral, evaluative questions in purely functional terms. However, it is our thesis that the persistence of prejudice can be attributed to its functions for society and various individuals and that the evaluative treatment of prejudice and discrimination—the persistent conclusion that they are evil—can only take us so far in the effort to understand and eradicate them. Whether or not prejudice can be regarded as good is independent of the conclusions reached in a functional analysis. Prejudice can be viewed by an individual or by society as a whole as an immoral act and therefore an unacceptable means, regardless of its relative costs and benefits for the maintenance of a given system.

Manifest and Latent Functions

Merton also distinguished between functions that are manifest (whose contribution to the stability of a system is intended and recognized) and latent positive functions (whose contribution to the stability of a system is neither intentional nor normally recognized by system participants). Manifest and latent dysfunctions are also, therefore, possible. Table 3.3 is an example of one way that the possible functional categories can be arranged.

Any one action, idea, or object may have a variety of conse-

Table 3.3 Functional Consequences and the Concept of Latency

	Manifest	Latent
Functional	Contributes to the stability of some system and is intended and recognized as doing so	Contributes to the stability of some system but is neither intended nor recognized as so doing
Dysfunctional	Detracts from the stability of some system and is intended and recognized as doing so.	Detracts from the stability of some system but is neither intended nor recognized as doing so

quences for a variety of systems. For example, the manifest function of a marriage ceremony is to legally unite a bride and groom, but one of the latent positive functions (in terms of maintaining the social structure of the larger family) is to provide an occasion for family members to come together socially. Another latent consequence of the marriage ceremony is to provide work for a variety of businesses such as caterers, dance bands, tent manufacturers (in some cases), tuxedo renters, and so on. Clearly these are not the normally recognized purposes or consequences for which wedding ceremonies officially exist, but they clearly contribute to the persistence of the celebration as we know it in much of America. As another example, the manifest function of television is to entertain and distribute information, but latent functions include the socialization of the audience to middle-class values, the development of a desire for certain products, and the provision of a form of baby-sitter for young children.

If we were to analyze the variety of consequences of a given object, action, or idea for a specific system, it would become apparent whether the consequences were manifest or latent and whether they were functional or dysfunctional. Here are brief example analyses of two very different societal phenomena. One is, we can agree, undesirable—war, and the other is more generally considered desirable—college.

Of course these sample analyses are very brief and incomplete. In fact, given the complexity of the social world, it seems extremely unlikely that *all* the consequences of even a fairly simple action or idea could be fully charted. For one thing, systems exist at several levels. In accordance with Merton's and Parsons' functionalism (Turner 1960:71), we can recognize a range of levels—(1) organism, (2) personality, (3) the social system and its various subgroups, and (4) the culture—for which any given item may have consequences. In addition, a given action can be functional for one system but dysfunctional for another.

System Levels

Organism The word "organism" refers to the human body as a system in relative equilibrium or physical health. War is manifestly dysfunctional at the level of the human organism because it kills

Table 3.4

Functional Analysis of College

	Manifest	Latent
Functional	1. Education. 2. Maturation. 3. Develop citizenship. 4. Broaden experiences. (These are the official claims in any college catalog, handbook or recruitment circular for the functions of a college education.)	1. Postpone entry into the work world. 2. Find a person to marry. 3. Have fun. 4. Train for entry into professional sports. 5. Provide jobs for professors. 6. Provide a market for textbooks.

Dysfunctional	1. Some colleges may be designed to intentionally promote changes in:
	   a. social structures
	   b. personalities
	(For colleges to have manifest dysfunctions they must officially have change as a goal.)
		1. Creates overqualification.
		2. Promotes independent and critical thinking which can lead to pressures for social change or disruption (dysfunctional when such change is unwanted by the society).
		3. Can be very costly to some segments of the society such as taxpayers.

Functional Analysis of War

	Manifest	Latent
Functional	1. Defend territory. 2. Take land. 3. Achieve independence. (Only manifest functions when these are the officially stated purposes of going to war.)	1. Strengthens the economy by, for example, increasing employment. 2. Stimulates inventions and technical innovations. 3. Population control. 4. Increases internal national cohesion. 5. Military structure expands and is strengthened. 6. Expands territory (a latent function only when this is not an officially stated goal of going to war). 7. Profitable for some industries, but not for others, for whom war is dysfunctional.
Dysfunctional	1. Death. 2. Suffering from injuries and other sacrifices made by certain members of the society—especially the poor. 3. Financial costs to much of the society, especially the poor and lower middle classes.	1. Forces us to kill in violation of our own religious and moral beliefs. 2. Relations with some nations, such as allies, may deteriorate. 3. Certain subgroups in society are alienated (such as Japanese Americans during WWII).

and maims both civilians and soldiers. However, for those soldiers who are not injured, war may actually have latent functions for their health if they have gone through strenuous basic training and are denied the unhealthful indulgences of peace-time diets and inactivity. Overall though, it would seem safe to assume that war is more dysfunctional than functional at the level of the organism.

Personality The personality level refers to our mental adaptive capacity, the ability to understand how to accomplish our daily tasks and how to make sense of the world (including the demands of other people) around us. Our mental well-being is considered stable, or in equilibrium, to the extent that we feel comfortable about our daily lives, confident and well-fitted to our surroundings. Disequilibrium or imbalance is apparent in feelings of insecurity, anxiety, lack of self-confidence, depression, or, in the extreme, the total inability to face the world or operate in it for other than physical reasons. In functional terms, we expect college to be functional for the personalities of students to the extent that it raises self-confidence and esteem and allows us to adapt better to the career or way of life we may have chosen. College may, however, have latent dysfunctions for those who wish to attend but are denied the opportunity to do so. They may feel deprived or inadequate or even inferior. War has been found to be dysfunctional for the personalities of returning soldiers, especially those returned from Viet Nam, who are finding it difficult to adjust to a civilian life in which there are fewer structured regimens for daily life and in which the sacrifices they made as soldiers are unrecognized, or even ridiculed, by their fellow citizens. The difficulties in adjusting mentally to civilian life after war are evident in high rates of alcoholism, drug addiction, and suicide.

Social System The social-structured level is probably the most complex and varied level of systems at which functional analyses are normally made. This is because social structures range in size and complexity from the simple, two-person group (a friendship, for example) to the society itself. Between are social structures and categories as varied as the family, economy, private business, government, a single governmental agency, a type of occupation, the military, the welfare system, and so on. If we include not just social structures, with their stable and well-defined sets of relationships and norms for behavior, but also all the subgroups (or even subcategories of people) in the society, the list of possible systems becomes endless. Thus, in the analysis of the functions of war we can guess that war contributes to the stability of the military structure and some industries, such as munitions, transportation, communication, some clothing manufacture, and so on. But for other types of business, such as pollution control, high-fashion clothing, cosmetics, leisure industries, and for subgroups such as minorities, the elderly and the poor, war is clearly dysfunctional.

Culture Last of all, the culture, that system of symbols and meanings that humans create to organize their lives at the most abstract level, may be thought of as another system for which war or college may have consequences. College education is normally thought of as functional for the culture because it helps perpetuate the values of progress, science, independence, profit, future-time orientation, and so on. To the extent that war, college education, or any other facet of society weakens such values (for example, the Viet Nam War may have weakened our respect for authority in America), they may be considered dysfunctional for the American culture as it was at the time.

Our analysis of the functions of prejudice and discrimination will focus on the personality and social-system levels, although some mention of the consequences of prejudice and discrimination at the organism and cultural levels will be made. Returning to the difficulty of completing a full, functionalist analysis, notice that in the foregoing illustrations, war and college each have some positive functions and some dysfunctions. The knowledge that even much simpler facets of human existence have simultaneous functions for one system and dysfunctions for others makes the analysis both richer and more difficult. For a student, studying for very long hours may be dysfunctional at the level of the organism (getting tired) but functional for the personality structure (providing confidence). When we decide to air a grievance in our family, to "have it out," we may be diminishing frustration at the level of the personality (functional) but simultaneously decreasing the stability of the bonds of the relationship (dysfunctional at the social-system level).

The Net Balance of Consequences and the Role of Power

The fact that there are such mixed sets of consequences and the fact that they may vary in the severity of their influence on systems allow us to appreciate Merton's idea of the "net balance of an aggregate of consequences." A given action, object, or idea may have extremely important consequences for a system or very minor ones. It may, if dysfunctional, throw a system slightly out of balance (like catching a cold)—a disruption with which the system deals quite easily—or it may totally destroy the system's equilibrium (like bashing a spinning top with a baseball bat). In the same way, an object may have extremely important functions for the operation of a system (such as the human heart, without which the organism does not operate at all) or rather more marginal contributions to make to the stability of the system. Our sense of smell contributes to the operation of the organism, but we can, with some diminished efficiency, live without it. We can call this the *concept of functional (or dysfunctional) importance.*

Now to Merton's idea of the net balance of consequences. We began the discussion of functionalism in order to deal with the question of why prejudice and discrimination persist; that is, if prejudice and discrimination are as disruptive to the operation of society and individuals as most of the existing literature has contended, then why have they not been extinguished, wiped out, the way we eliminate other uniformly costly behaviors? If prejudice is dysfunctional for all systems, at all levels, then would we not expect it to be actively fought by those whose stability it disrupts, or at least, to wither away like some vestigial or nonfunctional structure? We have models for such a process from the biological world. A popular example is the vermiform appendix, which, having lost its (likely) function in the digestion of raw meats, has become nonfunctional. Through disuse, it has withered, as have other nonfunctional or marginally functional structures of the body, such as small toes and the muscles that direct the positioning of the outer ear.

But is there a similar process in the system operation of human psychological, social, and cultural orders? Can a social structure "select for" certain behaviors that would enhance its stability? Can the personality? And even if some segment of a larger society, such as a minority population, benefited from a given idea or behavior, could they actually influence its existence? Or, even more importantly in this case, *could a behavior perceived as dysfunctional for such a segment of society be extinguished by them?*

It is our contention that actions, ideas, and objects can be analyzed in terms of the consequences they have for a variety of human systems. The particular actions and ideas with which we are concerned are prejudice and discrimination. Most often attributed to flaws in human character such as fear, greed, weakness, and so on, prejudice and discrimination have been assumed to be dysfunctional for all systems. We believe that *prejudice and discrimination have persisted because they contribute to the stability of a number of structures in human social and psycholgoical order and that these systems have acted (or have failed to act) in order to contribute to the persistence of prejudice and discrimination to the benefit of their own stability.* Although prejudice and discrimination are clearly overwhelmingly dysfunctional for a variety of other systems (such as minorities at both the social and psychological levels), these systems lack the power to influence the existence of prejudice and discrimination in America. In order to conceptualize in functionalist terms the relationships between these systems, we can begin with Merton's concept of the net aggregate of consequences, which later will need to be altered.

If we want to establish a net balance for a given behavior, we need to know a few things: (1) For what systems does the behavior have consequences? (2) For each system are the consequences functional or dysfunctional and to what degree (functional importance)? In theory, we could make out a kind of balance sheet on which all the functions and dysfunctions of a given behavior could be listed and the systems so influenced identified along with the functional (or dysfunctional) importance of each consequence. One would imagine that if the final tally of the functions versus dysfunctions came out overwhelmingly positive, the systems for which the behavior was positive would act to perpetuate, or even strengthen, the existence of the behavior involved. Similarly, if the balance sheet for the behavior came out strongly dysfunctional (the behavior is dysfunctional for many more systems than those for which it is functional), then those systems for which it is dysfunctional would act to weaken or extinguish the behavior. However, some systems have no influence over the persistence of behaviors that influence that system's stability. They have no mechanism for strengthening or weakening the structures, actions, or beliefs in society. The key is power. Power allows a system (whether an individual, subgroup, or social structure) to exercise influence out of proportion to its numbers, even to the detriment of others.

How much power does each system need in order to do something about the existence of any behavior? As an illustration, think of the consequences of a teacher giving his or her class a surprise exam. Let's assume that the only systems influenced by this behavior are the mental well-being of the students and that of the teacher. Let's also assume (as students have told us) that surprise exams are dysfunctional for students (reducing confidence, raising anxiety and frustration, and so on) but functional for the teacher, enhancing the teacher's sense of control and power and implying his or her expertise in the subject being taught. If there are 40 students in the class and 1 teacher, then at first glance it might look like the dysfunctions of giving a surprise exam greatly outweigh the functions. But such exams are given over the objections of even larger classes of students. The answer lies in the power of the students versus the power of the teacher to do anything about it. Power exists independent of numbers. The group that has at its disposal the will and the mechanism (such as legislation) can influence the fate of a behavior, object, or idea out of proportion to the number of people in that group. Think, for example, of the existence of racial apartheid in South Africa, which has persisted in spite of its overwhelmingly negative consequences for the more than 85 percent of the population which is black. Often a teacher has so much more power than his or her students that he or she can, if it is important enough, compel them to suffer some extremely dysfunctional experiences. Greatly outnumbered in the system sense, more powerful actors can cause such behaviors as spot quizzes to persist. Thus *the idea of the net aggregate of consequences must be greatly adjusted to take into account the role of power in determining the persistence of functions and the extinction of dysfunctions,* even to the detriment of a variety of other individuals, subgroups, or social systems.

In the remainder of this book we will focus on the system-maintaining functions that prejudice and discrimination have for a variety of systems. We will focus on the personality and social-system levels, with only brief mention of the functions of prejudice and discrimination at the organism and cultural levels. Further, we will concentrate on the functions for the personalities and social structures of majority-group members, largely because they are the people for whom the most positive consequences of prejudice and discrimination accumulate and because they are the people with the most power to influence the existence of a given idea or behavior. We will briefly discuss some of the surprising positive consequences of prejudice and discrimination for *some* minority-group members, in spite of the fact that prejudice and discrimination are overwhelmingly *dys*functional for minority-group members.

Lastly, because we believe that up to this point prejudice and discrimination have been treated as solely dysfunctional and that their dysfunctions have been more than adequately identified, we will not continue to emphasize these components of the functionalist model. And because it is so rare to find anyone who contends openly and intentionally that prejudice is functional, *and ought to be* (we strongly believe that it is functional but ought not to be), we will not focus on the manifest functions of prejudice and discrimination. Figure 3.3 is a diagram of how this book will analyze prejudice and discrimination in functionalist terms.

As we discuss the positive, or system-maintaining functions of discrimination and prejudice, keep in mind that the power of the various systems for which discrimination and prejudice are functional differ greatly in terms of their ability to contribute to the maintenance of discrimination and prejudice. For example, although we will identify some functions for *minority-group* members, it is clear that discrimination and prejudice remain overwhelmingly dysfunctional for them. Nevertheless, the fact that minority groups lack the power to do anything about this situation means that ultimately nothing will be done to extinguish those attitudes and behaviors that harm them.

Similarly, we will be discussing the functions of discrimination and prejudice for a number of other social systems (e.g., economic and occupational) and psychological systems of *majority-group* members. One important distinction between social systems is the difference between richer, more powerful members of the majority (what might be called upper-class, business-operating, white males) and less wealthy, middle-, and lower-middle-class majority-group members (those white males who do not own businesses and so must work for others, including both blue- and white-collar employees). We believe that there is a strong tendency for those in the lower segment of the majority group to benefit from discrimination and prejudice *at the level of the personality*. Prejudice makes them "feel better" about their difficulties. It allows them to displace aggression, protect self-esteem, and reduce uncertainty. In contrast, the upper segment of the majority group is much more likely to benefit *at the level of the social structure*. They reap eco-

Figure 3.3 A diagram of prejudice and discrimination in functionalist terms.

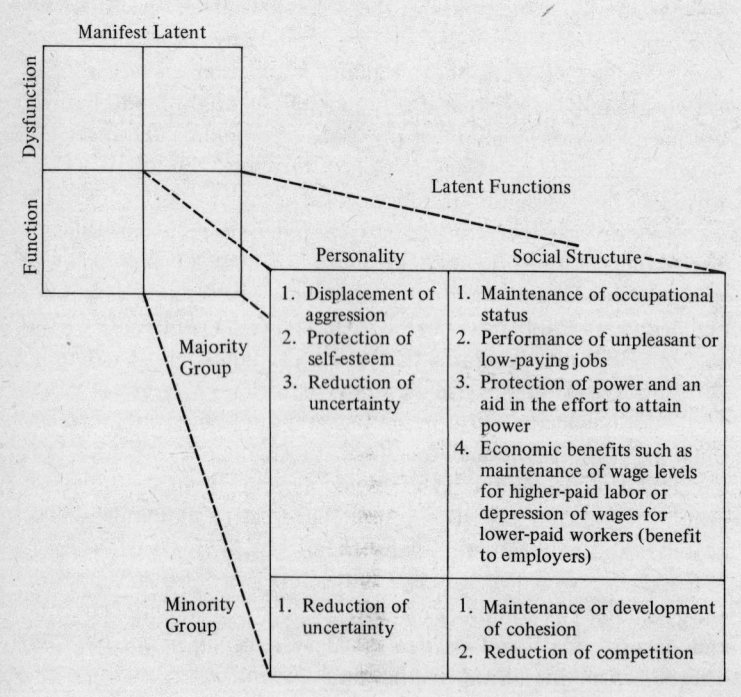

	Personality	Social Structure
Majority Group	1. Displacement of aggression 2. Protection of self-esteem 3. Reduction of uncertainty	1. Maintenance of occupational status 2. Performance of unpleasant or low-paying jobs 3. Protection of power and an aid in the effort to attain power 4. Economic benefits such as maintenance of wage levels for higher-paid labor or depression of wages for lower-paid workers (benefit to employers)
Minority Group	1. Reduction of uncertainty	1. Maintenance or development of cohesion 2. Reduction of competition

nomic benefits in the form of paying lower wages, controlling production costs, protecting their advantaged power position, acquiring land, and so on. Although white laborers do sometimes benefit in terms of protection of their jobs and wage levels and in not having to do the low-paying and unpleasant jobs of life, their benefits are largely psychological. So when we say that discrimination and prejudice are functional, it must always be kept in mind that the group for whom they are functional may or may not be in a position to do anything about extinguishing or maintaining their existence. Benefits for the most powerful members of the society, those who distribute the bulk of the occupational opportunities, do a great deal more to cause discrimination and prejudice to persist than do those psychological benefits that make less powerful majority-group members feel better.

NOTES

1. Merton also identified the concept of *nonfunctional consequences* in which an object, action, or idea has no consequence for the stability of a given system. This idea emphasizes that although many systems are functionally interrelated, they do not overlap entirely.

Chapter 4
Personality Functions of Discrimination and Prejudice for the Majority Group

Sartre once wrote, "If the Jew did not exist, the anti-Semite would invent him" (1965:13). Nowhere can the functional nature of discrimination and prejudice be seen more clearly than in the gains that accrue to the personality of a majority-group member who harbors negative feelings and beliefs regarding a minority. In its ego-defensive consequences, prejudice provides a safe outlet for displaced aggression and aids in the maintenance and enhancement of self-esteem. With reference to its knowledge function, prejudice is capable of reducing the myriad uncertainties, both emotional and cognitive, to which all of us are exposed in the course of our everyday affairs (Katz, 1960).

To be sure, such payoffs have their costs as well; for instance, the defensive energy expended by bigoted individuals to safeguard their self-image may jeopardize their chances to find a long-term, more effective adaptation. In this connection, one is reminded of a student so busy convincing himself of his superiority that he does not study and fails his examinations. Moreover, the use of prejudice as a factor in interpersonal perception will likely give a distorted and unrealistic view of others, a view that can mislead individuals seeking to fulfill their goals.

Yet the immediate positive functions of prejudice for the maintenance of the personality of a majority-group member can hardly be exaggerated. Prejudice sustains the personality in the face of deprivation or external threat and helps to structure a highly complex, otherwise chaotic, social environment. We cannot understand the nature of prejudice without taking account of such personality functions. A good place to begin is to examine the nature of displaced aggression.

Displacement of Aggression

There is an old story, which has probably replayed countless times throughout history, concerning a frustrated, belittled, and hostile worker who submits passively to the daily indignities dished out by his tyrannical boss, while he "takes it out" on his wife by shouting obscenities or periodically beating her. This is a clear-cut example of what is known as *displaced aggression.* The frustrations imposed by a powerful figure (in this case, a tyrannical boss) creates in the worker feelings of intense anger and hostility, which he safely displaces or redirects to an innocent target, his wife. To the extent that she takes the blame for a matter not of her making, the worker's wife becomes a scapegoat for her husband.

Frustration and Aggression

In *Frustration and Aggression,* Dollard, Doob, Miller, Mowrer, and Sears are convinced that *aggression is the inevitable consequence of frustration:*

More specifically the proposition is that the occurrence of aggressive behavior always presupposes the existence of frustration and, contrariwise, that the existence of frustration always leads to some form of aggression. From the point of view of daily observation, it does not seem unreasonable to assume that aggressive behavior of the usually recognized varieties is always traceable to and produced by some form of frustration. But it is by no means so immediately evident that, whenever frustration occurs, aggression of some kind and in some degree will inevitably result. In many adults and even children, frustration may be followed so promptly by an apparent acceptance of the situation and readjustment thereto that one looks in vain for the relatively gross criteria ordinarily thought of as characterizing aggressive action. It must be kept in mind, however, that one of the earliest lessons human beings learn as a result of social living is to suppress and restrain their overtly aggressive reactions. This does not mean, however, that such reaction tendencies are thereby annihilated; rather it has been found that, although these reactions may be temporarily compressed, delayed, disguised, displaced, or otherwise deflected from their immediate and logical goal, they are not destroyed. [1939:1-2.]

Whether or not frustration and aggression are inextricably bound together, we have compelling reason to believe that the myriad frustrations of everyday life tend to increase aggressive motivation (Henry and Short, 1954; Palmer, 1960; Rule and Percival, 1971). What is more, there may be certain releasing cues whose presence in a situation assures that aggression will be expressed (Berkowitz and Geen, 1967). For example, we know that frustrated individuals are more likely to be aggressive in bars or at football games than in churches (Goldstein, 1975). We also have evidence to suggest that frustrated people are more inclined to be violent when a gun is present in the situation (Berkowitz and LePage, 1967). Just as clearly, hostility or aggression cannot always be directed against the true source of a frustration, for the source may be vague and difficult to identify or much too powerful for safe attack. In order to blow off steam, then, an individual who has experienced frustration may attempt to locate a more vulnerable and visible enemy against whom his hostility can be directed with relative impunity (see Figure 4.1). Lacking the resources for retaliation, American minorities have traditionally served as targets for the displaced aggression of the majority group (see also Box 4.1). In this regard, blacks have made especially desirable scapegoats, for not only were they powerless to strike back but they had adequate visibility as well. Until 1930, for example, the frequency with which blacks in the South were lynched increased as the value of southern cotton declined (Hovland and Sears, 1970). See Figure 4.2. To blow off the steam that accompanies increased frustration, southern whites apparently found it useful to focus the blame for their economic hardships on blacks, though by no stretch of the imagination could blacks have been responsible for the price of cotton or the level of economic depression in the South. For similar reasons, the Depression of the 1930s saw the birth of 114 organizations that spent their time and money in spreading anti-Semitism (Rose, 1958). And, on a wider scale, the Depression period brought a substantial increase in nativist activity aimed at the total exclusion of potential immigrants as well as the wholesale deportation of recent arrivals. As a more current example, the shortage of energy and economic recession that characterized much of the period of the 1970s and early 1980s were accompanied by a sharp rise in anti-Semitic incidents as well as renewed activities of the Ku Klux Klan (King, 1979).

There seems to be an element of scapegoating in the phenomenon known as *elder abuse*. The vulnerability of elderly persons who are physically disabled and dependent on their adult children makes them candidates for the displaced aggression of their younger caretakers. Abused elders typically suffer from severe physical impairments; their abusers frequently experience economic frustration and stress. The result shows up as physical or

Figure 4.1 The relationship between frustration and aggression.

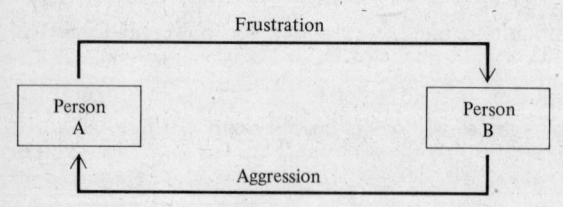

psychological abuse: bruises and welts, beatings, lack of personal care and supervision, verbal assault, fear, and isolation (Block and Sinnott, 1979).

Early experimental evidence for the existence of displaced aggression was provided by Miller and Bugelski (1948), who required 31 men in a vocational training camp to take a series of

---

Box 4.1

Limitations of the Frustration–Aggression Hypothesis

The frustration-aggression hypothesis (Dollard et al., 1939) has guided much of the research into the social psychology of aggression conducted over the past few decades. Despite the criticism that has been leveled against it, this hypothesis continues to provide a valuable focal point for the study of various forms of aggression, including prejudice. However, most social scientists presently agree that frustration is not the only nor the most powerful cause of aggression (Geen, 1972).

The scapegoat or displaced aggression hypothesis has additional problems, though it too has been the subject of much research. As Berkowitz (1962) reminds us, aggression is not always displaced but is frequently directed against the perceived source of frustration. Displacement of aggression may be more likely to occur, however, if the frustrator is powerful or difficult to locate (Williams, 1947) or when the frustration is accidental, beyond the control of the frustrator, or carried out in a socially acceptable manner (Burnstein and Worchel, 1962; Geen, 1972). Moreover, the weakest target is not always the recipient of displaced aggression. Frequently, the scapegoat may be selected for his or her similarity to the actual source of the frustration (Berkowitz, 1962). The scapegoat may also be relatively strong, if he or she is chosen in order to restore self-esteem to the victim of frustration (White and Lippitt, 1960). Finally, displaced aggression does not always occur in experiments designed to test for its presence (Rosnow, Holz, and Levin, 1966; Stagner and Congdon, 1955) and may be associated with certain personality types (Adorno et al., 1950).

The scapegoat phenomenon is clearly represented in the meaning of the bumper sticker below that supposedly appeared during the energy crisis of the 1970s:

138 The Functions of Discrimination and Prejudice

> HELP END THE ENERGY CRISIS:
> BURN A JEW

Figure 4.2 Relation of lynchings to a composite economic index (Ayres).

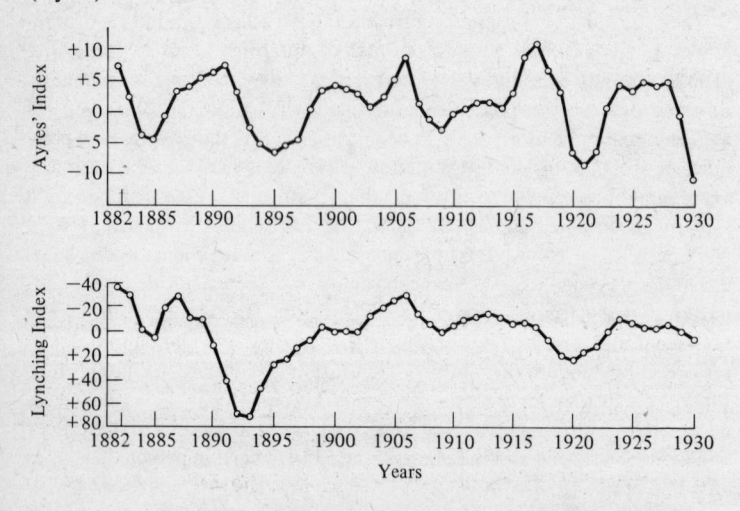

Source: Carl I. Hovland and Robert R. Sears, 1970, "Minor Studies of Aggression: Correlation of Lynchings with Economic Indices." *Journal of Psychology* (Winter): 304.

lengthy and difficult examinations that prevented them from visiting the local movie house where the most interesting event of the week was taking place. Both before and after these exams were administered by Miller and Bugelski, they measured the attitudes of their subjects toward Japanese and Mexicans. This was done by having the men check a list of ten desirable and ten undesirable traits as being either present or absent in the average Mexican or Japanese. The results of the study were as expected by the investigators: The men regarded Mexicans and Japanese less favorably after the frustrating examination than prior to it. Specifically, from pretest to posttest, there was a significant decrease in the number of favorable items checked and a slight increase in the number of negative items checked.

The findings of Miller and Bugelski have been replicated several times since 1948, either by means of paper-and-pencil questionnaires in which subjects express their aggressive feelings (Cowen, Landes, and Schaet, 1959) or, more behaviorally, as the tendency of a subject to administer an intense electrical shock to another naive subject (Holmes, 1972). At the same time, social scientists have taken note of the fact that frustration cannot always be accurately conceptualized or measured in absolute terms. George Bernard Shaw recognized this when he astutely noted, "It is not enough to succeed. One's friends must fail." Hence, the notion of *relative deprivation,* a concept that focuses on the level of achievement attained by an individual *relative* to the standard that he or she employs as a basis of comparison.

Relative Deprivation and Prejudice

Not all forms of frustration are obvious. As a result, the concept of relative deprivation has been useful for the purpose of identifying frustration and its sources. For instance, Bettelheim and Janowitz (1964) uncovered no relationship between income level or socioeconomic status and intensity of anti-Semitism but found that downwardly mobile men—individuals who had moved lower in terms of socioeconomic status by comparison with their previous civilian employment—expressed greater hostility toward Jews than did men stable with respect to socioeconomic status. For these men, loss of occupational status apparently constituted a frustration sufficiently intense to generate considerable ethnic hostility.

Other research has indicated that feelings of relative deprivation are not necessarily indicated by conventional measures of frustration. In a particular survey, for instance, it was found that supporters of 1968 presidential candidate George Wallace, with whom issues of race were often associated, were surprisingly well-off: More specifically, individuals having annual family incomes between $7,500 and $10,000 were much more likely to support Wallace than those who had family incomes under $5,000 (Pettigrew, Riley, and Vanneman, 1972). Yet frustration was very much a factor among Wallace supporters. In the first place, Wallace-ites tended to have *status inconsistency* (high income but low education), a condition thought to produce much psychological stress and tension (Eitzen, 1970). Moreover, Wallace supporters clearly tended to feel relatively deprived in social-class terms when they compared the economic gains of their group—the working class—to those of white-collar workers. Thus, Wallace-ites more than supporters of Nixon or Humphrey would agree that "in spite of what some people say, the condition of the average man is getting worse not better." In reference to George Wallace's constituents, Pettigrew, Riley, and Vanneman wrote, "We had a picture of solid, fairly comfortable, fairly well-educated persons displaying psychological characteristics—political alienation, fear, distrust, racial bias—that generally are found most intensely among the worst-educated and most poverty-stricken segments of the population" (1972:49).

Protection of Self-Esteem

Though prejudice against the members of a minority group may often occur as a result of a need to get rid of the aggression that accompanies frustration, prejudice can have a more profound and complex meaning for the personality of a prejudiced person. It is a method of defending self-image, whereby, for the majority member, a minority group becomes a *negative reference group,* or a point of comparison against which the values, abilities, or performances of the majority member can be regarded as superior.

Social Comparison and Self-Esteem

Indeed, some psychologists have argued that virtually all displaced aggression is of an ego-defensive nature, having as its primary objective the restoration of an individual's self-esteem or status (White and Lippitt, 1960). This may be particularly true with respect to the development of prejudice. By the use of a minority as a negative reference group, an individual need not acknowledge truths about him or herself or about threatening aspects of his or her environment. As noted by Daniel Katz, "When we cannot admit to ourselves that we have deep feelings of inferiority we may project those feelings onto some convenient minority group and bolster our egos by attitudes of superiority toward this underprivileged group" (1960:172). Examples of this are easy enough to find in everyday life: the out-of-shape middle-aged man or woman who feels better about being out of breath in comparison with "those old codgers who can barely walk" or the man who lords it over the secretarial pool in a "macho" display of his own self-worth.

Several experimental studies have yielded support for the view that individuals employ negative reference groups in an effort to maintain or restore self-esteem. In this regard, Hakmiller (1966) reported that subjects exposed to a high-threat condition (having been given negative information about themselves) were more likely than subjects in a low-threat condition to make *downward comparisons* with individuals regarded as clearly inferior with respect to the performance being compared. For Hakmiller, this finding reflects the operation of defensive social comparison, "the function of comparison in this situation of sustaining or reasserting the favorability of the individual's self-regard" (1966:37). In a more recent study, Wilson and Benner (1971) set out to examine the notion that individuals having high self-esteem would choose a "comparison other" to maximize the information they obtain about themselves, whereas individuals who have low self-esteem would seek instead to avoid a potentially threatening comparison. After receiving their scores on a "leadership test," Wilson and Benner's subjects were given the opportunity to compare their leadership ability with that of another student. The expectation was clear: Subjects with low self-esteem should want to compare themselves with someone lower in ability and should avoid a high-scoring "comparison other." Results of the study by Wilson and Benner tended to support their prediction. In a public condition, significantly more high-self-esteem males chose the highest scorer as a "comparison other" than did low-self-esteem males. For female subjects, self-esteem influenced choices of "comparison other" in a private condition, where sex-related competition was minimal.

If defensive social comparison requires the availability of an "inferior" reference group, then the presence of a negatively regarded minority group such as blacks, Puerto Ricans, Mexican-Americans, or Jews may represent an ideal situation for a majority-group member. Social scientists have long stressed the importance of excessive concern with the attainment of higher status as a cause of prejudice (Blalock, 1967; Kaufman, 1957; Williams, 1964). Dollard, in his perceptive analysis of life in a small southern town, clearly identified the manner in which white southerners gained status and self-esteem by virtue of their position in the traditional pattern of race relations found in the Deep South:

In the North a man may have a prestige position because he has money, or is learned, or is old; the novelty in the South is that one has prestige solely because one is white. The gain here is very simple. It consists in the fact that a member of the white caste has an automatic right to demand forms of behavior from Negroes which serve to increase his own self-esteem. To put it another way, it consists of an illumination of the image of the self, an expansive feeling of being something special and valuable. It might be compared to the illusion of greatness that comes with early stages of alcoholization, except that prestige is not an illusion, but a steadily repeated fact. [1937:174.]

The phenomenon of defensive social comparison with a minority-group member was experimentally explored by Levin (1969) who exposed his subjects, a group of 180 college students, either to relative deprivation or to relative satisfaction regarding their performance on a bogus test of achievement during a regular class period. In the relative-deprivation condition, the students were led to believe their examination scores fell far below that of "the average student in similar groups of undergraduates." In contrast, students in the relative-satisfaction condition were told their scores were substantially higher than that of "the average student." Immediately after receiving their examination grades, all subjects answered the following paper-and-pencil measure of prejudice against Puerto Ricans:

> Directions: Place an "X" in one position between the adjectives of each scale (e.g., ___ : ___ : ___) to indicate how well these adjectives apply in general to Puerto Ricans. Your evaluation should reflect what you believe *many* of the members of this particular group tend to be (what the average Puerto Rican is like), and *not* necessarily what 100% of them are.

PUERTO RICANS

	1	2	3	4	5	6	7	
reputable								disreputable
knowledgeable								ignorant
intelligent								stupid
industrious								lazy
kind								cruel
clean								dirty
straightforward								sly
reliable								unreliable

Levin found that exposure to relative deprivation yielded a more negative evaluation of Puerto Ricans (as indicated by the tendency to place a check mark closer to negative adjectives) than did relative satisfaction (see Figure 4.3), but only among certain subjects. Specifically, subjects affected by relative deprivation were *relative evaluators,* individuals who tended to rely heavily on a social frame of reference for the measurement of success in fulfilling their goals.

These were persons who, as indicated by their scores on a paper-and-pencil measure of relative evaluation, were likely to evaluate their personal performances relative to the productivity or achievement of other persons or groups. By contrast, subjects who did not become more prejudiced under relative deprivation were *self-evaluators,* individuals who relied upon their other personal performances, past or present, as a standard of comparison (i.e., personal improvement). A questionnaire survey of the students who participated in this study revealed that relative evaluators scored higher than self-evaluators on measures of authoritarianism, conflict, and competitiveness. Moreover, as compared with self-evaluators relative evaluators were significantly more likely to prefer careers in profit-making and money-oriented occupations. To summarize these findings, then, prejudice against Puerto Ricans increased under relative deprivation but only among individuals initially predisposed toward making social comparisons and employing negative reference groups or individuals in order to maintain or bolster their self-image.

The Authoritarian Personality

The foregoing conception is not without precedence in the literature of social science. During the 1940s, at a time when fascism and anti-Semitism were of major concern to social scientists and laypeople alike, Adorno et al. (1950) set out to examine systematically the possible existence of a deep-lying personality predisposition for directing aggression to minority groups. In their research, Adorno and his collaborators amassed a good deal of evidence for the pres-

Figure 4.3 The mediating influence of relative evaluation on the relationship between relative deprivation and prejudice.

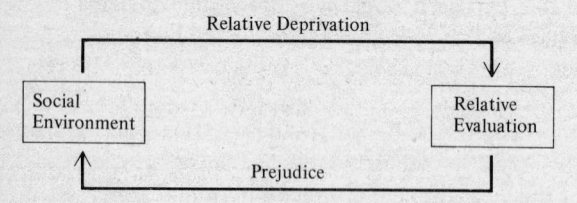

ence of an *authoritarian personality structure,* a configuration of functionally interrelated personality characteristics in which prejudice plays an important part.

The symptoms of authoritarianism were identified by the F (potentiality for fascism) Scale, a series of opinion items to which individuals were asked to express their agreement or disagreement. Below are the nine characteristics in the authoritarian syndrome and an item from the F Scale to illustrate each one. An affirmative response to any item indicates authoritarianism.

1. *Conventionalism.* This characteristic involves a rigid commitment to conventional, middle-class values and goals—a disposition to feel anxious by the very expectation that such values and goals might be violated by others.
Example Item: "Obedience and respect for authority are the most important virtues children should learn."
2. *Authoritarian Submission.* This involves an exaggerated need to submit to moral authorities of the in-group.
Example Item: "Young people sometimes get rebellious ideas, but as they grow up they ought to get over them and settle down."
3. *Authoritarian Aggression.* This is the tendency to condemn and punish individuals who are suspected of violating conventional, middle-class values.
Example Item: "Homosexuals are hardly better than criminals and ought to be severely punished."
4. *Anti-Intraception.* This entails opposition to subjective, imaginative, "tender-minded" phenomena.
Example Item: "When a person has a problem or worry, it is best for him not to think about it, but to keep busy with more cheerful things."
5. *Superstition and Stereotypy.* Both of these involve a narrowness of consciousness. In the case of superstitiousness, there is a tendency to perceive responsibility for the individual's fate in outside forces beyond his control. With respect to stereotypy, the tendency is to think in rigid, oversimplified categories.
Example Item: "Some people are born with an urge to jump from high places."

6. *Power and Toughness.* This characteristic includes an alignment of the individual with power figures—a preoccupation with strength versus weakness, dominance versus submission, and an exaggerated assertion of power and toughness.
Example Item: "People can be divided into two distinct classes: the weak and the strong."

7. *Destructiveness and Cynicism.* This involves a generalized resentment and hostility toward humans.
Example Item "Human nature being what it is, there will always be war and conflict."

8. *Projectivity.* This characteristic entails the belief that wild and dangerous events occur in the world, a projection onto the external world of unconscious emotional impulses.
Example Item: "Wars and social troubles may some day be ended by an earthquake or flood that will destroy the whole world."

9. *Sex.* This involves an exaggerated concern with the sexual behavior of other people.
Example Item: "The wild sex life of the old Greeks and Romans was tame compared to some of the goings-on in this country, even in places where people might least expect it."

According to Adorno et al., the origin of the authoritarian personality is located in the early socialization experiences of the child, particularly, in harsh and punitive forms of discipline and clearly defined family roles. The authoritarian child is expected to be weak and to submit to the desires of his parents; the parents, in turn, assume a dominant posture in their relations with the child. As a result, an authoritarian child makes only a superficial identification with his parents, actually harboring much latent hostility and resentment toward them. The outcome of such childhood experiences has relevance for an understanding of prejudice: Authoritarians finally come to treat others in the manner that their parents treated them. As adults, they maintain a general contempt for the allegedly inferior and weak members of their society; they come to despise such diverse groups as blacks, foreigners, Puerto Ricans, Catholics, and Jews. In this manner, authoritarians bolster their self-esteem, avoid painful truths about themselves, and clarify their perceptions of the world.

In 1975 Chapko and Lewis found that authoritarians were especially likely to approve of the behavior and attitudes of All in the Family's Archie Bunker—the same Archie Bunker who consistently reacts to threats to his self-esteem by bigoted outbursts: Polish jokes directed against his son-in-law, angry orders to his wife to bring him a beer, outbursts about the inferiority of blacks and Jews, and, in one episode, hostility toward old people. In this instance, an old man who had "escaped" from a nursing home is brought to the Bunker home by Archie's wife. Archie demands that the old man be sent back, because that's where older people belong, since they can't do anything for themselves anyway. See Box 4.2 for further discussion of the relationship between authoritarianism and prejudice.

Box 4.2

Limitations of the Authoritarian Personality

One of the most widely employed concepts of prejudice can be found in the work of the "Berkeley Group," which produced *The Authoritarian Personality* (1950). Several hundred research projects, many focusing on the relationship between authoritarianism and prejudice, have followed the publication of the original work, and the body of research continues to grow. At the same time, however, critics of this work have focused on several of its major deficiencies and limitations. We shall review a few of these here.

1. *Only the politically reactionary segment of authoritarianism was studied.* Research into authoritarianism was conducted at a time when fascism was of major concern to both social scientists as well as laypeople. As a result, authoritarianism became equated with commitment to fascist ideology and anti-Semitism. As Rokeach (1960) subsequently determined, however, authoritarianism may also be found among radicals, liberals, and middle-of-the-roaders.

2. *A tendency toward acquiescence can partially account for the relationship of authoritarianism to prejudice.* The F Scale was constructed so that agreement with any of its items would indicate authoritarianism. In order to obtain a low authoritarianism score, then, an individual would have to disagree with the statements in the F Scale. However, social scientists have discovered the presence of so-called yeasayers and naysayers, individuals who tend to agree or disagree with any statement on any scale, regardless of its specific content (Couch and Keniston, 1960). Therefore, agreement with F Scale items may indicate a general disposition to agree as well as (or instead of) general authoritarianism.

3. *A third variable may partially explain the apparent relationship between authoritarianism and prejudice.* When the effect of such variables as "concern with achieving high status" (Golden, 1974; Kaufman, 1957) or "anomie" (Srole, 1956) is held constant, the relationship between authoritarianism and prejudice diminishes.

By the use of a statistical procedure known as partial correlation, Kaufman (1957) examined the intensity of the relationship between authoritarianism and prejudice both before and after he controlled for [or held constant] the influence of status concern. The original correlation of .53 [fairly strong] between authoritarianism and prejudice [before controlling for status concern] dropped sharply to .12 when the effect of status concern was held constant. As a result, Kaufman suggested that the correlation between authoritarianism and prejudice can be explained at least in part by the mutual association of these variables with status concern. Also on the basis of partial correlation, Srole (1956) similarly concluded that anomie [a psychological state characterized by personal disorganization and alienation from group life] may account for much of the relationship between authoritarianism and prejudice.

4. *The authoritarian personality fails to give adequate recognition to cultural forms of prejudice.* For the authors of *The Authoritarian Personality,* prejudice is psychologically pathological. Yet regional and societal differences in prejudice occur that probably cannot be explained on the basis of authoritarian predispositions. If, for example, the residents of Georgia are found to be more prejudiced against blacks than are the residents of Rhode Island, this does not necessarily mean that they are more "authoritarian." Middleton (1976) found, in this regard, that residents of the South had a much higher level of antiblack prejudice than did residents of other regions of the United States; however, the regions differed only slightly with respect to anti-Semitism, anti-Catholic prejudice, and authoritarianism. Different

cultural norms may be operating to produce differences in prejudice. Any adequate conception of prejudice must therefore consider social, structural, and cultural differences as well (Simpson and Yinger, 1972).

Note: Many of the deficiencies of the original thesis of authoritarianism can be overcome. For example, revised versions of the F Scale have been constructed to minimize the influence of acquiescence (Christie, Havel, and Seidenberg, 1958) and to measure left-wing authoritarianism (Rokeach, 1960). There is also growing realization that authoritarianism is but one of the many factors associated with prejudice—a factor that interacts with sociocultural variables to determine the nature of intergroup relations in a society.

Reduction of Uncertainty

To this point, we have examined the ego-defensive functions of prejudice for the personality of a majority-group member. We turn our attention now to the part played by prejudice in structuring the perceived world of the majority-group member. We begin with the mass media.

Mass Media Stereotypes

In 1946 Berelson and Salter identified the stereotyped portrayals of minority characters in short stories as a convenient method of "getting the character across" to an audience (1946:187). As later explained by O'Hara, the prejudicial treatment of characters serves to frame a mass communication message in terms that are meaningful to the members of American society:

It enables the mass communicator to frame his messages with the least amount of lost motion, and it enables the receiver to comprehend what is being communicated with equal speed and facility. He is given situations and characters that have become familiar to him. . . . There is, therefore, little lost motion on either side of the fence. [1961:194.]

Nowhere is there a better example of the effective use of stereotypes to facilitate characterization than in the "Amos and Andy

Show," a popular radio and television program that for decades routinely depicted derogatory but *familiar* images of black Americans. In *Confessions of a White Racist,* Larry King analyzes the characterizations of "The Amos and Andy Show":

Who does not readily recognize the white man's nigger as represented by the cast? Lawyer Calhoun pretended to a literacy so obviously impossible in a black man that he could only spout quasi-legalisms in the most unintelligible terms; Andy was a *cum laude* graduate of the School of Memorable Malapropisms as well as an inordinately sly dog among coveys of loose black ladies; "Lightnin'" from his office-boy station was so lazy he only reluctantly expended the energy required to breathe; George (Kingfish) Stevens embodied the sum qualities of all "bad niggers" everywhere—a con man who naturally preferred ill-gotten gains to honest labors, a philanderer even under the cold Black Maternalism eye of wife Sapphire, a circus nigger who dug parading in colorful lodge uniforms while pretending to ludicrous titles. Among regulars on the show only Amos was a good nigger, a white nigger, a nigger who might be trusted in the presence of the white man's money or his sister. He alone had a steady job or wanted one; he sometimes tried to persuade his black brothers to higher moral paths; he even paid his bills and told his children bedtime stories. Yes, Amos was what all his brothers might have become if only the black man had not been famed for excesses of larceny or so few brains. [1969:5.]

The reliance of media stereotypes on the familiar and the simple can be seen in their portrayal of the linguistic difficulties of American minorities. For example, blacks have traditionally been depicted as indiscriminately substituting the "d" sound for "th." Thus, a black might be viewed as saying "dis" and "dat" as in "lift dat bale" or "dis is de place." In a similar way, the Mexican has been characterized as handicapped by his use of the double "e." A Mexican character might typically say "theenk" rather than "think"; "peenk" rather than "pink." By contrast, the American Indian has been depicted as devoid of any English at all, his linguistic ability generally limited to "ugh," "kemo sabe," or some monosyllabic grunt.

The only exception to this rule is a line famed for its durability over the years. If you fall asleep during the Late Show and suddenly awaken to the words "go in peace my son," it is either an Indian chief bidding his son good-bye as the boy heads for college or a Roman Catholic priest forgiving Paul Newman or Steve McQueen for killing a hundred men in the preceding reel. [Deloria, 1970:37.]

Women and the elderly seem to fare no better than blacks and native Americans when it comes to their portrayals by the mass media. Female characters on family-oriented television programs are typically depicted in dependent, frivolous, and demeaning roles (Tedesco, 1974). In soap operas, they are disproportionately represented among the victims of psychiatric disorders (Cassata, Skill, and Boadu, 1979), and, in prime-time television drama, men outnumber women about three to one (Gerbner, Gross, Signorielli, and Morgan, 1980). Despite the fact that more than 50 percent of the labor force consists of women, magazine and television advertisements portray women away from the world of work: "The fact is that when a woman appears in an ad today, she is usually a housewife, pictured in the home, helping to sell some product found in the kitchen or bathroom" (Culley and Bennett, 1976).

As revealed in his study of characters appearing in prime-time network television drama between 1969 and 1971, Aronoff (1974) reports that the aged comprised less than 5 percent of all characters, about half of the proportion that they actually occupied in the population of the United States at that time. What is more, when they did appear as dramatic characters, the aged tended to be depicted as evil, unsuccessful, and unhappy: "In a world of generally positive portrayals and happy endings, only 40 percent of older male, and even fewer female, characters are seen as successful, happy, and good" (Aronoff, 1974:87).

Television commercials have similarly ignored or stereotyped the aged. For example, a content analysis by Francher (1973) determined that only 2 out of 100 television commercials contained older characters. The focus of attention was on "the Pepsi Generation"—young and attractive characters who were featured in order to promise youthful appearance or behavior. As Hanaver (1976) recently noted, "It's the rare wrinkled face—and never a wrinkled hand—that appears on television ads. Even the denture glues go for younger folks; the laxative ladies seldom go beyond middle age, if that, and judging from the ads, no one over 35 ever cleans house except 'Aunt Bluebelle'" (p. 12).

Simplifying the World

Just as it works in the context of mass communication, so prejudice operates in the lives of many people to "define the situation," provide order and clarity, and reduce the cognitive and emotional uncertainties of everyday experiences. Every individual has the need "to give adequate structure to his universe" (Katz, 1969:170). How this is done may vary a good deal from one individual to another.

Unfortunately, when an individual has an extreme need to simplify the world and uses prejudice to do it, it does not seem to matter who the target of that prejudice may be. For example, Kogan (1961) asked 482 undergraduate students for their agreement–disagreement with a number of statements concerning attitudes toward ethnic minorities, blacks, the mentally ill, the blind, the deaf, and the crippled. He found that subjects who held unfavorable attitudes toward old people also tended to be prejudiced toward the members of ethnic, mentally ill, and physically disabled minorities. These data support the contention that "there is a general trend for subjects to be positively or negatively disposed toward a wide variety of groups deviating in some respect from a hypothetical norm of similarity to self" (Kogan 1961:53).

Kogan also asked his subjects to respond to Srole's (1956) Anomie Scale, whose items have previously been found to be correlated with prejudice against ethnic minorities. His results suggest that subjects unfavorably disposed toward the aged are also more likely to be anomic, that is, to feel helpless in the face of powerful social forces, incapable of finding meaning in their lives, and insecure about what is expected of them.

One thing is clear, however: individuals do not always define one another exclusively on the basis of cues that they receive in social interaction. Undoubtedly, there are times when interpersonal attitudes must be formed in the absence of detailed information about another person. For instance, a prospective employer might have to form a judgment of the abilities of a job applicant after having interviewed him or her for only a short period of time.

Culturally supported prejudices provide ready-made expectations in terms of which individuals can be categorized. What people often do is to fill the gap in their knowledge of others with oversimplified and distorted preconceptions, many of which are based on group membership. Thus, a prospective employer who knows little about a black job applicant, save from his limited contact in an interview situation, might use an antiblack stereotype in order to form a conclusion regarding the applicant's abilities (Katz, 1960).

Although stereotyped categories narrow the amount of information necessary for action to occur, they also expand the scope of available information (Ehrlich, 1972). Thus, the prospective employer who evaluates an applicant on the basis of his or her "blackness" immediately gains much information about characteristics that the applicant presumably shares with other members of his or her race. This is what author Langston Hughes (Chapman, 1968) had in mind for his fictional character, Simple, when he wrote:

" . . . being white and curious, my boss keeps asking me just what does THE Negro want. Yesterday he tackled me during the coffee break, talking about THE Negro. He always says 'the Negro,' as if there was not 50–11 different kinds of Negroes in the U.S.A.," complained Simple. "My boss says, 'Now that you-all have got the Civil Rights Bill and the Supreme Court, Adam Powell in Congress, Ralph Bunche in the United Nations, and Leontyne Price singing in the Metropolitan Opera, plus Dr. Martin Luther King getting the Nobel Prize, what more do you want? I am asking you, just what does THE Negro want?" 'I am not the Negro,' I says, I am *me*." [1968:106–107.]

What happens in reaction to a person's race also seems to happen in response to his or her age. Rosen and Jerdee (1976) asked 142 undergraduate business students to play the role of a division manager by making a series of decisions about the fate of a male employee involved in an "on-the-job" incident. In each of six incidents, the employee's age was experimentally manipulated by specifying his age (for example, 61 years old versus 32 years old) or by describing him as a "younger" or an "older" employee. For example, to examine the influence of age on perceptions of untrainability, Rosen and Jerdee depicted as either 30 years old or 60 years old a computer programmer whose technical skills had become obsolete. Subjects were asked to decide whether to terminate the programmer or to retrain him. Results obtained by the investigators confirmed their hypothesis that stereotypes about physical and mental decline in older workers contribute to on-the-job discrimination against them. When the employee was described as an older person, subjects were significantly less likely to recommend that the company provide him with selection, promotion, and training opportunities. Instead, they were likely to suggest ignoring him or firing him as an appropriate managerial response.

Intolerance of Ambiguity

Prejudiced people seem to be especially intolerant of cognitive and emotional ambiguities (Martin and Westie, 1959; Steiner and Johnson, 1963; Triandis and Triandis, 1972). According to Adorno et al. (1950), this aversion of prejudiced individuals is a generalization of their intolerance of the affectual ambivalence that exists when both love and hate are felt for a parent. Prejudiced people desire absolute and unequivocal feelings about themselves and others; aided by a series of stereotyped polarities—black versus white, strong versus weak, hero versus villain—they suppress awareness of their own weaknesses and the weaknesses of their parents. Instead, their aggression is externalized. Members of the majority group are glorified and idealized, whereas culturally designated out-groups become targets for displaced hostility.

As adults, prejudiced individuals may be inaccurate *role takers,* people who are not capable of accurately estimating qualities of others from cues given in interactional settings. In this connection, Scodel and Mussen (1953) instructed pairs of strangers consisting of an authoritarian and a nonauthoritarian subject to discuss together several topics related to mass communication and then to estimate how they thought the subject with whom they had been interacting would respond to a series of attitude questions. The authoritarian subjects tended to perceive their nonauthoritarian peer as holding attitudes and personality characteristics similar to their own, whereas the nonauthoritarian subjects were better able to judge their peer accurately in terms of attitudes and personality. Similarly, Koenig and King (1962) found that students opposed to racial integration were less accurate in predicting the responses of others on campus than were students who expressed attitudes favorable to racial integration.

Experimental evidence for the presence of extreme intolerance of ambiguity in prejudiced people was uncovered by Block and Block (1951), who tested 65 college students over 100 trials as follows: Each subject was placed in a darkened room where he or she was asked to view a pinpoint of light until he or she saw it move and to estimate the distance that the light had traveled. Actually, these subjects were exposed to the "autokinetic phenomenon": The pinpoint of light was in fact stationary, but it gave the illusion of movement when viewed in a totally darkened room. Block and Block reported that students who had scored high on the Ethnocentrism Scale—a measure of general prejudice—were quicker than those who scored low on this scale to establish a norm for themselves regarding the movement of the light. More specifically, the prejudiced or ethnocentric subjects quickly reported the light as moving in a constant direction and to a constant number of inches from one trial to another, whereas the subjects low in prejudice could better tolerate not having a clear-cut answer and took much longer to establish a norm regarding the movement of the light.

Rokeach (1952) found that similarly very prejudiced subjects were afraid to admit defeat when confronted with the challenging task of correctly matching names with the faces of strangers. Whereas prejudiced subjects made numerous erroneous guesses, subjects with less prejudice more often admitted being confused and were less willing to take wild guesses.

In another test, Quanty, Keats, and Harkins (1975) found that anti-Semitic subjects were more willing to label a face Jewish on the basis of limited information than were unprejudiced subjects. When asked to identify a number of photographs as Jewish or non-Jewish, the anti-Semites thought that they saw more Jews but were also more inaccurate than their unprejudiced counterparts: "They seem more concerned with correctly identifying Jews than they are with falsely labeling a person Jewish" (Quanty, Keats, and Harkins, 1975: 454).

Summary

Nowhere can the functional nature of discrimination and prejudice be seen more clearly than in the gains that accrue to the personality of a majority-group member who harbors negative feelings, beliefs, and action tendencies regarding a minority. In particular, discrimination and prejudice can be employed to displace aggression, protect self-esteem, and reduce uncertainties.

There is compelling reason to believe that the myriad frustrations of everyday life tend to increase aggressive motivation. Just as clearly, aggression cannot always be directed against the true source of frustration, for the source may be vague and difficult to identify or too powerful for safe attack. In order to blow off steam, then, an individual who has experienced frustration may try to locate a more vulnerable and visible enemy against whom his or her hostility can be directed with relative impunity. Lacking the resources for retaliation, American minorities have frequently served as targets for the *displaced aggression* of the majority group.

Though prejudice against the members of a minority group may occur as a result of a need to get rid of the aggression that accompanies frustration, prejudice can also have a more profound and complex meaning for the personality of a prejudiced person. It is a method of defending self-image, whereby a minority group becomes a *negative reference group* for the majority member—a point of comparison against which the opinions, abilities, or performances of the majority member can be regarded as superior. Some psychologists have argued that virtually all displaced aggression is actually of an ego-defensive nature, having as its primary objective the restoration of an individual's self-esteem or status. By using a minority group as a negative reference group, an individual need not acknowledge truths about him or herself or about threatening aspects of his or her environment.

There may be certain individuals who are especially predisposed toward making social comparisons and employing negative reference groups in order to maintain or to bolster their self-image. During the 1940s, a group of social scientists set out to examine the possible existence of a deep-lying personality predisposition for directing aggression to minority groups. They amassed a good deal of evidence for the presence of an *authoritarian personality structure,* a syndrome of functionally interrelated personality characteristics in which prejudice plays an important part. As a result of harsh and punitive forms of discipline in early socialization, the authoritarian personality comes to have a general contempt for the allegedly inferior and weak members of society and in the process bolsters his or her self-esteem and avoids painful truths about him or herself.

Aside from its ego-defensive functions as previously discussed, prejudice also plays a part in structuring the perceived world of the majority-group member. Prejudice operates in the lives of majority-group members to define situations, provide order and clarity, and reduce the cognitive and emotional uncertainties of everyday experiences. Culturally supported prejudices provide ready-made expectations in terms of which individuals can easily be categorized. Prejudiced individuals may be incapable of accurately estimating qualities of others from the cues given in interactional settings and seem to be especially intolerant of cognitive and emotional ambiguities.

In the next chapter, we again find ourselves addressing the question of whether and how discrimination and prejudice are functional, but at an entirely different level. This time, we turn our attention to the social functions of discrimination and prejudice.

Chapter 5
Social Functions of Discrimination and Prejudice for the Majority Group

Discrimination and prejudice may be understood, in part, as an expression of latent forces that operate in order to fulfill the psychological needs of bigoted individuals. As suggested in the last chapter, these needs may involve the displacement of aggression, the protection of self-esteem, or the reduction of cognitive and emotional uncertainties.

Personality functions of discrimination and prejudice are important psychologically, but we must also examine their *social* functions for the majority group—those consequences of a political or an economic nature that aid in the maintenance of the majority group *qua* group and of its advantaged position in a society. We address ourselves now to the consequences of discrimination and prejudice for: (1) acquiring and maintaining economic advantages,

(2) performing unpleasant or low-paying jobs, and (3) maintaining power.

Acquisition and Maintenance of Economic Advantages

Intergroup hostility tends to increase as competition for scarce resources becomes more intense. Sherif and his collaborators (1961) demonstrated the link between competition and intergroup hostility in a series of experiments that took place in an isolated summer camp for 11- and 12-year-old boys. After a period of time together, the boys attending the camp were separated into two groups and placed in different cabins. When each group of boys had developed a strong sense of group spirit and organization, Sherif arranged for a number of intergroup encounters—a tournament of competitive games such as football, baseball, tug-of-war, and a treasure hunt—in which one group could fulfill its goals only at the expense of the other group. Though the tournament began in a spirit of friendliness and good-natured rivalry, it soon became apparent that negative intergroup feelings were emerging on a large scale. The members of each group began to name-call their rivals, completely turning against members of the opposing group, even members whom they had selected as "best friends" upon first arriving at the camp.

Intergroup Competition

Sherif's findings shed light on the nature of majority–minority relations: When the maintenance or enhancement of the status of the majority group depends on the continued subordination of a minority, then we might expect that intergroup competition will become translated into prejudice and discrimination. Indeed, some of the most visible benefits of prejudice for the majority group have a rational economic basis. Such benefits occur as the minority-group member attempts to secure a share of the scarce resources of his or her society. For example, there appears to be a direct relationship between the occurrence of anti-immigrant nativist activity and the incidence of economic depression.

The Native American party of the 1830s, the Know-Nothing Order of the 1850s, the American Protective Association in the last two decades of the nineteenth century, and the scores of anti-alien, 100 percent American groups in the 1930s—these all show the tendency to try to bolster a shaky economic situation by prejudice against recent immigrant groups. [Simpson and Yinger, 1972:116].

Large-scale economic problems such as the depressions of 1893 and 1907 served to solidify the opposition to further immigration from Italy, setting the stage for acceptance of stereotypes of Italians as "organ-grinders, paupers, slovenly ignoramuses, and so on" (LaGumina, 1973). Dollard (1938) has shown that local, white Southerners became more hostile toward German newcomers to their town as economic conditions worsened and competition for jobs increased. In a similar way, Chinese immigrants to nineteenth-century America tended to be regarded as "honest," "industrious," and "peaceful" as long as jobs remained plentiful. But when the job market tightened and the Chinese began to seek work in mines, farming, domestic service, and factories, a dramatic increase in anti-Chinese sentiment emerged. They quickly became stereotyped as "dangerous," "deceitful," "vicious," and "clannish." Whites who felt themselves in competition for jobs accused the Chinese—just as they accused other immigrant groups—of undermining their standard of living (Sung, 1967).

According to van den Berghe, competition yields many of the conditions necessary for the development and maintenance of the prejudice associated with complex, industrialized societies that are based on large-scale manufacturing and a capitalist economy. Under such structural arrangements, the roles of majority and minority members are ill-defined and in a state of flux. Majority-group members feel themselves in direct competition with members of minority groups. There is concern for status, and antagonism prevails: "Competition, real or imaginary, for status, for jobs, for women, etc., or the threat of competition, poison race relations" (1966:60–61).

Such is not the case in traditional societies, where a rather simple division of labor and an agricultural base require only minimal and latent forms of competitiveness, mobility, and status concern. Moreover, when it occurs in the traditional context, competitiveness rarely develops as a motivating force of everyday life and is generally built into the rigid status definitions of the system (e.g., castes).

The Economic Dimension

Probably the most powerful forces that determine and perpetuate majority–minority relationships are economic. The corporate and labor sectors of the economic structure shape opportunity in everyone's lives. In fact, if any one segment of the society has the power to influence the persistence or elimination of an action, object, or idea (such as discrimination), it is likely to be this one. The relationship between economic structures and the distribution of opportunity has been studied under the label of political economy. What are the political dimensions of group membership, work, production, pay levels, consumption, and so on? If discrimination and prejudice have some consequences for majority and minority groups in terms of their economic well-being, what are these consequences? In order to deal with such questions, it is necessary to identify who could possibly benefit or lose from the existence of discrimination and prejudice.

Opportunity on a Continuum

One view claims (naively, we believe) that the economic structure exists on a sort of continuum along which all individuals are distributed; that is, everyone brings to the marketplace of the economy a given amount of "human capital." This is the measure of the skills and knowledge that allow (or cause) one's productive capacity. The more skills and knowledge one possesses, the more productivity and, presumably, the more opportunities to earn one has: "Individuals with little education, training, and skills have low marginal productivities and earn low incomes. With very little human capital, they earn poverty incomes. Blacks who have less capital than whites earn less" (Thurow, 1969:66).

Of course, in order to understand why some people earn less than others, it is also vital to understand the origins of their levels of human capital. It is one thing to list the raw materials of productivity, such as education and motivation, and quite another to identify discrimination, for example, as the source of their unequal distribution. Sometimes this analysis is not made, and "human capital" is used as a given fact. The continuum notion allows classical economists to assume that businesses make "rational" decisions based only on a person's productivity, independent of his or her group membership. Accordingly, everyone is seen as an equal before businesses' rational economic judgment, and only one's capacity to contribute to a particular economic enterprise is at issue: What can you produce?

One example of the belief that businesses are not biased (except about productivity) is evident in a brief paper by economist Thomas C. Schelling (1972). Schelling suggests that when analyzing employment discrimination, prejudice ought not to be discussed. He argues that distinctions between workers are objectively not subjectively made by employers on the basis of net productivity, or "utility functions." He then proceeds to tell of the costs and benefits of hiring "greens" as opposed to "blues" in one theoretical organization. (This device, presumably, keeps race from muddying the rationality of the issues.) Greens, we are told, live on the other side of a boundary that makes their labor more costly in a number of ways: They must travel farther to their place of work, walk across the lawns of blues (doing damage), and there is a labor import duty to be paid. Given all these costs, the net pay to greens is inevitably less. Notice that Schelling pays no attention to how and by whom businesses are located, housing denied or made available to each group, or import duties levied and spent. His focus is on making it seem purely rational, in business terms, that greens earn less than blues. Nothing personal, you see, just business rationality. But he clearly ignores all the background decisions that made such distinctions inevitably profitable for both businesses and blue workers only. One more example, just to make the fallacy clearer: "Greens—and the analogy now may be with people who have prison records—are known to steal from the firms they work for." This, of course, Schelling wishes to make clear to us, is a cost to the employer, increasing the undesirability of employing greens. According to Schelling, the same costs occur even if such criminal tendencies are *mistakenly* imputed to greens. Such evaluations are anything *but* group-neutral. There are so many unexamined conditions preceding the decisions of employers that their rationality is totally blind to the existence of discrimination in the society.

Reich (1971) has recognized the danger of this approach. He says that conventional economists:

> presume that they can analyze the sources of pure wage discrimination without simultaneously analyzing the extent to which discrimination also affects the factors they hold constant. But such a technique distorts reality. The various forms of discrimination are not separable in real life. Employers' hiring and promotion practices, resource allocation in city schools, the structure of transportation systems, residential segregation and housing quality, availability of decent health care, behavior of policemen and judges, foremen's prejudices, images of blacks presented in the media and the schools, price gouging in ghetto stores—these and the other forms of social and economic discrimination interact strongly with each other in determining the occupational status and annual income, and welfare, of black people. [1971:184.]

If employers see individuals as existing on some sort of group-blind continuum of productive merit, such "rational" employment decisions do nothing to eliminate the massive effects that other discriminations have on the earning potential of minority-group members once they reach the job market. In fact, such decisions by employers further institutionalize these discriminations and amplify their effect.

Opportunity Bifurcated

A second view of the economic structure is a sort of bifurcated perspective. It sees a process whereby groups contend with one another for economic opportunity, one on one. According to this view, when groups are *in competition with one another* for opportunities over which neither has control, prejudice and discrimination are developed in order to enhance the ability of either group to win the struggle. This process has already been illustrated in the example of Sherif's experiment. When one group has an advantaged position, however, prejudice and discrimination are used in order to *protect* its superior hold on the opportunities in question (Vander Zanden, 1966). This is the case of the "haves" discriminating against the "have nots" to keep them from becoming a threat.

Opportunity and the Split Labor Market

But the fact that the wealthiest people in society do not seem, at least on the surface, to be bigots coupled with the character of American employment bring forth a third model for describing the distribution of economic opportunity. This is called the *split labor market theory* (Bonacich, 1972). According to this view, the economic structure has the following components: employers and laborers. Laborers are *split* into two levels, higher-paid labor and lower-paid, or marginal, labor. Employers have as one of their main goals the reduction of labor costs in order to increase profits. Higher-paid labor has better working conditions, more job security, and is more organized. Cheaper labor is worse off in all these categories (Bonacich, 1972).

The question of who benefits from discrimination now becomes more elaborate and, as we will show, clearer. Within the split labor market approach there are two main interpretations of the data concerning who benefits from discrimination. The only thing about which they agree is that the bottom segment (blacks, women, and other minorities) consistently loses.

Table 5.1 compares the two main approaches. Bonacich (1972, 1976) argues that employers lose from discrimination, higher-paid workers benefit, and it is the higher-paid workers who do the actual discriminating. (Among others who have found that white workers benefit from discrimination against blacks are Glenn, 1963, 1966 and, more recently, Beck, 1980). She claims that higher-paid laborers, by processes called *exclusion* and *caste,* protect their jobs and their pay level from encroachment by cheaper laborers. When they

Table 5.1 A Comparison of Two Versions of the Split Labor Market Theory

	Bonacich	Reich
Employers	Lose (−)	Gain (+)
Higher-paid labor	Gain (+)	Lose (−)
Cheap labor	Lose (−)	Lose (−)

are powerful enough, higher-paid workers can keep cheaper labor out of the market entirely (exclusion), thus protecting their jobs and their level of pay. When they are not this powerful, higher-paid workers must settle for keeping the number of lower-paid workers to a minimum and restricted to the worst jobs (caste). In either case, Bonacich claims that such actions are costly for employers, for they diminish, or eliminate altogether, the employer's ability to take advantage of lower-paid labor.

A second version of this view (Becker, 1957) agrees with Bonacich that employers lose from discrimination and that higher-paid workers benefit. But Becker adds to this scheme the belief that both employers and workers have a "taste for discrimination"—a preference not to associate with lower-paid workers (blacks in Becker's analysis)—and that in order to indulge this "taste," they act so as to deny them jobs. In the terms that we used when we discussed the relationship between discrimination and prejudice, Becker suggests that the attitude precedes the behavior in this case: The "taste" for discrimination leads to the hiring preferences. For the white worker, the discrimination has benefits, but for the employer, such practices have economic costs, which, according to Becker, ultimately should lead to the end of discrimination. How the "tastes" for discrimination are to be eliminated in employers remains unclear.

In contrast with Bonacich and Becker—who agree that higher-paid laborers benefit while employers lose from discrimination against lower-paid laborers—Reich (1970) argues that employers benefit and both higher- and lower-paid laborers lose from discrimination: "The economic consequences of racism are not only lower incomes for blacks, but also higher incomes for the capitalist class coupled with lower incomes for white workers" (p. 185). Reich claims that in addition to the wage effects of discrimination, racism also weakens the entire working class by promoting competition and class divisions among them:

Wages of white labor are lessened by racism because the fear of a cheaper and underemployed black labor supply in the area is invoked by employers when labor presents its wage demands. Racial antagonisms on the shop floor deflect attention from labor grievances related to working conditions, permitting employers to cut costs. Racial divisions among labor prevent the development of united worker organizations both in the workplace and in the labor movement as a whole. As a result, union strength and union militancy will be less, the greater the extent of racism. [1971:187.]

Thus, the main mechanisms whereby discrimination benefits employers and costs workers at both levels are: (1) the reduction of wages for higher-paid workers and, to an even greater extent, for lower-paid workers (which is why there are two minus signs for cheaper labor in the column for Reich's theory in Table 5.1) and (2) the reduction of the power of workers in general to organize in their own interests against those of employers. According to Reich, there are also secondary mechanisms by which discrimination costs workers at both levels and ultimately benefits employers:

The second mechanism we shall consider concerns the allocation of expenditures for public services. The most important of these services is education. Racial antagonisms dilute both the desire and the ability of poor white parents to improve educational opportunities for their children. Antagonism between blacks and whites drives wedges between the two groups and reduces their ability to join in a united political movement pressing for improved and more equal education. Moreover, many poor whites recognize that however inferior their own schools, black schools are even worse. This provides some degree of satisfaction and identification with the status quo, reducing the desire of poor whites to press politically for better schools in their neighborhoods. [1971:187.]

To the extent that discrimination by either employers or higher-paid laborers contributes to the weakening of the position of workers in general (either by direct, wage and working-condition effects or by lessening their "human capital"), then discrimination will continue to benefit employers. This theory has been called "divide and conquer." If I have a position worth defending (in goods, power, status, or so on), then it is to my advantage to divide my potential competitors against one another, thus deflecting the energies they could direct against me, and turning them against one another. If, in addition to keeping them from uniting against me, their hatred of one another allows me to play them off against one another in the job market, so much the better. Far from doing anything to reduce the hatreds that perpetuate such a situation, I am likely to do whatever is necessary to cause it to persist.

One example of the application of Reich's model to the analysis of discrimination is Goldberg's (1971) work on the exploitation of women. She contends that although capitalists did not invent the family structure, "capitalism actively promotes the isolated family unit and the woman's role in it, through such propaganda devices as the glorification of motherhood, in order to facilitate its economic exploitation of both men and women" (Goldberg, 1971:113). Women are disproportionately found in the lower sector of the split labor market, employed at lower wages in much more insecure positions than are men. They also are disproportionately found in part-time jobs, the pay rate for which is also low. They are always available to fill the seasonal or other temporary labor needs of businesses and, when necessary, to threaten male workers whose demands on management become too extreme (Deckard and Sherman, 1974).

Resolving the Issue of Who "Benefits" from Discrimination

The debate about who benefits from discrimination puts business in opposition to higher-paid labor. When blacks or women are paid less, hired only for temporary or insecure jobs, promoted less, or not hired at all, the question has been whether capitalists or laboring majority-group members (whites males) gain. But there are two ways to resolve the issue, the outcomes of which satisfy the questions asked by a functionalist analysis such as ours.

First of all, from the perspective of minority-group members, there is no debate at all. Whichever model you choose, Bonacich's or Reich's, minority-group members lose. Discrimination is overwhelmingly dysfunctional for blacks, women, and other minority-group members. In functional terms, discrimination against minority groups is positively functional for majority-group members, whether they be capitalists whose profit margins benefit from discrimination or higher-paid, unionized, white males whose job security and wages benefit. For minority-group members, whether benefits accrue to the lower segment of the majority group or to the upper segment, the balance of the consequences of discrimination still comes out so that discrimination and prejudice are likely to persist (see Box 5.1).

The second resolution of the debate focuses on the conditions under which the benefits of discrimination go to each segment of the majority group. This can be an important issue when we realize that, although majority-group members have more power than minority-group members to influence the persistence of discrimination and prejudice, the greatest concentration of power is in the upper (business-operating) segment of the majority group. They

---

BOX 5.1

Minority Subordination and Majority Status

In a rigorous study of the relationship between minority subordination and majority occupational status, Glenn has similarly argued that a tradition of prejudice must be regarded as more than "merely a self-perpetuating carry-over from a past era which will certainly and rapidly disappear once the Myrdalian 'vicious circle' is broken" (1963: 447–448). In order to investigate his contention that the presence of self-interest continues to reinforce the existence of prejudice, Glenn investigated distributions of white income and occupational status for 151 large metropolitan areas during 1950, hypothesizing that occupational gains among whites would be higher where the relative size of the black population was greater. Glenn's findings generally confirmed his hypothesis. Whites did in fact experience important occupational gains from the continued subordination of large numbers of blacks, gains that included greater occupational prestige, better working conditions, as well as authority and independence on the job.

Examining data based on the 1960 census, Glenn (1966) found that similarly many whites living in southern urbanized areas received important occupational benefits from the presence of a large and subordinated black population. Such benefits to whites in southern localities with large black populations included more favorable occupational status, higher employment rates, and greater incomes than those obtained by whites in other southern localities.

control the vast bulk of the resources from which opportunity is distributed, especially in the occupational structure.

Just as the labor market can be seen as split into two sectors, business can also be divided into sectors, namely, the competitive and monopoly sectors. The competitive areas of business work on relatively narrow profit margins and must control costs in order to survive in competition with one another. Those businesses involved in monopoly capitalism, however, can support very high profit margins precisely because they are in control of the marketplace, and therefore, their control over production costs need not be tight. Competitive business, therefore, must hire cheap labor in order to survive (Bluestone, 1972), whereas the monopolies can afford to hire more expensive, unionized, majority-group labor. Monopolies can pass labor costs along to the consumer, but competitive businesses cannot. It is in competitive capitalist enterprises that minority-group workers are concentrated (Deckard and Sherman, 1974). Therefore, discrimination in the job market benefits higher-paid workers in the monopoly capitalism sector. Their higher labor costs get passed on to the consumer (including, of course, every other segment of the society), and these businesses can maintain high profit margins without hiring cheaper labor. Thus, in the competitive business sector, discrimination benefits capitalists.[1]

In sum, then, a number of important economic and occupational benefits are derived for majority-group members from the persistence of discrimination and prejudice. Baran and Sweezy (1966) summarize some of them as follows:

(a) Employers benefit from divisions in the labor force which enable them to play one group off against another, thus weakening all. Historically, for example, no small amount of Negro migration was in direct response to the recruiting of strikebreakers. (b) Owners of ghetto real estate are able to overcrowd and overcharge. (c) Middle and upper income groups benefit from having at their disposal a large supply of cheap domestic labor. (d) Many small marginal businesses, especially in the service trades, can operate profitably only if cheap labor is available to them. (e) White workers benefit by being protected from Negro competition for the more desirable and higher paying jobs. [1966:263–264.]

In this section we have focused on the benefits of discrimination in terms of profits, wages, and job security. But, as Baran and Sweezy point out, a number of other functions accrue to majority-group members as a consequence of the creation of a relatively permanent underclass of poor people. We will discuss at some length during this chapter such consequences, especially the acquisition and maintenance of land and power, and the performance of unpleasant or low-paying jobs. But just as Baran and Sweezy have noted, poor people can be taken advantage of by slumlords, among others. Their poverty provides them with no choices. Thus, they must shop in their own neighborhoods because their transportation is limited. They are also trapped into paying high prices for inferior goods. Gans (1972), for example, has identified a number of "the positive functions of poverty": For example, the poor create jobs for those who serve their needs (e.g., social workers and planners); they stand as an example of what failure is like; they provide a market for inferior goods such as used goods, day-old bread, and so on; they are practice subjects for doctors and lawyers in training; they provide the idle rich with targets for their charitable activities, and they act as a buffer, absorbing "the economic and political costs of change and growth in American society" (Gans, 1972:283).

Once discrimination and prejudice are seen in functionalist terms, it is quite easy to stack up impressive lists of such functions for majority-group members. We have decided to focus on just a few of the more important consequences. In this section, for example, we have limited our attention to the occupational and land-control functions of discrimination and prejudice. We urge those interested in this functionalist approach to analyze other consequences that will further our understanding of the net aggregate of the consequences of discrimination and prejudice.

Mexicans, American Indians, and the Acquisition of Land

In the history of American society, intergroup competition for scarce resources has often taken the form of organized efforts to secure land and extend political boundaries. Prejudice has played a central role in the acquisition of property, for it has served to justify the ruthless, illegal tactics that were so frequently employed.

The experience of Mexican-Americans provides a case in point. After being stereotyped by Anglo-Americans as "treacherous, childlike, primitive, lazy, and irresponsible," Mexican-Americans found themselves manipulated by politicians, lawyers, and land-grabbers alike. Despite the 1848 Treaty of Guadalupe-Hidalgo, which guaranteed Mexicans the right of full citizenship, land-owning Mexican families found their titles in jeopardy and their land and cattle stolen or taken from them by fraud. Furthermore, they could not count on the courts for protection (Jacobs and Landau, 1971).

American Indians were severely mistreated at the hands of land-hungry white Americans who eagerly accepted the view that Indians were "treacherous and cruel savages who could never be trusted." The negative stereotype served a purpose: As long as the Indians were needed for their agricultural expertise, their military assistance, or their skill as trappers, white Americans tended to regard them in a favorable light and to permit their culture to maintain itself, but when large-scale campaigns became directed toward securing the lands occupied and settled by Indians, the negative stereotype emerged in full force and the rules applicable to dealings between "civilized peoples of the world" were suspended. After all, if the central business of the Indian "savage" was to "torture" and "slay," then the central business of the white man must have been to gradually eliminate the Indian "savage" (Jacobs and Landau, 1971).

In some cases, of course, the process of elimination was anything but gradual. By 1825, some thirteen thousand Cherokees maintained their homes in the southeastern region of the United States. They occupied 7 million acres of land, owned prosperous farms, and were at peace. However, this situation was radically altered by the discovery of gold in the hills of Georgia. In order to gain possession of the rich Cherokee-owned lands, white Americans—with the help of the Georgia legislature, President Andrew Jackson, the U.S. Congress, the Supreme Court, and the military—found it "necessary" to drive the Cherokees beyond the Mississippi. In the Cherokee removal of 1838, Indians were rounded up and taken away; their homes were burned; their property was seized; many were herded into stockades; and thousands died (Berry, 1965).

Such thinking on the part of white Americans also led to the passage of the Dawes General Allotment Act of 1887, which took two-thirds (90 million acres) of the tribal lands previously granted to American Indians by treaty. "It does not take much sophistication to find a rationale for acquiring 90 million acres of land, especially when the owner cannot do anything to protect his property, and besides, wasn't even an American citizen" (Burnette, 1971:82).

Competition and Antiblack Prejudice

Antiblack sentiment in American society has run a similar course, generally becoming most intense among groups that have stood the most to lose from the equal treatment of blacks. It is not surprising that southern white slave owners who enjoyed the economic and social rewards of the plantation sought to preserve the institution of slavery. What is less obvious, perhaps, is that the nearly three-fourths of the southern whites who owned no slaves also profited from slavery (albeit indirectly) and, therefore, were no less willing to see it abolished. For the nonslaveholder, slavery was a method of limiting the competition from blacks and providing whites with highly visible membership in a superior caste (Stampp, 1956).

After the Civil War, the presence of whites in direct competition with ex-slaves for jobs assured the perpetuation of the myth that blacks were somehow innately ill-equipped for precisely the same skilled work they had competently performed before Emancipation (Bonacich, 1972; Harris, 1964). This was true, even though an absolute level of segregation and humiliation of blacks did not set in until the turn of the twentieth century, long after decades of racial conflict and competition led by a "relaxation of the opposition" to racism had established a firm hold on the character of our society (Woodward, 1955).

Dollard's (1937) "gains" theory of race relations represents an early attempt to understand the consequences of prejudice against blacks for the occupational status of white workers. In his classic study of a southern community, Dollard observed that local whites gained occupationally from the presence of institutionalized forms of prejudice. Thus, as compared with their black counterparts in the community, whites in Southerntown generally got higher returns for their work and secured a disproportionately large share of goods and services. (See Box 5.2.)

In light of the relationship between minority-group subordination and majority-group occupational status, it may not be surprising to learn that anti-black sentiment in contemporary American society continues to be most visible, if not most pronounced, among white working-class individuals, for these are the very individuals

---

BOX 5.2

Prejudice and Fear of Competition

The emotional impact of the fear of competition from blacks was clearly expressed in the following letter from a southern white workingman who wrote at the turn of the twentieth century:

> All the genuine Southern people like the Negro as a servant, and so long as he remains the hewer of wood and carrier of water, and remains strictly in what we choose to call his place, everything is all right, but when ambition, prompted by real education, causes the Negro to grow restless and bestir himself to get out of that servile condition, then there is, or at least there will be, trouble, sure enough trouble, that all the great editors, parsons, and philosophers can no more check than they can now state the whole truth and nothing but the truth, about this all-absorbing, far-reaching miserable race question. There are those among Southern editors and other public men who have been shouting into the ears of the North for twenty-five years that education would solve the Negro question; there is not an honest, fearless, thinking man in the South but who knows that to be a bare-faced lie. Take a young Negro of little more than ordinary intelligence, even, get hold of him in time, train him thoroughly as to books, and finish him up with a good industrial education, send him out into the South with ever so good intentions both on the part of his benefactor and himself, send him to take my work away from me and I will kill him. [Franklin and Starr, 1967:25.]

who are most anxious to protect their small amounts of power and status and *feel* most threatened by the possibility of racial equality. As Blauner (1972) suggests, 1.3 million white workers would have to be downgraded occupationally, in order to equalize the job distributions of blacks and whites. Moreover, racial equality would mean that the white working class—more than any other group in our society—would have to share its schools, neighborhoods, and political influence with blacks (Rossi, 1972). Such data go far to explain why working-class individuals are most likely to be attracted to groups such as the Ku Klux Klan (Vander Zanden, 1960) and to contribute in large numbers to a white backlash in the presence of civil rights activities (Rossi, 1972).

More recently, Cummings (1980) showed that white ethnic workers in the lower segment of the labor market (those filling lower-paid, less-secure jobs) who are in direct competition with blacks for employment are more racially bigoted than are white ethnics who work in the better-paid and more-secure segment of the labor market. Once again we see that as competition increases, intolerance for minority groups also increases. In contrast, workers in the primary (higher) segment of the labor market are not in direct competition with blacks and so show less bigotry toward them.

Performance of Unpleasant or Low-Paying Jobs

Up to this point, we have been concerned with only a single dimension of the contribution to the majority group made by the presence of prejudice: As a result of their forced subordination, the absence of competition from members of minority groups helps to reserve the statuses with prestige and economic reward for members of the majority group. However, the flip side of this economic function must be given its due emphasis, namely, that prejudice justifies placing members of the minority in a position to serve the majority group, whether by taking low-paying jobs or by performing important tasks that the majority does not itself elect to perform.

The Jews in Medieval Europe

The history of the Jews provides an appropriate illustration. During the Middle Ages, European Jews were systematically excluded from such respectable activities as farming, owning land, and joining the guilds of craftsmen. Instead, Jews were generally restricted to the despised occupation of lending money at interest—an activity absolutely forbidden to the Christian majority on religious grounds—which was regarded as essential by the church and the nobility as a source of outside financing for building, farming, waging war, or engaging in political affairs. Powerless to protest or retaliate in an effective manner, Jews often played this necessary but stigmatizing role for the majority group.

In order to understand the reason why the Jews were the only group to perform the essential money-lending service, we must understand the attitude of the medieval church toward it. As viewed by the church, the lending of money for interest was sinful regardless of the amount of interest charged or the purpose for which money was borrowed. Thus, a Christian who today receives 5 percent interest on his savings account would have been committing a mortal sin during the Middle Ages. As non-Christians, however, Jews were a different story altogether. In the view of the medieval church, Jews were already headed for hell; their participation in money lending could add little to the eternal punishment that awaited them in the hereafter (Dimont, 1962).

The Immigrant Experience

Prior to the Immigration Quota Act of 1924, immigration was an essential source of labor for the economic development of the United States. Until the early part of the nineteenth century, important numbers of European immigrants continued to come from England, France, and Germany. These were mostly farmers and artisans who brought their marketable skills and capital in order to seize on more attractive opportunities in the New World.

But the nature of immigration changed considerably after 1840, when sizable groups of landless peasants from Ireland and Germany arrived in the United States. Lacking either resources or skills, most of these immigrants had only their labor to sell and therefore managed to secure a marginal existence for themselves and their families. The distribution of immigrants by area of the United States was directly related to the presence of opportunities for unskilled labor.

Immigration from Ireland and Germany persisted at a respectable level beyond the turn of the twentieth century at the same time that new sources of immigration began to mount in importance. After 1870, economic problems in Scandinavia brought a large and growing number of Scandinavians to the shores of America. And only a decade later, the same social and economic changes in eastern and southern Europe resulted in an increasing volume of emigration to the United States and elsewhere. Between 1880 and World War I, large numbers of Italians and eastern European Jews entered the United States. Smaller groups of newcomers also arrived from Greece and Rumania, and from the Slavic and Baltic nations. Like those before them, the members of these immigrant groups were predominantly peasants without skills or money who were forced to enter the lowest levels of the American labor market.

Upon their arrival, these immigrants were faced with the unenviable task of getting work immediately in order to sustain their lives. They had little choice, for they desperately needed jobs and could not afford to negotiate wages, hours, or working conditions. As a result, many immigrants were exploited by employers who found a willing labor pool for poor pay and miserable working conditions. What is more, a growing prejudice against these newcomers often developed to justify their continued exploitation, keeping them tied to lowly positions in the economic order (Handlin, 1962).

The impact of immigration on America's expanding industrialism cannot easily be exaggerated:

Without the immigrants America could not have found quickly enough the manpower to build the railroads, mine the coal, man the open-hearth steel furnaces, and run the machines. Moreover, while most of the immigrants were pushed into the unskilled, backbreaking jobs, enough of them were skilled—carrying over techniques from a European industrialism which had made an earlier start—so that the Great Migration was not only one of people but of talents, skills, and cultural traditions. [Lerner, 1972:114.]

The Impact of Slavery

Slavery in the antebellum South gives more brutal but decisive testimony of the economic importance of prejudice, a factor that permitted justifying the enslavement of millions of human beings in order to provide cheap labor for an expanding agricultural economy. The American version of slavery may have derived its initial impetus from an acute labor shortage existing in Colonial America that could not be resolved adequately by means of European manpower. At least half of the white European immigrants to Colonial America paid their passage to the New World by obligating themselves as servants for periods of from 2 to 7 years (Stampp, 1956). When sources of white labor threatened to dry up, however, America shifted its attention to Africa:

> The master could not sustain white servitude without risking the eventual cutoff of Europeans coming to the New World. But with no such possibility existing with respect to Africans, since few blacks were voluntarily entering the colonies anyway, the color line soon developed into a conspicuous, distinguishing feature between free and slave labor. Through this course, according to Oscar Handlin, the inferiority associated with servitude transferred to the color black; virtual lifetime bondage became the lot only of Negroes. The arrangement, moreover, provided an economic incentive for aggressive recruitment of slaves from the black continent.[2] [Wilhelm, 1970:127.]

Southerners could have turned entirely to free white labor, but they would have sacrificed the several advantages that only slavery could have provided. In the first place, an average white laborer was paid more than the cost of investing in and maintaining his or her enslaved counterpart. Second, the slave owner was far better able to exploit black women and children. Third, a master could require his slaves to work longer hours under more difficult conditions without having to negotiate with his workers or with their organizations. Finally, slave ownership was a symbol of status that identified the master with a privileged social class in the South (Stampp, 1956).[3]

In the southern colonies, a few powerful people, predominantly planters, shared a need for numerous slaves who could be trained and controlled for profitable exploitation (Noel, 1968). As a result, the vast majority of southern slaves filled the roles of field hands and domestic servants, though smaller numbers of slaves were employed as needed in saltworks, mines, railroad construction, textile mills, and in other occupations that required specialized skills (Logan, 1954). Also as a result of the need for exploitable labor, slavery soon came to be regarded as a kind of "white man's burden," as a moral and religious obligation on the part of white southerners that was divinely ordained and ultimately beneficial to the "uncivilized" and "inferior" black slave (Comer, 1972; Genovese, 1969).

Contemporary American Society

The economic exploitation of black Americans continued long after the resolution of the Civil War. The continued presence of institutionalized forms of prejudice against blacks assured that many southern whites would go on avoiding the dirty work of their communities—work requiring heavy manual labor or the performance of monotonous tasks and paying low wages (Dollard, 1938).

The same phenomenon has been observed to occur in other parts of the United States, where the nature of the minority selected to perform unpleasant or low-paying jobs is determined by the historical presence of its members in the population of that area. For example, the economy of eastern Oklahoma depends on its sizable population of Cherokee Indians to provide an inexpensive and permanent labor supply for the low-paying manual work of the region. In the 1960s, Cherokee median per capita income was approximately $500. "In some areas, Cherokees live in virtual peonage; in others, straw bosses recruit Cherokee laborers for irregular work at low pay" (Wahrhaftig and Thomas, 1969:195).

The changing character of California's farm workers similarly illustrates the influence of sheer availability on the fate of minority Americans. California Indians were the state's first farm workers, coming on the scene at a time when agricultural production was essentially limited to cattle and wheat. But a subsequent influx of Chinese immigrants soon changed the nature of farm work in California. By 1870, as work on the transcontinental railroad was coming to an end, Chinese laborers turned for work to California's farmlands. The availability of this large supply of Chinese labor was an important factor in the shift in California's agricultural patterns from livestock and wheat to fruits and vegetables, crops which required larger amounts of hand labor.

The supply of Chinese labor for California agriculture was sharply reduced when, in 1882, Congress suspended Chinese immigration. Shortly thereafter, however, the Japanese government decided to lift its ban on emigration, and sizable numbers of workers from the rice paddies of Japan began to appear in California. Until the early decades of the twentieth century, when anti-Japanese prejudice appeared in full force, the Japanese were a major source of farm labor in California. After 1910, however, the turmoil of a revolution in Mexico persuaded tens of thousands of rural Mexicans to flee to the safety and security of the United States. From that time to the present day, Mexicans have continued to represent the most important source of farm labor in California (London and Anderson, 1970).

Present-day attitudes and norms regarding minority Americans still reflect the existence of a need to fill low-paying and unpleasant jobs: As Glenn's (1966) data indicate, black subordination in the 1960s helped to reduce the cost of labor to employers, especially in the South. The presence of large numbers of blacks in the population of a locality increased the availability of domestic help to southern white housewives and helped to reduce the cost of operatives and laborers to many southern employers. (See Box 5.3.)

BOX 5.3

The Effects of Educational Tracking

"Ability grouping" is a method of educational tracking whereby students are sorted into homogeneous groups on the basis of "their ability to perform classroom tasks" such as reading or arithmetic. With respect to higher education, ability grouping may determine whether or not a child can enter college or, if the child does receive an extended education, whether or not he or she is able to attend a prestige school. Howe and

Lauter (1972) argue that ability grouping helps to ensure that low-paying and unpleasant occupations are supplied with manpower while white, middle-class children are being prepared to fill the technological and professional needs of our society. In the following excerpt from "How the School System Is Rigged for Failure," Howe and Lauter present evidence for their view:

> Ability grouping has been operating effectively to limit competition with the children of white, middle-class parents who, on the whole, have controlled the schools. In New York City in 1967, for example, nonwhites, the vast majority of them poor, made up 40 percent of the high school population; they constituted about 36 percent of students in the "academic" high schools and about 60 percent of those tracked into "vocational" high schools. In the Bronx High School of Science and in Brooklyn Tech, elite institutions for which students must qualify by examination, "nonwhites" totaled only 7 and 12 percent of the students, respectively.
>
> But the real effects of tracking can better be seen in the statistics of students in the academic high schools. A majority of blacks and Puerto Ricans fill lower tracks, which lead them—if they stay at all—to "general" rather than "academic" diplomas. Only 18 percent of academic high school graduates were black or Puerto Rican (though they were, as we said, 36 percent of the academic student population); and only one-fifth of that 19 percent went on to college, as compared with 63 percent of whites who graduated. In other words, only 7 percent of the graduates of New York's academic high schools who went on to college were black or Puerto Rican. The rest, for the most part were tracked into non-college-preparatory programs, left school with what amounted to a ticket into the Army. [1972:232–233.]

Maintenance of Power

The power leadership of a society may owe part of its capacity for survival to the presence of institutionalized forms of discrimination and prejudice against minority groups. Throughout history, various minorities have been selected by the majority group as "servants of power."

Court Jews and Renegade Christians

The position of Jews in seventeenth- and eighteenth-century Germany provides a case in point. The Jews held only a marginal position in the social structure of the larger German society, having no citizen rights or legal protections and being widely despised and persecuted by the German people. As a result, German Jews, taken from the squalor of the ghetto, found themselves at the mercy of the Germanic absolutist rulers who utilized them as instruments for maximizing their power in society. As servants of power to these rulers, court Jews became advisors, collaborators, bankers, and financiers:

Jewish financiers and entrepreneurs supplied the armies of their prince, financed his wars, arranged new loans and settled old debts. They supplied the jewels for the prince's wife and his mistresses, but they also were innovators in building up trade and industry in defiance of guild restrictions. At times they monopolized the trade in silver, salt, or tobacco. They built silk, ribbon, cloth, and velvet factories in Prussia; they were chief tax collectors and diplomatic representatives, financial administrators and bankers, but above all confidants of the prince.[Coser, 1972:578.]

As Coser (1972) points out, renegade Christians were similarly employed by fourteenth- and fifteenth-century Turkish sultans who sought to maintain and extend their power over their Muslim subjects. Taken as youths and converted to the Muslim faith, these nonnative Christians became important human resources for the sultan's staff, serving in both civilian and military capacities as courtiers, administrators, and military officers. Renegade Christians provided Turkish rulers with a loyal and ambitious staff. Being the slaves of a single ruler as well as outsiders from the standpoint of the native population, they were totally dependent on the sultan, who, in turn, became freed from reliance on the support of his native Muslim population.

The Safety-Valve Function

The consequences of discrimination and prejudice for maintaining power are sometimes directly visible to the members of a society; other times, however, such consequences take indirect and subtle forms that are dependent on the operation and interplay of both psychological as well as sociological mechanisms. As shown in Chapter 4, the tendency to find a scapegoat, or to displace aggression, may become incorporated into the personality dynamics of an individual, often providing for the immediate gratification of his or her irrational ego-defensive needs and desires. Among highly prejudiced people, there seems to be an extreme unwillingness to attribute blame to the dominant sources of power in society. In an effort to compensate for feelings of weakness and inferiority, prejudiced individuals instead seek to identify themselves with powerful individuals and groups, typically attributing their frustrations to members of minority groups (Berkowitz, 1962).

On a collective level, scapegoating may serve as a *safety valve* whereby feelings of hostility are diverted to substitute objects, thereby protecting the leaders of a group from becoming the recipients of aggression (Coser, 1956). This phenomenon has been observed in the confines of the small-group laboratory. Burke (1969) has shown, for example, that the displacement of hostility on a low-status member of a small group can become a mechanism whereby the task leader escapes the hostility of other group members.

Outside the experimental laboratory, the safety-valve function of scapegoating often protects powerful individuals in a society from the unmitigated hostility of its members. According to Sherman, at least part of this function is carried out by dividing the members of society along majority–minority lines, so that interests shared by both groups become obscured and hostility is directed downward in the system of social class, rather than toward a common opponent located at the top:

For example, no one is more oppressed or poverty-stricken than the white sharecropper of the South (except the black sharecropper). But he has always fought against his natural allies, and supported the wealthy white Southerners to the extent that they not only monopolize Southern politics but achieve the chairmanship of most congressional committees by seniority. Similarly, the white worker is set against the black worker, so that unionization is prevented altogether in many Southern areas, and each can be used as a strikebreaker against the other. The same kind of divide and rule tactic is used in Northern cities. [1972:180–181.]

McWilliams (1948) has argued that the anti-Semitism that emerged in full force during the closing decades of nineteenth-century America originated in significant part with wealthy industrial tycoons who utilized prejudice as a tactic for diverting attention from their greedy labor practices and for maintaining power and wealth. Under the active encouragement of these tycoons, anti-Semitism became a "mask for privilege" that quickly spread in scope to encompass wider and wider sectors of American society.

According to Featherstone (1976), busing the powerless to achieve desegregated schools is a recent creation of the rich and powerful who hope that violence between blacks and whites will serve their own ends. During the early years of busing in northern cities, local and national leaders frequently led the opponents of busing to believe that they would be able to reverse the federal desegregation orders and win their battle against busing. Such official support for organized resistance resulted in "an updated Northern version of the old Southern alliance of planters and blacks against poor whites, which never really profited anyone except the elites" (Featherstone, 1976). Thus, despite an urgent need for poor city dwellers to join together in more inclusive political units, blacks and whites only drew farther apart.

Rigid social structures such as totalitarian societies seem to be especially dependent for their existence on the safety-valve function of scapegoating (Coser, 1956). The institutionalization of anti-Semitism in Nazi Germany provides an appropriate example: The Jews were widely viewed by the members of German society as being directly responsible for the severe economic problems that plagued them. In an experimental context, Lippitt and White (1958) similarly report that children who participated in an autocratic group atmosphere tended to express their hostility against one of the children in their group or against members of out-groups rather than against the authoritarian leader.

Summary

In this chapter, we have examined the social functions of discrimination and prejudice for the majority group—those consequences of a political or economic nature that help the majority group to maintain its advantaged position in a society. The emphasis has been on intergroup conflict. As Weber (Gerth and Mills, 1946) long ago suggested, the structured inequalities of a society may involve differences between individuals with respect to the dimensions of status, economic resources, and power. Thus, the present chapter has focused on the consequences of discrimination and prejudice for: (1) acquisition and maintenance of economic advantages, (2) the performance of unpleasant or low-paying jobs, and (3) the maintenance of power.

When the maintenance of the status of the majority group depends on the continued subordination of a minority, then intergroup competition tends to be translated into discrimination. Indeed, many of the most visible benefits of discrimination and prejudice for the majority group have a rational economic basis, occurring as the minority-group member seeks to secure a share of the scarce resources of his or her society. This has been true historically for many of the minorities in America, including Germans, Chinese, and blacks. For Mexican-Americans and American Indians, prejudice against them has been associated with organized efforts on the part of white Americans to secure land and extend political boundaries.

There is evidence to suggest that the relationship between minority-group subordination and majority-group occupational status applies to contemporary American society as well. For example, localities with large black populations have more favorable occupational status among whites. Moreover, antiblack sentiment in our society continues to be most pronounced among those individuals who are most anxious to protect their small amounts of power and status.

The flip side of the economic function of discrimination and prejudice must be given its due emphasis. Prejudice justifies placing members of the minority in a position to serve the majority group, whether by taking low-paying jobs or by performing important tasks that the majority does not itself elect to perform.

Examples of the importance of this function can be found throughout history. During the Middle Ages, European Jews were generally restricted to the despised but essential occupation of lending money at interest. Immigrant labor was essential to a rapidly expanding American industrialism. In the antebellum South, millions of human beings were enslaved in order to provide cheap labor for an expanding agricultural economy. As a contemporary example, the presence of large numbers of blacks in a locality ensures that domestic help will be available to white housewives and helps to reduce the cost of laborers to white employers. The historical presence of such minorities as Chinese, Japanese, and Mexicans has influenced the character of California agriculture.

The power leadership of a society may owe part of its capacity for survival to the presence of discrimination and prejudice against minorities. Throughout history, various minority groups have been chosen as "servants of power." The position of Jews in seventeenth- and eighteenth-century Germany provides a case in point. Certain German Jews became advisors, collaborators, bankers, and financiers to Germanic absolutist rulers. In a similar way, renegade Christians were employed by fourteenth- and fifteenth-century Turkish sultans who sought to maintain and extend their power over their Muslim subjects.

The consequences of discrimination and prejudice for maintaining power may take more indirect and subtle forms. On a collective level, scapegoating may serve as a *safety valve* whereby feelings of hostility are diverted to substitute objects, thereby protecting the leaders of a group from becoming the recipients of aggression. At least part of this function is carried out by dividing the members of society along majority–minority lines, so that interests shared by both groups become obscured and hostility is directed downward in the system of social class, rather than toward a common opponent located at the top.

Up to this point, we have examined the consequences of discrimination and prejudice for majority-group members. In the following chapter, we turn our attention to the functions of discrimination and prejudice for the minority group, the very individuals against whom hostility has been directed.

NOTES

1. Although we are primarily concerned with the relationship between majorities and minorities in the United States, it is also clear that American businesses have work done outside this country, usually in

order to take advantage of cheaper labor in the Third World. It is possible to see monopoly capitalism as competitive among the giants for resources (including labor) on a worldwide scale. Thus, even though profits within the United States can be kept high by monopolies and expensive labor can be tolerated in some areas, in others, such as in the manufacture of electronic circuitry, Third World laborers can be employed to do work for which automated technology does not yet exist or is too expensive and which majority-group workers are unwilling to do at Third World rates. (Fröbel, Heinrichs, and Kreye, "The Tendency Towards a New International Division of Labor," *Review* I, 1 (1977); 73–88.)
2. For a period of time, American Indians also were enslaved by the white colonials. However, several factors determined that the general trend of policy toward American Indians would be against their enslavement. First, their adaptation to plantation life was impeded by cultural factors. Second, Indians could often escape to the protection of their own tribes located in proximity to the plantation. Third, early white settlers feared neighboring Indians and sought their friendship more than their labor. As a result, a predominantly Negro ancestry became the requirement for enslavement (Stampp, 1956).
3. Though slavery benefited a small group of masters, the economic profitability of slave labor for the South as a whole is a debatable issue that involves the relative advantages and disadvantages of one-crop agriculture, soil exhaustion, and long-run differences between agriculture and manufacturing, to mention only a few of the relevant issues.

Chapter 6
Functions of Discrimination and Prejudice for the Minority Group

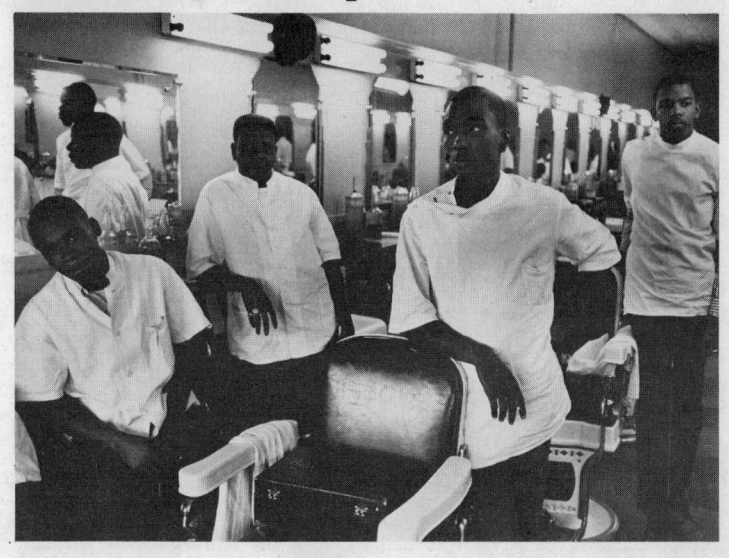

The functions of discrimination and prejudice frequently manifest themselves as positive consequences for the members of a majority group either at the personality level or at the level of group maintenance. From this standpoint, elements within the majority group clearly represent the major obstacle to progress toward full equality for a minority group. Subordination could not be sustained for any length of time or with any effectiveness if it were not for the presence of important majority-group interests and needs that are being served (or are perceived as being served) by the maintenance of discrimination and prejudice.

Having examined the range of such functions for the majority group, we turn our attention now to the consequences of discrimination and prejudice for minority-group members, the very people against whom the hostility of the majority group has been directed. What are the secondary gains and special opportunities that exist in a minority group by virtue of the hostility that confronts it? How do certain members of a minority group come to "take advantage of the disadvantages" that have been imposed on them? The implications of this inquiry for our purposes are clear: To the extent that such minority-group functions of discrimination and prejudice actually occur, there may be certain resistances to total equality located within the minority group itself, resistances that operate to reinforce and support the interests of the majority group and that must be identified and overcome in order to reduce the level of prejudice in a society. This chapter has been organized around the following consequences for the minority group: (1) the reduction of competition, (2) the maintenance of solidarity, and (3) the reduction of uncertainty.

Reduction of Competition

To acknowledge the presence in a minority group of opposition to equality is to recognize that discrimination can transcend lines of ethnicity and link itself to interests apart from those of race, religion, or national origin. For Rose (1951), the willingness of minority-group members to turn to personal advantage the hostility directed against them may indicate the presence of group self-hatred. This occurs when personal desires for political or economic gain conflict with the needs and interests of the group as a whole.

Frazier recognized the presence of such economic and political gains among certain black Americans when he wrote about "the Negro's vested interest in segregation." According to Frazier, it was primarily the middle-class black—the businessman, teacher, social worker, physician, and clergyman—who benefited from the impact of segregation and discrimination, for it was he or she who enjoyed the advantage of being guarded from competing with his or her white occupational counterpart. Preferring the security achieved by a monopoly of occupations within the segregated black community, certain black professionals and businesspeople adopted ambivalent attitudes toward the possibility of integration and created rationalizations about the peculiar needs of black Americans or about prejudice against blacks in nonsegregated occupational settings:

> Thus, Negro physicians may advocate separate hospitals on the grounds that in them they would have more opportunities to develop their skill and to serve their "own people." But this, too, is only a rationalization because there is abundant evidence that the standard of medical care in segregated hospitals, where Negro physicians are supposed to have every professional opportunity, is lower than in unsegregated institutions. It is scarcely necessary to point out that to abolish segregation would create technological unemployment for Negroes who secure a living from the existence of segregation. [1951:335.]

How accurate were Frazier's observations regarding the attitudes of some black professionals? Are such individuals actually hesitant to compete with their white counterparts? In order to shed light on these and related questions, Howard interviewed a sample of 100 black male physicians, dentists, lawyers, and teachers regarding their attitudes toward competition with whites. These were the very individuals who might have had some interest in maintaining the relatively closed system of competition that accompanies prejudice and segregation against blacks, for it provides them with a virtual monopoly of services to other blacks.

Howard's respondents were asked to indicate their agreement or disagreement with a series of items including hypothetical situations such as the following:

> Dr. J, who is a white physician, opened an office in an all-Negro neighborhood about 6 months ago. Recently, he advised a white physician friend to open an office in the same neighborhood. The white friend decided to open the office. Negro physicians in the neighborhood heard about the decision of Dr. J's friend and urged him not to open the office. They advised him on several desirable locations in all-white neighborhoods. How do you feel about the advice of the Negro physicians? [1966:23.]

Howard's findings lend support to the observations made earlier by Frazier: These black professionals were less than enthusiastic about the notion of intergroup competition; their general position being only *slightly* in agreement with open competition with whites. This ambivalence of black professionals toward open competition applied across the board to the members of all four sample groups—physicians, dentists, lawyers, and teachers.

Howard refers to the source of ambivalence among black professionals as the "Negro dilemma": Their commitment to the democratic goal of free competition prevented them from becoming strongly opposed to competition with whites; yet, their economic and social interests in segregation inhibited the development of very favorable attitudes toward such competition.

Maintenance of Solidarity

In the nineteenth century, Simmel (1955 translation) suggested that an external threat could reduce the tensions and strengthen the solidarity within a group. An everyday example of this phenomenon is provided by Sherif's study of the production of intergroup conflict among 11-year-old campers. Competition and conflict between the two groups of boys resulted in "renewed efforts at in-group coordination, planning new tactics or engaging in acts directed against the out-group, and the like . . ." (1956:311). The common purpose supplied by intergroup friction quickly submerged internal discord, so that negative feelings and beliefs could be focused on the members of the rival group.

Intergroup conflict has long been thought to contribute to group cohesiveness in many contexts:

The confrontation between police and protesters in Chicago had a divisive effect on the community and the society, but it solidified group feeling within the police department and also served to unify the protesting factions. A religious sect that breaks away from an established Church to initiate some type of reform is likely to become increasingly close-knit as conflict develops with the larger group. A society fighting for its very existence against a common enemy, as Great Britain did during World War II, often exhibits a powerful sense of determination and will to resist as individuals subordinate their personal interests to the welfare of their country. [DeFleur, D'Antonio, and DeFleur, 1971:58.]

In a similar way, it can be said that the internal cohesion of a minority group is frequently enhanced as a result of an external threat to it. It would appear, for instance, that anti-Semitism has had a profound influence on the internal solidarity of the Jews, frequently isolating them from the non-Jewish population and strengthening their determination to preserve their religious identity. (See Box 6.1.) This is the phenomenon that Theodor Herzl had in mind when he asserted, "We are a people—the enemy makes us a people."

From the standpoint of some observers, the Jews would probably not have maintained themselves as Jews historically without the continued presence of considerable hostility from the Christian world (van den Haag, 1969). It may also be the case that the rapid rate of Jewish upward mobility in the United States can be regarded, at least in some part, as a defensive reaction to anti-Semitism. More specifically, it may be seen as a compensatory mechanism whereby economic achievement is assigned a high value by Jewish Americans who seek to escape their socioeconomically and culturally marginal position in society. In a similar way, the relative success of Japanese Americans in regard to their quest for increased socioeconomic status may have been aided by the presence of the same hostility which was often used against them by white Americans (Caudill and Vos, 1966).

The cohesiveness of a minority may decline as an external threat to the group decreases. Thus, Jews in America continue to participate rather extensively in activities related to the survival of Judaism (Lazarwitz, 1970), whereas Israeli Jews may be losing their Jewish identity in favor of an association with the State of Israel. The transference of ethnic identity from Judaism to Zionism seems to reflect the impact of a perceived and actual threat to the persistence of the Jewish state from its hostile neighbors (Hofman, 1970) as well as the unique presence of a Jewish majority group in Israeli society that no longer confronts hardship, hostility, or hatred based on its *religious* identity.

As seen, prejudice directed against a minority group often exerts pressure for group cohesiveness and pride, forces emphasis on its history and achievements, and brings about the development of

BOX 6.1

Out-Group Hostility and In-Group Pride

Group solidarity frequently takes the form of in-group pride and hostility toward members of the majority group. Harry Golden's account of his early impressions of Christians provides an interesting illustration:

> My first impressions of Christianity came in the home, of course. My parents brought with them the burden of the Middle Ages from the blood-soaked continent of Europe. They had come from the villages of Eastern Europe where Christians were feared with legitimate reason.
>
> When occasionally a Jewish drunk was seen in our neighborhood, our parents would say, "He's behaving like a Gentile."
>
> For in truth, our parents had often witnessed the Polish, Romanian, Hungarian, and Russian peasants, gather around a barrel of whiskey on Saturday night, drink themselves into oblivion, "and beat their wives." Once in a while the rumor would spread through the tenements that a fellow had struck his wife, and on all sides we heard the inevitable, "Just like a Gentile."
>
> Oddly enough, too, our parents had us convinced that the Gentiles were noisy, boisterous, and loud—unlike the Jews. It is indeed strange how often stereotypes are exactly reversed.
>
> If we raised our voices, we were told, "Jewish boys don't shout." And this admonition covered every activity in and out of the home: "Jewish boys don't fight." "Jewish boys don't get dirty." "Jewish boys study hard."
>
> It wasn't until I was in school and was subjected to the influence of Gentile teachers and met Gentile social workers and classmates that I began to question these generalizations. Then I began to read and I found myself finally dismissing all prejudice from my mind. I still had a vague idea that the Jews were *very* special with God, but I discarded the notion that He was disinterested in or hostile to the Gentiles. [1962:210.]

organizations that further its interests. Yet external threat may sometimes diminish rather than heighten the morale of group members. For instance, if a minority group has previously experienced severe deprivation of group identity, the external pressure of discrimination and prejudice from the majority group tends to demoralize its members and heighten intragroup conflict. Thus, in the collective experience of black America, prejudice and discrimination have contributed to a diminution of group solidarity, leading to rejection and escape more than to any sense of group spirit. It was not until the expectations of black Americans had risen sufficiently that group solidarity could be regarded as a widespread response to antiblack hostility (Yinger, 1961). In the recent experiences of black America, group solidarity and pride have been an important dimension of the broader phenomenon of "black power," in which mistrust of whites, racial separation, black capitalism, violence, and community control have played a part (MacDonald, 1971). See Box 6.2.

BOX 6.2

Black Power in Reaction to Discrimination and Prejudice

Group-unifying elements of "black power" have been represented in the following statement by Stokely Carmichael and Charles V. Hamilton:

> Black people must redefine themselves, and only *they* can do that. Throughout this country, vast segments of the black communities are beginning to recognize the need to assert their own definitions, to reclaim their history, their culture; to create their own sense of community and togetherness. There is a growing resentment of the word "Negro," for example, because this term is the invention of our oppressor; it is *his* image of us that he describes. Many blacks are now calling themselves African-Americans, Afro-Americans or black people because that is *our* image of ourselves. When we begin to define our own image, the stereotypes—that is, lies—that our oppressor has developed will begin in the white community and end there. The black community will have a positive image of itself that

it has created. This means we will no longer call ourselves lazy, apathetic, dumb, good-timers, shiftless, etc. Those are words used by white America to define us. If we accept these adjectives, as some of us have in the past, then we see ourselves only in a negative way, precisely the way white America wants us to see ourselves. Our incentive is broken and our will to fight is surrendered. From now on we shall view ourselves as African-Americans and as black people who are in fact energetic, determined, intelligent, beautiful and peace-loving. [1967:37–38.]

Reduction of Uncertainty

Just as it operates to structure the world of the majority-group member, so prejudice can help to define the situation of the minority-group member who seeks to create a degree of psychological security out of an otherwise unfriendly, if not threatening, social environment. Given the nature of such conditions in society, it is not surprising that, as a well-known journalist has recently asserted, "segregation is an affliction, but for many it is a crutch as well" (Silberman, 1964:11).

The role expectations and prescriptions for subordinated groups in a society represent the burden of oppression for those individuals who must fulfill them. But all expectations and prescriptions also lend a psychologically comfortable level of predictability to the social relationships in which such individuals are involved, in some cases producing a kind of "social inertia," a compromise between the desire for equality of opportunity, on the one hand, and the need for certainty, on the other.

Many individuals may have a desire to achieve a *defined status* within a group; they may actively seek to arrive at a clear-cut social position for themselves, whether it be defined as high or low in the eyes of others (Prosterman, 1972). Viewed in this way, it becomes easier to understand why Helen Lynch (1972), a woman writing for a large Boston newspaper, would declare that "equality would be a demotion." For this columnist, "equal status with the men in my life" would be an undesirable end!

An important consequence of prejudice in its capacity to reduce uncertainty is to locate the source of problems experienced by a minority-group member in the social system rather than in his or her own inadequacy. In this regard, Cloward and Ohlin have argued that "when external barriers to the achievement of success-goals and their influence on the criteria of evaluation are clearly apparent, it is much more likely that persons who fail to achieve their aspirations will attribute failure to the social order rather than to themselves" (1960:121).

In the context of black–white relations, the availability of a system-blame explanation of personal shortcomings that clearly has a good deal of validity may keep many blacks from suffering a great loss of self-esteem. For individuals who locate the source of their problems in personal inadequacy, failure results in low self-regard. In contrast, individuals who ascribe their failure to the system tend to withdraw their loyalty from the system and attack it in either a direct or indirect manner (McCarthy and Yancey, 1971). It is significant to note that, despite the well-known sociological truism that blacks suffer from low self-esteem, recent evidence instead suggests that black Americans do not have lower self-esteem, and may even have higher self-esteem, than whites (Heiss and Owens, 1972; Yancey, Rigsby and McCarthy, 1972). In support of this contention, Parker and Kleiner (1968) have shown that mental illness tends to be less severe among those blacks who perceive "being a Negro" as a barrier to achievement. Moreover, the relatively low suicide rate among black Americans may indicate the presence of "external restraints" in the form of a well-defined set of expectations from which blacks have lacked the freedom to deviate (Henry and Short, 1954).

Summary

Opposition to full equality for American minorities can be located for the largest part in elements of the majority group that perceive their interests or needs as depending on the continuance of discrimination and prejudice against the members of a minority. So far-reaching is the hostility of the majority, however, that it often overlaps the boundaries that separate majority from minority. In such circumstances, certain elements of a minority may identify their interests or needs with the maintenance of the status quo and come to resist the idea of full equality for the members of their own group.

We emphasize once again that the resistances within the minority group are minimal and secondary when compared with those found within the majority, which, by definition, has a greater capacity to realize its will. We stress also that the minority group contains within it major forces for the breakdown of prejudiced attitudes and institutions. Clearly, for example, many individuals and groups within the black community have provided the major thrust of important civil rights activities over the last few decades, activities that could lead to significant progress toward achieving equality.

On the whole, discrimination has been culturally, if not physically, debilitating in its consequences for minority groups. Yet we must also recognize the presence of vested interests and special opportunities among certain elements of minority groups specifically having to do with the reduction of competition, the maintenance of solidarity, and the reduction of uncertainty—secondary gains that remain dependent on the continuance of discrimination against members of the minority group.

To acknowledge the presence in a minority group of opposition to equality is to recognize that hostility can transcend lines of ethnicity and link itself to interests apart from those of race, religion, or national origin. Such economic and political gains may occur among certain black Americans, namely, middle-class black businesspeople, teachers, social workers, physicians, and clergymen, who have been guarded from competition with their white occupational counterparts. As a result, such black professionals and businesspeople may adopt ambivalent attitudes toward the possibility of integration and create rationalizations about the peculiar needs of blacks in America.

The consequences of discrimination and prejudice for the minority group can be less deliberate. In the nineteenth century, Simmel suggested that an external threat could reduce the tensions and strengthen the solidarity within a group. It would appear that anti-

Semitism has had a profound influence on the internal solidarity of the Jews, frequently isolating them from the non-Jewish population and strengthening their determination to preserve their religious identity.

Discrimination and prejudice directed against a minority group often exert pressure for group cohesiveness and pride, force emphasis on its history and achievement, and bring about the development of organizations that further its interests as a group. Yet external threat may also have the opposite effect, especially in a minority group that has experienced severe deprivation and loss of group identity. Thus, in the collective experience of black America, hostility has contributed to a diminution of group solidarity, leading to escape and retreat more than to any sense of group spirit. It was not until the expectations of black Americans had risen sufficiently that group solidarity could be regarded as a widespread response to antiblack prejudice and discrimination.

Just as it operates to structure the world of the majority-group member, so prejudice can help to define the situation of the minority-group member who seeks to create a degree of psychological security out of an otherwise unfriendly, if not threatening, social environment. An important consequence of prejudice in its capacity to reduce uncertainty is to locate the source of problems experienced by a minority-group member in the social system rather than in his or her own inadequacy. In the context of black–white relations, the availability of a system-blame explanation of personal shortcomings that *clearly has a good deal of validity* may keep many blacks from suffering a great loss of self-esteem.

In the final chapter, we focus our attention on the nature, or essential characteristics, of American society. Using a functional framework, we attempt to identify possible determinants of discrimination and prejudice and to link them to the consequences discussed in previous chapters.

Chapter 7
Discrimination and Prejudice in American Society

Scholars focusing on the dysfunctional consequences of discrimination and prejudice have rightly drawn the attention of social science as well as society to the costly and morally unacceptable impact of bigotry. But they have done little to explain the tenacious hold of discrimination and prejudice on the members of our society or to provide meaningful suggestions for their reduction.

As we have seen, discrimination and prejudice can be treated as *independent variables,* causal factors that have certain consequences for society and its members (see Figure 7.1). From a broader perspective, however, discrimination and prejudice also act as *intervening variables* between important psychological and sociocultural forces, on the one hand, and individual responses, on the other, or between the factors responsible for the maintenance of discrimination and prejudice and the functions that discrimination and prejudice perform (see Figure 7.2). Specifically, our focus has been on such causal factors as: (1) frustration–aggression, (2) threat to self-esteem, (3) need to reduce uncertainty, and (4) competition for power, status, and wealth.

Figure 7.1 Discrimination and prejudice as independent variables.

Independent Variable (Cause) → Dependent Variables (Consequences)

Discrimination and Prejudice →

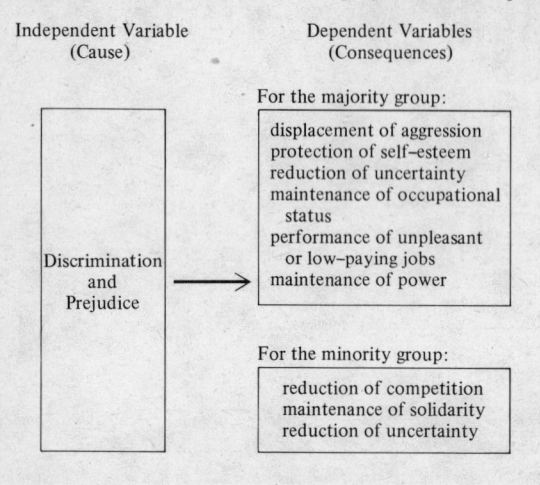

For the majority group:
- displacement of aggression
- protection of self-esteem
- reduction of uncertainty
- maintenance of occupational status
- performance of unpleasant or low-paying jobs
- maintenance of power

For the minority group:
- reduction of competition
- maintenance of solidarity
- reduction of uncertainty

Figure 7.2 Discrimination and prejudice as intervening variables.

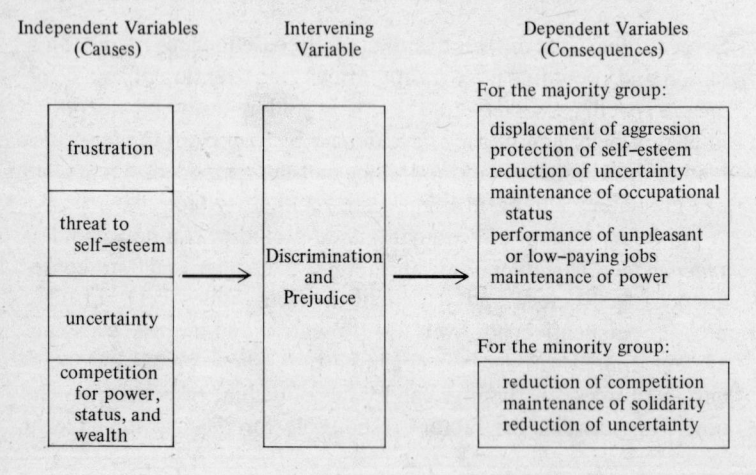

Independent Variables (Causes):
- frustration
- threat to self-esteem
- uncertainty
- competition for power, status, and wealth

→ Intervening Variable: Discrimination and Prejudice →

Dependent Variables (Consequences)

For the majority group:
- displacement of aggression
- protection of self-esteem
- reduction of uncertainty
- maintenance of occupational status
- performance of unpleasant or low-paying jobs
- maintenance of power

For the minority group:
- reduction of competition
- maintenance of solidarity
- reduction of uncertainty

We now ask: What are the sociocultural characteristics that interact with, support, or underlie such causal factors as frustration, threat to self-esteem, uncertainty, and competition? What factors make it possible for discrimination and prejudice to persist in our society? What is it about the character of our society that helps to sustain the functional nature of discrimination and prejudice? In this regard, we choose to stress the operation in our society of *competitiveness* and *rapid social change* as characteristics of particular relevance.[1]

Competitiveness and Prejudice in American Society

To characterize American society as competitive may be to understate the obvious. Foreign observers have frequently noted the admiration of Americans for competitive effort and for the acquisition of wealth (Torrence and Meadows, 1958). Social scientists have similarly concluded that American society emphasizes competitive success and the competitive grading of its members (Williams, 1965). Horney described American social relationships in the following way:

The isolated individual has to fight with other individuals of the same group, has to surpass them and, frequently, thrust them aside. The advantage of the one is frequently the disadvantage of the other ... competitiveness, and the potential hostility that accompanies it, pervades all human relationships.... It pervades the relationships between men and men, between women and women, and whether the point of competition be popularity, competence, attractiveness or any other social value, it greatly impairs the possibilities of reliable friendship. [1937:285–286.]

The current emphasis on wealth goes hand in hand with an orientation toward competition. More than ever, money seems to be a convenient symbol of success and failure in that it fixes the individual's *relative* position in regard to his or her contemporaries. In particular, money can be regarded as an adult equivalent of the grades received by a schoolchild (Gorer, 1964). A relatively high income—like A's on a report card—is a visible indicator that an individual has "made it" in relation to his or her fellows.

It would be a mistake to regard extreme competitiveness as characteristic of all societies. Cross-cultural studies of the development of competitive behavior have been conducted with thousands of children from more than 20 subcultures, including those located in the United States, Belgium, Canada, Holland, Israel, Korea, and Mexico. The findings of such studies indicate, for example, that Anglo-American children tend to be more competitive than Mexican-American children, who, in turn, tend to be more competitive than Mexican rural children (Kagan and Madsen, 1971). Also of interest is the finding that Anglo-American children engage in rivalry even though it may be irrational to do so in terms of self-interest; that is to say, Anglo-American children are willing to forfeit their own prizes if it also means depriving their competitors of rewards (Nelson and Kagan, 1972).

If our society is particularly competitive, then we might expect newcomers from a traditional, ancestral culture to become increasingly more competitive the more they are assimilated into American society. Just such a finding has been obtained regarding Chinese-American students who become more competitive as they become better incorporated into American life and as their attitudes and interaction patterns draw them closer to Anglo-Americans (Levin and Leong, 1973).

We know that competitive tendencies in a child begin at home. For instance, the findings of Minturn and Lambert (1964) indicate that the mothers of American children are especially likely to encourage their children to direct their aggressiveness toward peers. Moreover, American mothers tend to reinforce their children *only* when they succeed; in contrast, mothers from noncompetitive cultures tend to reward their children whether or not they achieve a desired result (Nelson and Kagan, 1972).

Zero-Sum Orientation and Prejudice

Implicit in the foregoing concept of competitiveness is a *psychology of scarcity,* an assumption that personal gains require the losses of others. Thus, competitive persons employ a *zero-sum orientation:* They view two or more individuals or groups as striving for the same scarce goals, with the success of one automatically implying a reduced probability that others will also attain their goals (Phillips, 1969). See Table 7.1.

In a similar way, Americans hold a zero-sum orientation to moral evaluations, with the individual gaining in moral worth only to the extent that others lose in moral worth, and vice versa (Douglas, 1970). This orientation engages the individual in a competitive struggle to upgrade him or herself and to downgrade others. Respectability demands deviance; good requires evil. As a result, the members of our society must construct and maintain a set of negative stereotypes of minorities, deviants, criminals, and the poor, and attempt to find public methods for stigmatizing such individuals. In some cases, it may be irrelevant whether or not competition between groups actually occurs. A minority group need not be perceived as posing a threat to the resources of the majority but merely as *deviating from its important norms and values.*

The American version of competitiveness has important implications for an understanding of the contributions that discrimination and prejudice make to the personality of the majority member, especially those contributions involving the displacement of aggression, the protection of self-esteem, and the reinforcement of personal values. The subjective position of lower-class whites provides a case in point: If they perceive blacks as having success, then lower-class whites may see themselves as failing. As a result, they experience a keen sense of relative deprivation and seek to "keep the Negro in his place" (Phillips, 1969:199). See Figure 7.3.

But the zero-sum orientation lies not only in the eyes of the beholder, it is also deeply ingrained in the institutional arrangements of our society. Therefore, the struggle for status, power, and

Table 7.1 Zero-Sum Orientation

Individual A gains five units of success	+5
Individual B loses five units of success	−5
	0

Figure 7.3 The role of discrimination and prejudice in protecting self-esteem.

Competitiveness (Zero-Sum Orientation) → Threat to Self-Esteem → Discrimination and Prejudice → Protection of Self-Esteem

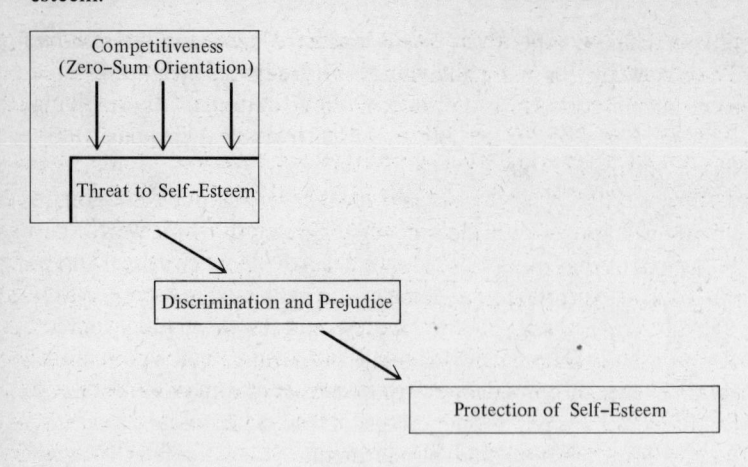

Figure 7.4 The functions of discrimination and prejudice for the majority and the minority in the face of competitiveness.

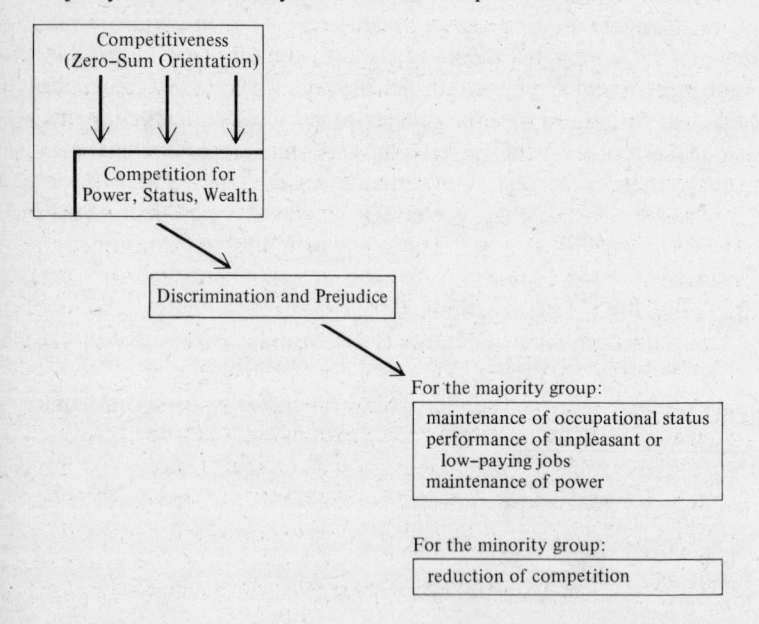

Competitiveness (Zero-Sum Orientation) → Competition for Power, Status, Wealth → Discrimination and Prejudice →

For the majority group:
- maintenance of occupational status
- performance of unpleasant or low-paying jobs
- maintenance of power

For the minority group:
- reduction of competition

class has an objective reality of its own that must be confronted in the decisions of everyday life, where it often occurs:

> A source of the problem is the kind of social structure where, as Horney puts it, the "advantage of the one (individual) is the disadvantage of the other." The businessman, in order to achieve his goal of success, frequently must climb over the backs of others. The basis for this kind of economic organization is the existence of scarcities in whatever it is that humans desire or value. Thus, if whatever is desired is in short supply, individuals must compete with one another for the available supply, and one man's gain is frequently another's loss.
> This structuring of scarce rewards is, of course, tied in with a stratification system where there are a limited number of positions at the top relative to the large number below them. For the individual to gain the highest rewards, he must oppose the interest of others who also desire them. With such opposed interests, it becomes more difficult for the individual to interact with his competitors in cooperative ways. [Phillips, 1969:415.]

The sizable payoff for the majority group is the protection of its privileged position in our society, a position that carries a disproportionate amount of power, status, and economic means. As far as the minority is concerned, competitiveness produces many of the conditions under which discrimination and prejudice create special opportunities and advantages for certain of its members. See Figure 7.4.

Social Change and Prejudice

Despite its importance as an explanatory variable, competitiveness does not exist in a social vacuum and should be properly regarded as but *one* of the sociocultural factors in the maintenance of prejudice. As noted by Allport (1954), rapid social change, like competitiveness, is another factor that characterizes our society and may be functionally related to the persistence of discrimination and prejudice.

In relatively stable, traditional societies, it is meaningful for an individual to rely on his or her previous achievements as a frame of reference for self-evaluation. Thus, a farmer might compare his or her annual crop yield against the results of previous years; a schoolchild might compare his or her academic performance from one year to the next; or, the profit from a family business might be evaluated on an annual basis.

Yet such comparisons with the past have meaning only to the extent that structural stability can be experienced and maintained, forming a common basis for the comparison of personal experiences. However, in a rapidly changing, highly differentiated society, prior achievements provide few meaningful reference points for the present or for the future. Under the conditions that characterize American society, standards of evaluation tend to differ from one role to another and from one time period to the next. Rapid change leaves its mark in the form of discontinuities between the events in our lives.

As a result, the members of American society have increasingly turned toward their contemporaries in the quest for new and more meaningful standards of evaluation. This "other-directedness" has contributed to the widespread use of relative evaluation whereby individuals strive to outdo others around them, whether at work, at school, or at play. Rapid change has created a need for *social* standards of evaluation, a need that many individuals are able to satisfy by comparing their achievements with those of their friends, classmates, or fellow employees.

In a very important sense, then, "keeping up with the Joneses" represents the presence and need for standards of evaluation as much as it represents the American brand of competitiveness. Because it contributes to relative evaluation, however, social change may help to provide conditions appropriate for the onset of zero-sum thinking which, in turn, leads to prejudice against minority-group members.

Stressful and disorienting aspects of rapid change have produced a kind of *future shock* that sweeps across the institutions of our society at an unprecedented rate. As noted by Toffler:

The final, qualitative difference between this and all previous lifetimes is the one most easily overlooked. For we have not merely extended the scope and scale of change, we have radically altered its pace. We have in our time released a totally new social force—a stream of change so accelerated that it influences our sense of time, revolutionizes the tempo of daily life, and affects the very way we "feel" the world around us. We no longer "feel" life as men did in the past. And this is the ultimate difference, the distinction that separates the truly contemporary man from all others. For this acceleration lies behind the impermanence— the transience—that penetrates and tinctures our consciousness, radically affecting the way we relate to other people, to things, to the entire universe of ideas, arts and values. [1970:17.]

If future shock actually occurs, then it must have some measurable impact on the individuals in our society. By means of a Social Readjustment Rating Scale (Holmes and Rahe, 1967), it is possible in fact to measure the adverse physiological impact of the occurrence of rapid change in an individual's life. The scale contains 43 life events that have been associated by means of extensive research with varying degrees of disruption in the life of the average person. Thus, "death of spouse" received 100 life-change units, indicating that it requires major social readjustment, whereas "minor violations of the law" received only 11 life-change units because it generally requires minor readjustment for an individual (see Box 7.1). Using the Social Readjustment Rating Scale, it has been determined that rapid change in the individual's role—as indicated by a clustering of life events and a high life-change score—frequently precedes the onset of disease and goes to determine its severity; that is, individuals who achieve high life-change scores during a short period of time (for example, by the death of a spouse, personal injury, and retirement all in 1 year) are especially likely to have an illness and to experience it in a severe form (Holmes and Rahe, 1967).

But the impact of future shock extends beyond the physiological functioning of the individual. There is impressive evidence as well of the adverse psychological effects of rapid social change. For example, Mangum (1973), using a modified version of the Social Readjustment Rating Scale, has recently determined that college students who undergo rapid changes in their role relationships tend to experience greater neurotic anxiety than do their counterparts

BOX 7.1

The Stress of Adjusting to Change

Events	Life-Change Units
Death of spouse	100
Divorce	73
Marital separation	65
Jail term	63
Death of close family member	63
Personal injury or illness	53
Marriage	50
Fired at work	47
Marital reconciliation	45
Retirement	45
Change in health of family member	44
Pregnancy	40
Sex difficulties	39
Gain of new family member	39
Business readjustment	39
Change in financial state	38
Death of close friend	37
Change to different line of work	36
Change in number of arguments with spouse	35
Mortgage over $10,000	31
Foreclosure of mortgage or loan	30
Change in responsibilities at work	29
Son or daughter leaving home	29
Trouble with in-laws	29
Outstanding personal achievement	28
Wife begins or stops work	26
Begin or end school	26
Change in living conditions	25
Revision of personal habits	24
Trouble with boss	23
Change in work hours or conditions	20
Change in residence	20

Change in schools	20
Change in recreation	19
Change in church activities	19
Change in social activities	18
Mortgage or loan less than $10,000	17
Change in sleeping habits	16
Change in number of family get-togethers	15
Change in eating habits	15
Vacation	13
Christmas	12
Minor violations of the law	11

Source: Jane E. Brody 1973 "Doctors Study Treatment of Ills Brought on by Stress." *The New York Times* (June 10): 20. © 1973 by The New York Times Company. Reprinted by permission.

---

who do not. High scorers on the scale were significantly more likely to report being bothered by "trembling hands," "nightmares," "sweating," and "nervousness." Using a similar measure of the stimulation that accompanies demands of readjustment to change, Constantini, Davis, Braun, and Iervolino (1973) found that rapid change was associated with tension, depression, anger, and fatigue.

At the basis of the stress that results from rapid social change may be the individual's need for structure and his or her intolerance of uncertainty, whether it be of a cognitive or an emotional nature. A rapidly shifting social environment fails to provide adequate anchors for the events in an individual's life, leaving him or her without a sense of security or order.

On this view, the absence of a clear-cut social structure in modern societies, the presence of overlapping and confusing roles that often lead to constant changes in status position vis-à-vis various groups within which the individual moves ... all intensely frustrate the built-in need to have a clearly defined position within the group. [Prosterman, 1972:125.]

As suggested earlier, one of the consequences of discrimination and prejudice for both the majority as well as the minority is the reduction of cognitive and emotional uncertainties. Victims of future shock often resort to supersimplification in order to reduce the ambiguities in their environment (Toffler, 1970). They may stereotype, prejudge, find unitary solutions for the problems that confront them, all in a desperate attempt to make sense out of disorder, to structure their world in a meaningful way, and to find a place for themselves in society. (See Figure 7.5.) Durkheim (1933) referred to such a state of disorder as *anomie,* a form of social pathology in which guidelines for behavior are missing and the individual is, in a sociological sense, very much alone.

Before turning from the topic at hand, we note again that social change does not necessarily result in increased discrimination and prejudice. Indeed, the historical circumstances of our own society suggest instead that a breakdown of traditional institutions has the effect of loosening the grip of prejudicial norms and attitudes. It is likely, therefore, that discrimination and prejudice increase under the impact of *both* extreme stability as well as extreme change in social structure. Obviously, the content of any change must be taken into consideration as well, though the *rate* of social change can be examined in order to determine its independent influence on the level or quality of hostility.

Figure 7.5 The role of discrimination and prejudice in reducing uncertainty.

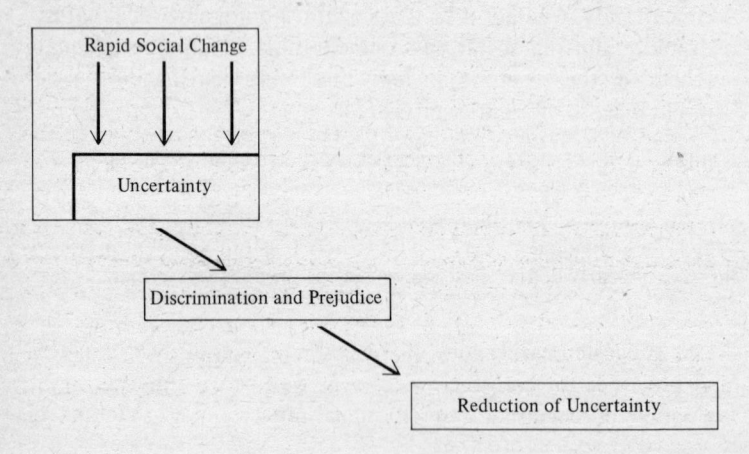

Prospects for the Reduction of Discrimination and Prejudice

How do we go about reducing discrimination and prejudice? On the basis of the present analysis, how can we intervene in an attempt to loosen the hold of hostility on our society and its members? At the most fundamental societal level, we might begin by directing our efforts toward achieving a more cooperative, less competitive culture, in which a zero-sum orientation and prejudice have less meaning for an individual's self-esteem or for his or her life-chances. Indeed, the recent decline in prejudice noted in Chapter 1 may be explained partially by the possibility that extreme competitiveness has also decreased. For example, the recent development of expressive, noncompetitive values among youth-oriented social movements such as the "beats" or the "hippies" may represent a larger process of "balancing" in American society as a whole, whereby our society, having been pushed more and more toward extreme competitiveness, is presently attempting to reduce the intensity of competitive values at all of its levels (Levin and Spates, 1970). This viewpoint has attained a good deal of popularity (Reich, 1970), though the supportive evidence is far from conclusive.

Moreover, given the extremely competitive nature of our society, it is not surprising that the acceptance of particular prejudices might rise and fall, depending on changes in their consequences for certain groups at particular points in time. For instance, the increasing purchasing power among black Americans as sought by the producers of competing goods and services may help to determine which barriers to equality will be lifted for the members of this minority (Lerner, 1957).

At the level of major institutional change, we suggest locating an institution in American society that presently serves as a focal point for the socialization of competitiveness. Specifically, we propose to focus our attention on the nature of formal education, a highly specialized social institution whose major function involves the transmission of the normative order from one generation to the next.

Though many investigators have studied the relationship between education and prejudice, relatively few continue to assert that formal education represents a powerful instrument for the reduction of prejudice. Selznick and Steinberg (1969) report finding an inverse relationship between anti-Semitism and amount of formal education, a relationship that could not be explained by differences in social class. Yet results claiming to demonstrate the impact of education on prejudice are extremely difficult to interpret and may demonstrate only that the educated members of our society have learned to express their prejudices publicly in subtle, more sophisticated ways, especially in the context of the paper-and-pencil questionnaires generally used by social science researchers (Stember, 1961).

Here we are not concerned with the impact of the *content* of formal education as it presently exists in American society. Unlike previous approaches, we propose instead to examine the *structure* of educational programs as a potent factor in the maintenance of competitiveness.

Psychologists and sociologists have long recognized that the structure of American education depends on social reinforcements for academic and athletic performance: Students tend to be encouraged in their efforts to exceed the achievement levels of classmates or friends. Competitiveness is emphasized, whereas personal improvement tends to be ignored (Coleman, 1963; Miller and Hamblin, 1963). American students come to be attracted to grading methods that can be structured toward explicit interpersonal comparisons (for example, "grading on the curve" and percentile scoring)—a preference that may be an outgrowth of the essentially competitive nature of middle-class American education and, more generally, of a socialization process in which competition is regarded as a basic virtue (Turner, 1960). See Box 7.2.

To illustrate the way in which schools foster interpersonal competition, Henry relates an incident from a fifth-grade arithmetic lesson involving a student named Boris. Boris is "patiently" and "quietly" humiliated by a teacher in the presence of his classmates because he has trouble reducing a fraction to its lowest terms. After concentrating her efforts on Boris for a minute or two, the teacher

BOX 7.2

Social Comparison in the Classroom

Failure and success in the classroom are frequently defined by students in regard to a grading mode that evaluates the achievements of any given student relative to the performance of his peers (e.g., by percentile scores) rather than relative to self-anchored performance criteria (e.g., by a student's own past performance). Children early come to have preferences for being evaluated vis-à-vis others and to direct their efforts toward the competitive struggle.

Thus, Levin and Levin (1973) hypothesized in a recent study that students who are graded with reference to the performance of other students ("you scored in the 80th percentile") would be more satisfied with their grading method than students graded with reference to their own past performance ("you got 50 percent correct on the 1st exam versus 80 percent correct on the 2nd exam"). The experimenters gave ninety-two undergraduate students a series of bogus vocabulary tests in multiple choice form that were immediately "scored by computer" and returned for the inspection of the students.

To provide a baseline against which they could evaluate their subsequent test performance, all students received a grade of approximately 50 percent on the first test in the series. On the second test, half of the students were given their grades in percent form (self-comparison of grades), while half were given their grades in percentile form (social comparison of grades). Whereas the percent form permitted students to draw comparisons with their grade on the first test but not with other students, the percentile form limited their comparisons to other students who had taken the same test.

As expected, social comparison of grades (e.g., "You scored in the 80th percentile") yielded significantly greater satisfaction with the assigned grading method than self-comparison of grades (e.g., "You got 80 percent correct"). This result was obtained whether or not the student was assigned a high score on his tests. Moreover, those students who were characterized as having competitive and manipulative personality styles (Machs) were particularly oriented to the performance of their contemporaries, significantly preferring the percentile method of receiving their grades on the series of tests.

then calls on another student, Peggy, who quickly offers the correct answer. The outcome is predictable:

> Boris's failure has made it possible for Peggy to succeed; his misery is the occasion for her rejoicing. This is the standard condition of the contemporary American elementary school. To a Zuñi, Hopi, or Dakota Indian, Peggy's performance would seem cruel beyond belief, for competition, the wringing of success from somebody's failure, is a form of torture foreign to those noncompetitive cultures. Yet Peggy's action seems natural to us; and so it is. How else would you run our world? [1969:205.]

The rewards given in educational contexts are capable of being structured so that competitiveness is minimized while achievement continues to be stressed. Some recognition of the need for such a change can be found in experimental studies of the effects of interpersonal competition on group achievement and cohesion. It has been shown, for example, that competition between students in a classroom actually generates subtle but significant interference with the efforts of each student by others in the group. The result is a reduction in the overall level of achievement and in the unity of the classroom (Deutsch, 1953). As demonstrated by Deutsch, a more effective alternative to interpersonal competition among students would be to structure the learning situation in such a way that group performance could be compared with and rewarded relative to other groups. When the competition is between classrooms, each student's achievement benefits the position of other members. As a result, the students in a group support the efforts of one another.

It is unfortunately true that the foregoing experiment merely substitutes one form of competition for another. Given the overwhelming presence of competitiveness, it is too often assumed that students cannot be achievement-oriented in noncompetitive educational settings. What frequently happens in the present educational structure is that individual improvement (self-evaluation) goes unrecognized and unrewarded in favor of interpersonal gain. Yet there may be a significant proportion of "noncomparers" for whom competitiveness is an alien frame of reference (Levin, 1969; Strauss, 1968). It is conceivable, as well, that a large number of students *would* be disposed to learn in a noncompetitive educational setting if it were made available to them as an alternative. Educational psychologists are presently exploring a number of reward structures that maintain, if not heighten, achievement and have the side effect of reducing the level of competitiveness as well. Such alternatives stress the need for individualized learning, open classrooms, or student-originated objectives (Gallagher, 1970; Lerner, 1971; Neill, 1960). But they currently tend to be utilized on a limited scale in order to reach "gifted" students, children with learning disabilities, or certain children from economically advantaged homes.

From the standpoint of the reduction of prejudice, one of the most promising alternatives to competitive education was demonstrated by social psychologist Elliot Aronson (1975) in his *jigsaw* teaching technique. Based on the principle of the jigsaw puzzle, Aronson gave each child a piece of information that had to be shared with other classmates in order to put the puzzle together:

For example, in the first classroom we studied, the next lesson happened to be on Joseph Pulitzer. We wrote a six-paragraph biography of the man, such that each paragraph contained a major aspect of Pulitzer's life: how his family came to this country, his childhood, his education and first jobs, etc. Next we cut up the biography into sections and gave each child in the learning group one paragraph. Thus, every learning group had within it the entire life story of Joseph Pulitzer, but each child had no more than one sixth of the story and was dependent on all of the others to complete the big picture. [1975:45.]

After the children went off alone to master their particular paragraph, they then rejoined the group to teach one another all parts of Pulitzer's biography. What they soon learned was that cooperation, not competition, was their only means to a good grade in the course. None of them could do well without the help of everyone else in their group.

Aronson tried his jigsaw technique for a period of 6 weeks in school systems that had recently been desegregated by race. His results were impressive: Compared with children in a traditional (competitive) fifth-grade classroom, the children in the jigsaw groups liked their black and white classmates better, expressed more positive attitudes toward school, had more favorable self-concepts, and performed at least equally well on their exams.

An effective movement away from extreme competitiveness probably requires major institutional and individual change. At another level, however, we might still seek to develop strategies for the reduction of discrimination and prejudice without also seeking to reduce competitiveness. Here, too, both psychological and sociological changes are required.

Regarding the personality functions of discrimination and prejudice, we might devise alternative means to maintain or enhance the self-esteem of an individual. At this time, personal and group forms of psychotherapy—to the extent that they can increase insight and self-acceptance on the part of an individual—may provide a springboard for individualized efforts to reduce prejudice. Personal psychotherapy tends to be most effective when its overriding concern is the formation of a healthy personality. The reduction of prejudice is frequently an important by-product.

Allport relates the experience of an anti-Semitic woman who served as the respondent in a lengthy, in-depth interview regarding her values, attitudes, and feelings. Having reviewed her previous experiences with Jews, she finally remarked, "The poor Jews, I guess we blame them for everything, don't we?" (1954:460). Her exchange with the interviewer increased her self-insight to the point where she could trace her hostility to its source and gain a new perspective on it.

Group therapy tends to be more efficient than its personal counterpart because several individuals can be aided simultaneously. Moreover, group therapy frequently operates to break down the support of prejudiced attitudes originating in the norms of the group. Haimowitz and Haimowitz (1950) provide some evidence for the influence of group therapy on the reduction of prejudice. As the individuals in their group began to feel less threatened and better able to cope with the actual source of their frustrations, they also became less hostile toward members of minority groups.

Rubin reports that sensitivity training was able to produce increased self-acceptance leading to a reduced level of prejudice. He notes that his study might just as easily have been concerned with the influence of psychotherapy on prejudice: "Each provides the elements of psychological safety, support, and opportunities for reality testing assumed necessary to effect an increase in an individual's level of self-acceptance and consequently, by our model, decrease his level of ethnic prejudice" (1967:238).

From the standpoint of this analysis, therapy may serve as a functional alternative to prejudice in that an individual's sense of worth can be protected or enhanced. As a significant long-term measure, however, the influence of therapy tends to be somewhat restricted. As noted earlier, therapy, even in its group form, is capable of reaching relatively few of those people who most need it. Moreover, individuals who undergo therapy continue to be influenced, as well, by the competitive social milieu in which they live.

Any slowdown in the rate of social change might contribute to an abatement in the overall level of discrimination and prejudice but would have destructive consequences as well. Certain changes are already long overdue; others might enhance the quality of life for all members of our society. Rather than retard the rate of change, we must seek to discover the conditions under which individuals in society can best adapt themselves to change in a way that their uncertainties do not interfere with their effectiveness or psychological comfort. In this regard, Toffler (1970) notes that creative strategies are needed in order to increase the adaptivity of the individual in his or her reaction to change. We must experiment with tactics to regulate the level of stimulation from our social milieu and to create educational or technological innovations in the socialization process to aid individuals who attempt to cope with rapid change. In this regard, Toffler suggests the development of "crisis counseling" for people who undergo a major life change and "coping classrooms" for people who pass through similar life transitions at the same time (e.g., prepared childbirth classes). Such tactics would provide social support for change and advance information regarding what lies ahead.

"Counteracting forces" have emerged spontaneously to offset the adverse effects of rapid social change. Some are large-scale social movements whose common denominator may involve an ability to order the events in the lives of their adherents and reduce anomie. Witness the recent popularity of the Children of God, transcendental meditation, and the Divine Light Mission, to mention but a few. What may frequently happen in such adaptive social movements, however, is that conventional stereotypes and traditional prejudices are laid aside in favor of new forms of in-group–out-group, we–they distinctions. The precise impact of such movements is, at the present time, unknown.

Up to this point, we have been concerned with alternatives for such personality functions as the reduction of uncertainty and the protection of self-esteem. Given the ubiquitous presence of competitiveness, it is extremely difficult to suggest viable alternatives for the social functions of discrimination and prejudice. It may be, as Tumin suggests, that the functional equivalents of disapproved phenomena such as poverty, prejudice, or mental illness "either are nonexistent or are even more repulsive than the actual problems themselves" (1965:385). This is what Gans (1972) concluded regarding the presence of poverty in American society: "Several of the most important functions of the poor cannot be replaced with alternatives, while some could be replaced, but almost always at higher costs to other people, particularly more affluent ones" (1972:286–287). It is unfortunately true that discrimination serves certain functions of a political or an economic nature that cannot easily be replaced. However, such functions may affect relatively small subgroups in our society and may be irrelevant, if not dysfunctional, to numerous others.

The foregoing discussion may have important implications for a minority group that seeks a strategy for reducing prejudice and discrimination. This can be seen most clearly perhaps in the recent history of black America. During the 1960s, significant numbers of black Americans increased their awareness of the positive functions, especially the economic functions, that prejudice and discrimination have served for some groups and individuals in society. Periodicals devoted to the black protest movement emphasized the "economic exploitation of the Negro by those who occupy the top rungs of power in our contemporary exploitative society" (*Freedomways*, 1962:230). Messages communicated by certain black leaders similarly stressed the belief that economic profit for white America resulted from the continuance of large-scale forms of racism (Foner, 1970). And trends in race relations were frequently explained in terms of the *costs* to white Americans of permitting improvements for blacks relative to the *costs* of policing and servicing black ghettos (Wright, 1971).

As a reflection of a changing group consciousness, emerging black leaders stressed the importance of developing group forms of *power* and *control* as opposed to relying on the good will of the majority. Huey Newton's column in the newspaper *The Black Panther* expressed in strong terms what was coming to be a popular point of view among black leaders and their constituents:

The oppressor must be harassed, until his doom. He must have no peace by day or by night. The slaves have always outnumbered the slavemasters. The power of the oppressor rests upon the submission of the people. When Black people really unite and rise up in all their splendid millions, they will have the strength to smash injustice. We do not understand the power in our numbers. We are millions and millions of Black people scattered across the continent and throughout the Western hemisphere. There are more Black people in America than the total population of many countries that now enjoy full membership in the United Nations. They have power and their power is based primarily on the fact that they are organized and united with each other. They are recognized by the powers of the world. [1971:426.]

It is important to inquire whether an emphasis on the power of a minority group actually represents the basis for an effective strategy for the reduction of prejudice and discrimination. The analysis in this work suggests that such an emphasis may indeed turn out to have greater effectiveness than any strategy whose major thrust relies on moral persuasion. If we are correct in our assertion that prejudice and discrimination provide gains for certain individuals and groups, then it seems unlikely that the recipients of such gains would be easily moved from their commitment to the status quo, regardless of the cogency of appeals to democracy, equalitarianism, humanism, or the like. It is more likely the case that efforts at moral persuasion would tend to be selectively perceived and distorted by those who are most anxious to protect their personality or social benefits. On the psychological level, for instance, social scientists who test the effectiveness of moral persuasion on prejudice report obtaining boomerang reactions to antiprejudice propaganda campaigns in which the persecution and victimization of minority-group members are stressed. What seems to happen is that the content of such propaganda—content that emphasizes the costs of prejudice to the *minority group*—actually *attracts* prejudiced persons who seek vicariously to satisfy their hidden desires for carrying out cruel forms of aggression on a scapegoat (Vander Zanden, 1972; Vidmar and Rokeach, 1974).

A number of television programs and series over the past decade have poignantly portrayed the plight of downtrodden minority groups in our society. Programs such as "Roots," "Holocaust," "The Autobiography of Jane Pittman," "King," "The Diary of Ann Frank," and "Against the Wind" may very well have raised the consciousness of the television audience regarding the history of American minorities. Sadly, however, they have probably accomplished little else than to feed the sadism of very prejudiced people. Rather than emphasize the costs of discrimination and prejudice to the minority group, it might be a more effective strategy to emphasize the costs of discrimination and prejudice to the *majority* group: the urban decay, crime and delinquency, international tension, civil disobedience, violence, and economic liabilities that discrimination and prejudice seem to breed and perpetuate.

Power may provide a focus of action for minority groups that seek an active role with respect to lessening the grip of discrimination and prejudice. Yet power itself can be effective only to the extent that it transcends the lines that separate majority from minority and minorities from one another. In particular, minority-group members who themselves lack adequate resources to realize their will must be concerned with developing *coalitions,* temporary alliances in which minority-group members can participate, in order to pursue a common objective. See Box 7.3.

Even militant old-age groups such as the Gray Panthers count on enlisting the aid and cooperation of the young in a shared struggle for human liberation and social change. Indeed, there may be certain issues around which young and old might effectively pool their resources and form temporary alliances. Therefore, programs designed *for* the aged should be carefully separated from those programs that *affect* the aged. The former (for example, Medicare and Supplemental Security Income) are aimed directly and exclusively at the problems of the elderly; the latter provide benefits for a broad range of individuals, including but not limited to the elderly (Gold, Kutza, and Marmor, 1976).

Support for programs *for* the aged may be difficult to secure from the members of younger populations, many of whom would prefer to deny the aging process in themselves and perceive the elderly as a competitive force. Even more detrimental is the exceptionalist scope of such age-entitlement programs, which tend to perpetuate the image of elders as constituting a group apart from other members of society. Consider, for example, benefits provided through programs under the Older Americans Act. Under Title IV of the Act, considerable research in the field of aging has been supported. Unfortunately, much of this research has focused on characteristics of the aged as reviewed in Chapter 2 rather than on characteristics of society that may be fundamentally responsible for

---

BOX 7.3

Conditions for Developing Minority Group Coalitions

Deutsch identifies several of the conditions under which a minority group (as a low-power group) is likely to succeed in locating allies:

> By definition, a low power group *is* unlikely to achieve many of its objectives unless it can find allies among significant elements within the high power group or unless it can obtain support from other ("third party") groups that can exert influence on the high power group. There is considerable reason to expect that allies are most likely to be obtained if: (1) they are sought out rather than ignored or rejected; (2) superordinate goals, common values, and common interests can be identified which could serve as a basis for the formation of cooperative bonds; (3) reasonably full communication is maintained with the potential allies; (4) one's objectives and methods are readily perceived as legitimate and feasible; (5) one's tactics dramatize one's objectives and require the potential allies to choose between acting "for" or "against" these objectives and, thus, to commit themselves to taking a position; and (6) those in high power employ tactics, as a counterresponse, which are widely viewed as "unfitting" and thus produce considerable sympathy for the low power group. [1971:226.]

the mistreatment of elders. Under the Older Americans Act, Title VII, group dining programs for older people have been developed. Even though such programs have obviously benefited numerous elders, they unfortunately fail to move beyond the goal of easing the adjustment of old people to their assigned role in our society and therefore can do little if anything to improve their situation.

In sharp contrast to programs *for* the aged, programs that *affect* the aged may be broadly perceived as benefiting young as well as old, and these should constitute the basis for the alliance between young and old. For example, the Medical Assistance Program (Medicaid) finances medical services for public assistance recipients. Only 20 percent of the Medicaid recipients are aged 65 and older, but they consume some 39 percent of the benefits. Another program that *affects* the aged is the Food Stamp Program—a negative income tax directed at reducing the cost of food. Eligibility for food stamps depends only on income and family size, not on age. In 1974, estimated food stamp benefits to the elderly totaled $95 million (Gold, Kutza, and Marmor, 1976). In the future, then, we might expect coalitions of young and old to come together for the sake of programs that *affect* the elderly, such as national health insurance or a guaranteed annual income.

In his discussion of black power and coalition politics, Rustin (1971) notes a tendency among spokespeople for black power to accept the historical myth that immigrant groups such as the Irish, the Jews, and the Italians were able to overcome adversities simply by sticking together as a group, making demands, and finally winning enough power to succeed. According to Rustin, the relative success of such groups depended on their ability to form alliances with other groups (as a part of political machines or of the trade union movement) and *not* on their ability singlehandedly to pull themselves up by their own bootstraps.

Blacks similarly have gained from alliances with white groups. This has occurred either when the members of both groups have had common interests or when whites have been aware that blacks could reciprocate favors or withhold detrimental actions against them. A modern example is provided by the institutionalization by the federal government of affirmative action policies that affect both blacks and women. Glenn may well be correct when he suggests that the strongest forces continuing to operate in support of black America are "self-interested actions of powerful whites that for one reason or another benefit the Negro cause" (1965:114). It remains to be seen, however, whether the strength of such forces will be capable of overcoming the resistance imposed by those in our society who continue to benefit from the persistence of prejudice and discrimination.

Summary

We have sought to move toward an explanation for the maintenance of discrimination and prejudice in our society. Discrimination and prejudice have been regarded both as *independent variables,* causal factors that have certain consequences for society and its members, and as *intervening variables* between important sociocultural forces, on the one hand, and individual responses, on the other. The major thrust of this chapter has been to determine why discrimination and prejudice are functional. And, in this regard, we have chosen to stress the operation of competitiveness and social change as sociocultural factors of particular relevance.

To characterize American society as competitive may be to understate the obvious. Competitiveness can be found in the admiration of Americans for the acquisition of wealth, in the structure of American education, and in American socialization practices.

Implicit in competitiveness is a *psychology of scarcity,* a *zero-sum orientation* whereby individuals assume that personal gains require the losses of others. This makes possible the contributions that discrimination and prejudice make to the personality of the majority-group member, especially those contributions involving the displacement of aggression and the protection of self-esteem: If, for example, a lower-class white perceives blacks as having success, then the lower-class white may see him or herself as failing. As a result, he or she experiences a sense of relative deprivation and attempts to "keep the Negro in his place."

But the zero-sum orientation lies not only in the eyes of the beholder; it is deeply ingrained in the institutions of society. The payoff for the majority group that results from prejudice and discrimination is sizable. It is the protection of its privileged position in our society—a position that carries a disproportionate amount of power, status, and economic means. Regarding the minority, competitiveness also creates many of the conditions under which special opportunities and advantages for certain of its members are produced.

Like competitiveness, social change is a factor that characterizes our society and may be functionally related to the persistence of discrimination and prejudice. In relatively stable, traditional societies, it is meaningful for an individual to rely upon his or her previous achievements as a frame of reference for self-evaluation. In contrast, standards of evaluation in a rapidly changing, highly differentiated society tend to differ from one role to another and from one time period to the next. As a result, the members of American society have turned toward their contemporaries in the quest for new, more meaningful standards of evaluation. Rapid change has created a need for social standards of comparison whereby individuals compare their achievements against those of their friends, classmates, or fellow employees. In the process, they strive to outdo others around them so that zero-sum thinking prevails.

The relationship between social change and prejudice can be seen in another way. Toffler has coined the term *future shock* to describe the stressful and disorienting consequences of rapid change for the individual, the kind of change that has swept across the institutions of our society. At the basis of this stress may be the individual's need for structure and his or her intolerance of uncertainty. A rapidly shifting social environment fails to provide adequate anchors for the events in an individual's life, leaving him or her without a sense of security or order. One of the consequences of prejudice for both the majority as well as the minority is to reduce cognitive and emotional uncertainties.

How do we go about reducing discrimination and prejudice? On the basis of this analysis, how do we intervene in an attempt to loosen the hold of discrimination and prejudice on our society and its members? At the most fundamental level, we might begin by directing our efforts toward achieving a more cooperative, less competitive culture, in which a zero-sum orientation and hostility have less meaning for the individual's self-esteem or his or her life-changes.

At the level of major institutional change, we propose focusing attention on the structure of American formal education, a highly specialized social institution whose major function concerns the transmission of the normative order from one generation to the next. Social scientists have long recognized that the structure of American education is largely based on the availability of social reinforcements for academic and athletic performance. Competitiveness is emphasized, while personal improvement tends to go unnoticed.

The rewards given in educational contexts can be restructured, so that competitiveness is minimized while achievement continues to be stressed. Educational psychologists are exploring a number of reward structures that may maintain achievement and have the side effect of reducing competitiveness as well.

An effective movement away from competitiveness requires major institutional and individual change. At another level, however, we might still seek to develop strategies for the reduction of prejudice, despite the persistence of competitiveness. Regarding the personality functions of discrimination and prejudice, we might devise alternative means to maintain or enhance the self-esteem of an individual. For example, personal and group forms of psychotherapy may provide a springboard for individualized efforts to reduce prejudice to the extent that they can increase insight and self-acceptance on the part of the individual.

Any slowdown in the rate of social change might contribute to an abatement in the overall level of discrimination and prejudice but would have destructive consequences as well. Rather than retard the rate of change, we must seek to discover the conditions under which individuals in society can best adapt themselves to it. We must experiment with tactics to regulate the level of stimulation from our social milieu and to create educational and technological innovations to aid individuals in their ability to cope with rapid change.

Up to this point, we have been concerned with alternatives for such personality functions as the reduction of uncertainty and the protection of self-esteem. Given the ubiquitous presence of competitiveness, it is extremely difficult to suggest viable alternatives for the social functions of discrimination and prejudice. It is unfortunately true that discrimination and prejudice serve certain functions of a political and economic nature that cannot easily be replaced.

The foregoing discussion may have important implications for a minority group that seeks a strategy for reducing prejudice and discrimination. The analysis in this work suggests that an emphasis on power may turn out to have greater effectiveness than any strategy whose major thrust relies on moral persuasion. If we are correct in asserting that prejudice provides gains for certain individuals and groups, then it seems unlikely that the recipients of such gains would be easily moved from their commitment to the status quo on the basis of appeals to democracy or humanism. Yet power itself can be effective only to the extent that it transcends the lines that separate majority from minority. Minority-group members who lack adequate resources to realize their will must be concerned with developing *coalitions,* temporary alliances in which minority-group members can participate in order to pursue a common objective.

NOTE

1. We should stress that neither characteristic is regarded as a *necessary* condition for prejudice but only for its particular *functional consequences*. For instance, competitiveness may turn out to be a prerequisite for the esteem-enhancing functions of prejudice but more or less unrelated to its capacity for reducing cognitive uncertainties. Similarly, prejudice can occur in the absence of rapid social change, even though change serves as a contributory factor in our society. It goes without saying that numerous variables contribute to the overall level of prejudice in any given social context. What deserves careful attention here is that certain contributory factors in the persistence of prejudice also act as antecedent conditions for the functions of prejudice.

References

Adorno, T. W., Else Frankel-Brunswick, Daniel J. Levinson, and Nevitt H. Sanford 1950 *The Authoritarian Personality.* New York: Harper & Row.

Allport, Gordon W. 1954 *The Nature of Prejudice.* Reading, Mass.: Addison-Wesley.

Antonousky, Aaron 1960 "The Social Meaning of Discrimination." *Phylon* (Spring): 81–95.

Armendáriz, Albert 1967 *The Mexican American: A New Focus of Opportunity.* Washington, D.C.: GPO.

Aronoff, Craig 1974 "Old Age in Prime Time." *Journal of Communication* 24: 86–87.

Aronson, Elliot 1975 "Busing and Racial Tension: the Jigsaw Route to Learning and Liking." *Psychology Today* 8: 43–45, 47–50.

Atchley, Robert C. 1980 *The Social Forces in Later Life.* Belmont, Calif.: Wadsworth.

Bachrach, Peter, and Mortón S. Baratz 1970 *Power and Poverty: Theory and Practice.* New York: Oxford University Press.

Banfield, Edward C. 1968 *The Unheavenly City Revisited.* Boston: Little, Brown.

Baran, Paul A. and Paul M. Sweezy 1966 *Monopoly Capital: An Essay on the American Economic and Social Order.* New York: Monthly Review Press.

Barcus, F. Earle and Jack Levin 1966 "Role Distance in Negro and Majority Fiction." *Journalism Quarterly* (Winter): 709–714.

Barker, Ernest, (ed.) 1962 *The Politics of Aristotle.* New York, Oxford.

Beck, E. M. 1980 "Discrimination and White Economic Loss: A Time Series Examination of the Radical Model." *Social Forces* (September) 59, No. 1: 148–168.

Becker, Gary S. 1957 *The Economics of Discrimination.* Chicago: The University of Chicago Press.

Bellisfield, Gwen 1972–1973 "White Attitudes Toward Racial Integration and the Urban Riots of the 1960's." *Public Opinion Quarterly* (Winter): 579–584.

Bem, Daryl 1970 *Beliefs, Attitudes and Human Affairs.* Belmont, Calif.: Brooks Cole.

Berelson, Bernard and Patricia Salter 1946 "Majority and Minority Americans: An Analysis of Magazine Fiction." *Public Opinion Quarterly* (Summer): 168–190.

Berger, M., and S. D. Rose 1977 "Interpersonal Skill Training with Institutionalized Elderly Patients." *Journal of Gerontology* 32: 346–353.

Berkowitz, Leonard 1962 *Aggression: A Social Psychological Analysis.* New York: McGraw-Hill.

Berkowitz, Leonard and R. Geen 1966 "Film Violence and the Cue Properties of Available Targets." *Journal of Personality and Social Psychology* 3: 525–530.

Berkowitz, Leonard and A. LePage 1967 "Weapons as Aggression-Eliciting Stimuli." *Journal of Personality and Social Psychology* 7: 202–207.

Berry, Brewton 1965 *Race and Ethnic Relations.* Boston: Houghton Mifflin.

Berry, Brewton, and Henry L. Tischler 1978 *Race and Ethnic Relations.* Boston: Houghton Mifflin.

Bettelheim, Bruno and Morris Janowitz 1964 *Social Change and Prejudice.* New York: Free Press.

References

Blalock, Hubert M., Jr. 1967 *Toward a Theory of Minority-Group Relations.* New York: Wiley.

Blassingame, John W. 1972 *The Slave Community.* New York: Oxford University Press.

Blauner, Robert 1972 *Racial Oppression in America.* New York: Harper & Row.

Block, J. and Jeanne Block 1951 "An Investigation of the Relationships Between Intolerance of Ambiguity and Ethnocentrism." *Journal of Personality* 19: 303–311.

Bluestone, Barry 1977 "The Characteristics of Marginal Industries." Pp. 97–102 in David M. Gordon (ed.), *Problems in Political Economy.* Lexington, Mass.: Heath.

Bogardus, Emory S. 1925 "Measuring Social Distance." *Journal of Applied Sociology* (March–April): 299–308.

Bonacich, Edna 1972 "A Theory of Ethnic Antagonism: The Split Labor Market." *American Sociological Review* (October): 547–559.

Breen, Leonard Z. 1960 "The Aging Individual." Pp. 145–164 in Clark Tibbitts (ed.), *Handbook of Social Gerontology.* Chicago: University of Chicago Press.

Brigham, Carl C. 1923 *A Study of American Intelligence.* Princeton, N.J.: Princeton University Press.

Brigham, John and Theodore Weissbach 1972 *Racial Attitudes in America.* New York: Harper & Row.

Brink, William and Louis Harris 1964 *The Negro Revolution in America.* New York: Simon & Schuster.

Brink, William and Louis Harris 1967 *Black and White.* New York: Simon & Schuster.

Brody, Jane E. 1973 "Doctors Study Treatment of Ills Brought on by Stress." *The New York Times* (June 10): 20.

Broverman, I. K., R. S. Vogel, D. M. Broverman, T. E. Clarkson, and P. S. Rosenkrantz 1972 "Sex-Role Stereotypes: A Current Appraisal." *Journal of Social Issues* 28: 59–78.

Burgess, Ernest W. (ed.), 1960 *Aging in Western Societies.* Chicago: University of Chicago Press.

Burke, Peter J. 1969 "Scapegoating: An Alternative to Role Differentiation." *Sociometry* (June): 159–168.

Burkey, Richard M. 1971 *Racial Discrimination and Public Policy in the United States.* Lexington, Mass.: Heath.

Burnette, Robert 1971 *The Tortured Americans.* Englewood Cliffs, N.J.: Prentice-Hall.

Burnstein, Eugene and Philip Worchel 1962 "Arbitrariness of Frustration and Its Consequences for Aggression in a Social Situation." *Journal of Personality* 30: 528–541.

Butler, Robert 1975 *Why Survive? Being Old in America.* New York: Harper & Row.

Campbell, Angus 1970 *White Attitudes Toward Black People.* Ann Arbor, Mich.: University of Michigan Press.

Carmichael, Stokely and Charles V. Hamilton 1967 *Black Power.* New York: Random House.

Cassata, Mary B., Thomas D. Skill, and Samuel O. Boadu 1979 "In Sickness and In Health." *Journal of Communication* 29: 73–80.

Caudill, William and George de Vos 1966 "Achievement, Culture, and Personality." Pp. 77–89 in Bernard E. Segal (ed.), *Racial and Ethnic Relations.* New York: Crowell.

Champlin, John 1970 "On the Study of Power." *Politics and Society* (November): 92–103.

Chapko, M. and M. Lewis 1975 "Authoritarianism and 'All in the Family'" *Journal of Psychology* 90: 245–248.

Chinoy, Ely 1961 *Society.* New York: Random House.

Chorover, Stephan L. 1973 "Big Brother and Psychotechnology." *Psychology Today* (October): 43–54.

Christie, Richard, Joan Havel, and Bernard Seidenberg 1958 "Is the F Scale Irreversible." *Journal of Abnormal and Social Psychology* (March): 143–159.

Clark, Kenneth B. and Mamie P. Clark 1958 "Racial Identification and Preference in Negro Children." Pp. 169–178 in Eleanor E. Maccoby, Theodore M. Newcomb, and Eugene L. Hartley (eds.), *Readings in Social Psychology.* New York: Holt, Rinehart and Winston.

Cloward, Richard A. and Lloyd E. Ohlin 1960 *Delinquency and Opportunity.* New York: Free Press.

Cole, Stewart G. and Mildred Wiese 1954 *Minorities and the American Promise.* New York: Harper & Row.

Coleman, James S. 1963 "Academic Achievement and the Structure of Competition." Pp. 212–229 in Neil J. Smelser and William T. Smelser (eds.), *Personality and Social Systems.* New York: Wiley.

Colfax, J. David and Susan Frankel Sternberg 1972 "The Perpetuation of Racial Stereotypes: Blacks in Mass Circulation Magazine Advertisements." *Public Opinion Quarterly* (Spring): 8–17.

Comer, James P. 1972 *Beyond Black and White.* Chicago: Quadrangle.

Comfort, Alex 1964 *The Process of Aging.* New York: New American Library.

References

Commission on the Cities in the '70's 1972 *Report*. New York: Praeger.

Condran, John G. 1979 "Changes in White Attitudes Toward Blacks: 1963–1977." *Public Opinion Quarterly* (Winter): 463–476.

Constantini, Arthur F., Jack Davis, John R. Braun, and Annette Iervolino 1973 "Personality and Mood Correlates of Schedule of Recent Experience Scores." *Psychological Reports* 32: 1143–1150.

Cook, Thomas J. 1970 "Benign Neglect: Minimum Feasible Understanding." *Social Problems* (Fall): 145–152.

Coser, Lewis A. 1956 *The Functions of Social Conflict*. New York: Free Press.

Coser, Lewis A. 1972 "The Alien as a Servant of Power: Court Jews and Christian Renegades." *American Sociological Review* (October): 574–581.

Couch, Arthur and Kenneth Keniston 1960 "Yeasayers and Naysayers: Agreeing Response Set as a Personality Variable." *Journal of Abnormal and Social Psychology* (March): 151–174.

Cowen, Emory L., Judith Landes, and Donald E. Schaet 1959 "The Effects of Mild Frustration on the Expression of Prejudiced Attitudes." *Journal of Abnormal and Social Psychology* (January): 33–38.

Culley, James D., and Rex Bennett 1976 "Selling Women, Selling Blacks." *Journal of Communication* (Autumn) 26, No. 4: 160–174.

Cumming, Elaine and William E. Henry 1961 *Growing Old: The Process of Disengagement*. New York: Basic Books.

de Beauvoir, Simone 1953 *The Second Sex*. New York: Knopf.

Deckard, Barbara and Howard Sherman 1974 "Monopoly Power and Sex Discrimination." *Politics and Society* Vol. 4, No. 4: 475–482.

DeFleur, Melvin L., William V. D'Antonio, and Lois B. DeFleur 1971 *Sociology: Man in Society*. Glenview, Ill.: Scott, Foresman.

Deloria, Vinc Jr. 1970 *We Talk, You Listen*. New York: Delta.

Derbyshire, Robert L., and Eugene Brody 1964 "Social Distance and Identity Conflict in Negro College Students." *Sociology and Social Research* (April): 301–314.

Deutsch, Morton 1953 "The Effects of Cooperation and Competition upon Group Process." Pp. 319–353 in D. Cartwright and A. Zander (eds.), *Group Dynamics*. New York: Harper & Row.

Deutsch, Morton 1971 "Strategies for Powerless Groups." Pp. 223–228 in Gary T. Marx (ed.), *Racial Conflict*. Boston: Little, Brown.

Dimont, Max I. 1962 *Jews, God and History*. New York: Signet.

Dollard, John 1937 *Caste and Class in a Southern Town.* New Haven, Conn.: Yale University Press.

Dollard, John 1938 "Hostility and Fear in Social Life." *Social Forces* (October): 15–26.

Dollard, John, Leonard W. Doob, Neal E. Miller, O. H. Mowrer, and Robert R. Sears 1939 *Frustration and Aggression.* New Haven, Conn.: Yale University Press.

Dorfman, D. D. 1978 "The Cyril Burt Question: New Findings." *Science* (September) 29, Vol. 201, No. 4362: 1177–1186.

Douglas, Jack D. 1970 *Deviance and Respectability.* New York: Basic Books.

Dunbar, Paul Laurence 1940 *The Complete Poems of Paul Laurence Dunbar.* New York: Dodd, Mead.

Durkheim, Emile 1933 *The Division of Labor in Society.* New York: Macmillan.

Edwards, Richard C., Michael Reich, and Thomas E. Weisskopf (eds.) 1972 *The Capitalist System.* Englewood Cliffs, N.J.: Prentice-Hall.

Ehrenreich, Barbara and Deirdre English 1978 *For Her Own Good: 150 Years of the Experts Advice to Women.* New York: Anchor Press.

Ehrlich, Howard J. 1973 *The Social Psychology of Prejudice.* New York: Wiley.

Eitzen, D. Stanley 1970 "Status Inconsistency and Wallace Supporters in a Midwestern City." *Social Forces* (June): 493–498.

El Gallo 1968 "La Raza Quiz." (March): 23.

Elshtain, Jean Bethke 1974 "Moral Woman and Immoral Man: A Consideration of the Public-Private Split and its Political Ramifications." *Politics and Society,* Vol. 4, No. 4: 453–473.

Eysenck, Hans J. 1971 *The I.Q. Argument.* New York: Library Press.

Faris, R. E. L. (ed.) 1964 *Handbook of Modern Sociology.* Skokie, Ill.: Rand McNally.

Feagin, Joe R. and Clairece B. Feagin 1978 *Discrimination American Style.* Englewood Cliffs, N. J.: Prentice-Hall.

Featherstone, J. 1976 "Busing the Powerless." *The New Republic* (May): 18–23.

Festinger, Leon 1957 *The Theory of Cognitive Dissonance.* New York: Harper & Row.

Figes, Eva 1970 *Patriarchal Attitudes.* New York: Stein & Day.

Fischer, David Hackett 1977 *Growing Old in America.* New York: Oxford University Press.

References

Flax, Michael J. 1971 *Blacks and Whites: An Experiment in Racial Indicators.* Washington, D.C.: The Urban Institute.

Foner, Philip S. (ed.) 1970 *The Black Panthers Speak.* Philadelphia: Lippincott.

Francher, J. S. 1973 "It's the Pepsi Generation ... Accelerated Aging and the Television Commercial." *Journal of Aging and Human Development.* 4: 245–255.

Franklin, John Hope and Isidore Starr (eds.) 1967 *The Negro in 20th Century America.* New York: Vintage.

Frazier, E. Franklin 1951 "The Negro's Vested Interest in Segregation." Pp. 332–339 in Arnold M. Rose (ed.), *Race Prejudice and Discrimination.* New York: Knopf.

Freedomways 1962 "The Economic Status of Negroes." (Summer): 230.

Freeman, Jo 1973 "Women and the American Scene: The Building of the Guilded Cage." Pp. 116–143 in Catherine R. Stimpson (ed.), *Discrimination Against Women: Congressional Hearings on Equal Rights in Education and Employment.* New York: Bowker.

Freeman, Jo 1979 "How to Discriminate Against Women Without Really Trying." Pp. 217–232 in Jo Freeman (ed.), *Women: A Feminist Perspective.* Palo Alto, Calif.: Mayfield.

Friedrichs, Robert W. 1973 "The Impact of Social Factors upon Scientific Judgement: The 'Jensen Thesis' as Appraised by Members of the American Psychological Association." *The Journal of Negro Education* (Fall): 429–438.

Frieze, Irene H., Jacquelynne E. Parsons, Paula B. Johnson, Diane N. Ruble, and Gail L. Zellman 1978 *Women and Sex Roles: A Social Psychological Perspective.* New York: Norton.

Gallagher, James J. 1970 *Teaching the Gifted Child.* Boston: Allyn & Bacon.

Gans, Herbert J. 1972 "The Positive Functions of Poverty." *American Journal of Sociology* (September): 275–289.

Geen, Russell G. 1972 *Aggression.* Morristown, N.J.: General Learning Press.

Genovese, Eugene D. 1969 *The World the Slaveholders Made.* New York: Pantheon.

Gerbner, George, Larry Gross, Nancy Signorielli, and Michael Morgan 1980 "Aging with Television: Images on Television Drama and Conceptions of Social Reality." *Journal of Communication* 30: 37–47.

Gerth, H. H. and C. W. Mills (eds.) 1946 *From Max Weber: Essays In Sociology*. New York: Oxford University Press.

Gerth, H. H. and C. W. Mills 1954 *Character and Social Structure*. New York: Harcourt Brace Jovanovich.

Gilbert, G. M. 1951 "Stereotype Persistence and Change Among College Students." *Journal of Abnormal and Social Psychology* (April): 245–254.

Glazer, Nathan and Daniel P. Moynihan 1963 *Beyond the Melting Pot: The Negroes, Puerto Ricans, Jews, Italians and Irish of New York City*. Cambridge, Mass.: MIT and Harvard University Press.

Glenn, Norval D. 1963 "Occupational Benefits to Whites from the Subordination of Negroes." *American Sociological Review* (June): 443–448.

Glenn, Norval D. 1965 "The Role of White Resistance and Facilitation in the Negro Struggle for Equality." *Phylon* (Summer): 105–116.

Glenn, Norval D. 1966 "White Gains from Negro Subordination." *Social Problems* (Fall): 159–178.

Gold, Byron, Elizabeth Kutza, and Theodore R. Marmor 1976 "United States Social Policy on Old Age: Present Patterns and Predictions." Pp. 9–22 in Bernice L. Neugarten and Robert J. Havighurst (eds.) *Social Policy, Social Ethics, and the Aging Society*. Washington, D.C.: U.S. Government Printing Office.

Goldberg, Marilyn Power 1971 "The Economic Exploitation of Women." Pp. 113–117 in David M. Gordon (ed.) *Problems in Political Economy: An Urban Perspective*. Lexington, Mass.: Heath.

Goldberg, Philip 1968 "Are Women Prejudiced Against Other Women?" *Transaction* 5: 28–30.

Golden, Harry 1962 *you're entitle'*. New York: Crest.

Golden, Patricia M. 1974 "Status-Concern, Authoritarianism, and Prejudice." Mimeo paper, Northeastern University.

Gordon, Milton M. 1964 *Assimilation in American Life*. New York: Oxford University Press.

Gorer, Geoffrey 1964 *The American People*. New York: Norton.

Gould, S. J. 1978 "Women's Brains." *Natural History* (October): 44–50.

Gould, S. J. 1979 "Wide Hats and Narrow Minds." *Natural History* (February): 34–37.

Gould, S. J. 1980 "Jensen's Last Stand." *New York Review of Books*. (May): 38–42.

Grabb, Edward G. 1980 "Social Class, Authoritarianism, and Racial Contact: Recent Trends." *Sociology and Social Research* 64, No. 2: 208–220.

Greeley, Andrew 1978 "After Ellis Island." *Harpers* (November): 16–22.

Greenwald, Herbert J. 1973 "Implications for Change Derived from a Theory of Hierarchical Dispositions." Mimeo paper.

Greenwald, Herbert J. and Don B. Oppenheim 1968 "Reported Magnitude of Self-Misidentification Among Negro Children—an Artifact?" *Journal of Personality and Social Psychology* (January): 49–52.

Haimowitz, Morris L. and Natalie R. Haimowitz 1950 "Reducing Ethnic Hostility Through Psychotherapy." *Journal of Social Psychology* (May): 231–241.

Hakmiller, Karl L. 1966 "Threat as a Determinant of Downward Comparison." *Journal of Experimental Social Psychology,* Supplement 1 (September): 32–39.

Haller, John S. Jr. 1971 *Outcasts From Evolution: Scientific Attitudes of Racial Inferiority, 1859–1900*. Urbana, Ill.: University of Illinois Press.

Hanaver, Joan 1976 "Senior Set Unhappy with TV's Mirror." *Patriot Ledger* (May 13): (12).

Handlin, Oscar 1962 *The Newcomers*. Garden City, N.Y.: Anchor.

Harris, Louis, and Associates 1975 *The Myth and Reality of Aging in America*. New York: National Council on Aging.

Harris, Marvin 1964 *Patterns of Race in the Americas*. New York: Walker.

Heer, David M. 1959 "The Sentiment of White Supremacy: An Ecological Study." *American Journal of Sociology* (May): 592–598.

Heiss, Jerold and Susan Owens 1972 "Self-Evaluations of Blacks and Whites." *American Journal of Sociology* (September): 360–370.

Henry, A. F. and J. F. Short, Jr. 1954 *Suicide and Homicide*. New York: Free Press.

Henry, Jules 1969 "American Schoolrooms: Learning the Nightmare." Pp. 202–209 in Richard C. Sprinthall and Norman A. Sprinthall (eds.), *Educational Psychology*. New York: Van Nostrand Reinhold.

Herrnstein, Richard J. 1971 "I.Q." *The Atlantic* (September): 43–64.

Hofman, John E. 1970 "The Meaning of Being a Jew in Israel: An

Analysis of Ethnic Identity." *Journal of Personality and Social Psychology* (July): 196–202.

Holmes, David S. 1972 "Aggression, Displacement, and Guilt." *Journal of Personality and Social Psychology* (March): 296–301.

Holmes, Thomas H. and Richard H. Rahe 1967 "The Social Readjustment Rating Scale." *Journal of Psychosomatic Research* 11: 213–218.

Horney, Karen 1937 *The Neurotic Personality of Our Time*. New York: Norton.

Hovland, Carl I. and Robert R. Sears 1940 "Minor Studies of Aggression: Correlation of Lynchings with Economic Indices." *Journal of Psychology* (Winter): 301–310.

Howard, David H. 1966 "An Exploratory Study of Attitudes of Negro Professionals Toward Competition with Whites." *Social Forces* (Summer): 20–27.

Howe, Florence and Paul Lauter 1972 "How the School System Is Rigged for Failure." Pp. 229–235 in Richard C. Edwards, Michael Reich, and Thomas E. Weisskopf (eds.), *The Capitalist System*. Englewood Cliffs, N.J.: Prentice-Hall.

Hoyenga, Katherine and Kermit Hoyenga 1979 *The Question of Sex Differences: Psychological, Cultural, and Biological Issues*. Boston: Little, Brown.

Hughes, Langston 1968 "Tales of Simple." Pp. 97–112 in Abraham Chapman (ed.), *Black Voices*. New York: Mentor.

Hyman, Herbert H. and Paul B. Sheatsley 1956 "Attitudes Toward Desegregation." *Scientific American* 195: 35–39.

Hyman, Herbert H. and Paul B. Sheatsley 1964 "Attitudes Toward Desegregation." *Scientific American* 211: 16–23.

Hyman, Herbert H. and Eleanor Singer (eds.) 1968 *Readings in Reference Group Theory and Research*. New York: Free Press.

Jacobs, Paul and Saul Landau with Eve Pell 1971 *To Serve the Devil*. Vol. I. New York: Vintage.

Jenson, Arthur R. 1969 "How Much Can We Boost IQ and Scholastic Achievement?" Pp. 1–123 in *Environment, Heredity, and Intelligence*. Harvard Educational Review Reprint Series No. 2. Cambridge, Mass.: Harvard University Press.

Jenson, Arthur R. 1980 *Bias in Mental Testing*. New York: Free Press.

Jones, James M. 1972 *Prejudice and Racism*. Reading, Mass.: Addison-Wesley.

Kagan, S. and M. C. Madsen 1972 "Experimental Analyses of Coop-

References

eration and Competition of Anglo-American and Mexican Children." *Developmental Psychology* 6: 49–59.

Kamin, Leon 1973 "War of IQ: Indecisive Genes." *Intellectual Digest* (December): 22–23.

Kamin, Leon 1974 *The Science and Politics of I.Q.* New York: Wiley.

Karlins, Marvin, Thomas L. Coffman, and Gary Walters 1969 "On the Fading of Social Stereotypes: Studies in Three Generations of College Students." *Journal of Personality and Social Psychology* (September): 1–16.

Katz, Daniel 1960 "The Functional Approach to the Study of Attitudes." *Public Opinion Quarterly* (Summer): 163–204.

Katz, David and Kenneth Braly 1933 "Racial Stereotypes of One Hundred College Students." *Journal of Abnormal and Social Psychology* (October–December): 280–290.

Katznelson, Ira 1973 *Black Men, White Cities*. New York: Oxford.

Kaufman, Walter 1957 "Status, Authoritarianism, and Anti-Semitism." *American Journal of Sociology* (January): 379–382.

Killian, Lewis M. 1968 *The Impossible Revolution*. New York: Random House.

King, Larry L. 1969 *Confessions of a White Racist*. New York: Viking.

King, Wayne 1979 "Vengeance for Raid Seen as Motive for 4 Killings at Anti-Klan March." *New York Times* (November 5): 1.

Knapp, Melvin J. and Jon P. Alston 1972–1973 "White Parental Acceptance of Varying Degrees of School Desegregation: 1965 and 1970." *Public Opinion Quarterly* (Winter): 585–591.

Knowles, Louis L and Kenneth Prewitt (eds.) 1969 *Institutional Racism in America*. Englewood Cliffs, N. J.: Prentice-Hall.

Koenig, Fredrick W. and Morton B. King, Jr. 1962 "Cognitive Simplicity and Prejudice." *Social Forces* (March): 220–222.

Kogan, Nathan 1961 "Attitudes Toward Old People: the Development of a Scale and an Examination of Correlates." *Journal of Abnormal and Social Psychology* 62: 44–54.

Kramer, Bernard M. 1949 "Dimensions of Prejudice." *The Journal of Psychology* 27: 389–451.

Kuhlen, Raymond G. 1968 "Developmental Changes in Motivation During the Adult Years." Pp. 115–136 in Bernice Neugarten (ed.), *Middle Age and Aging*. Chicago: University of Chicago Press.

La Gumina, Salvatore J. 1973 *Wop!* San Francisco: Straight Arrow.

Lam, Margaret M. 1936 "Racial Myth and Family Tradition-Worship Among Part-Hawaiians." *Social Forces* (March): 149–157.

Lazarwitz, Bernard 1970 "Contrasting the Effects of Generation, Class, Sex, and Age on Group Identification in the Jewish and Protestant Communities." *Social Forces* (September): 50–59.

Leibowitz, Lila 1973 "Perspectives on the Evolution of Sex Differences." Paper presented at the American Anthropological Association Meetings.

Lerner, Janet W. 1971 *Children with Learning Disabilities*. Boston: Houghton Mifflin.

Lerner, Max 1957 *America as a Civilization*. Vol. II. New York: Simon & Schuster.

Lerner, Max 1972 "People and Places." Pp. 103–119 in Peter I. Rose (ed.), *Nation of Nations*. New York: Random House.

Levin, Jack 1969 "The Influence of Social Comparison on Displaced Aggression." Paper presented at the Eastern Psychological Association Meeting. Philadelphia.

Levin, Jack and William J. Leong 1973 "Comparative Reference Group Behavior and Assimilation." *Phylon* (September): 289–294.

Levin, Jack and William C. Levin 1980 *Ageism: Prejudice and Discrimination Against the Elderly*. Belmont, Calif.: Wadsworth.

Levin, Jack and James L. Spates 1970 "Hippie Values: An Analysis of the Underground Press." *Youth and Society* (September): 59–73.

Levin, William C. and Jack Levin 1973 "Social Comparison of Grades: The Influence of Mode of Comparison and Machiavellianism." *Journal of Social Psychology* 91: 67–72.

Levine, Daniel U. and Jeanie K. Meyer 1977 "Level and Rate of Desegregation and White Enrollment Decline in a Big City School District." *Social Problems* (April) 24: 451–462.

Levy, Sheldon G. 1972 "Polarization in Racial Attitudes." *Public Opinion Quarterly* (Summer): 221–234.

Lewis, Oscar 1968 "The Culture of Poverty." Pp. 187–200 in Daniel P. Moynihan (ed.), *On Understanding Poverty*. New York: Basic Books.

Lindblom, Charles E. 1977 *Politics and Markets*. New York: Basic Books.

Lippitt, Ronald and Ralph K. White 1958 "An Experimental Study of Leadership and Group Life." Pp. 496–510 in Eleanor E. Maccoby, Theodore M. Newcomb, and Eugene L. Hartley (eds.), *Readings in Social Psychology*. New York: Holt, Rinehart and Winston.

Lippmann, Walter 1922 *Public Opinion*. New York: Harcourt Brace Jovanovich.

Littleton, Arthur C. and Mary W. Burger 1971 *Black Viewpoints*. New York: Mentor.

Logan, Rayford W. 1954 *The Betrayal of the Negro*. New York: Collier.

London, Joan and Henry Anderson 1970 *So Shall Ye Reap*. New York: Crowell.

Lynch, Helen 1972 "Equality Would Be a Demotion." *Sunday Herald Traveler (Pictorial Living)* (October 15): 4.

McCarthy, John D. and William L. Yancey 1971 "Uncle Tom and Mr. Charlie: Metaphysical Pathos in the Study of Racism and Personal Disorganization." *American Journal of Sociology* (January): 648–672.

Maccoby, Eleanor and C. N. Jacklin 1974 *The Psychology of Sex Differences*. Stanford, Calif.: Stanford University Press.

Maccoby, Eleanor, Theodore M. Newcomb, and Eugene L. Hartley 1958 *Readings in Social Psychology*. New York: Holt, Rinehart and Winston.

MacDonald, Kenneth W. 1971 "The Relationship of Classical Predictors of Prejudice to Attitudes Toward Black Power." Unpublished M.A. thesis, Kent State University.

McManus, J. T., and Louis Kronenberger 1946 "Motion Pictures, the Theater, and Race Relations." *Annals of the American Academy of Political and Social Science* (March): 152–157.

McWilliams, Carey 1948 *A Mask for Privilege: Anti-Semitism in America*. Boston: Little, Brown.

Mangum, Paul L. 1973 "Role Change, Intolerance of Ambiguity, and Psychological Stress." Unpublished M.A. thesis, Northeastern University.

Martin, James and Frank Westie 1959 "The Tolerant Personality." *American Sociological Review* 24: 524–531.

Martinez, Thomas M. 1969 "Advertising and Racism: The Case of the Mexican-American." *El Grito* (Summer): 2.

Marx, Gary T. (ed.) 1971 *Racial Conflict*. Boston: Little, Brown.

Megargee, Edwin I. and Jack E. Hokanson (eds.) 1970 *The Dynamics of Aggression*. New York: Harper & Row.

Meier, August and Elliot M. Rudwick 1966 *From Plantation to Ghetto*. New York: Hill & Wang.

Merton, Robert K. 1957 *Social Theory and Social Structure*. New York: Free Press.

Metzger, Paul L. 1971 "American Sociology and Black Assimilation: Conflicting Perspectives." *American Journal of Sociology* (January): 627–647.

Middleton, Russell 1976 "Regional Differences in Prejudice." *American Sociological Review* 41: 94–116.

Miller, L. Keith and Robert L. Hamblin 1963 "Interdependence, Differential Rewarding and Productivity." *American Sociological Review* 28: 768-778.

Miller, Neal E. and Richard Bugelski 1948 "Minor Studies of Aggression: The Influence of Frustrations Imposed by the In-Group on Attitudes Expressed Toward Out-Groups." *Journal of Psychology* 25: 437-442.

Miller, Walter 1958 "Lower Class Culture as a Generating Milieu of Gang Delinquency." *Journal of Social Issues* XIV, No. 4: 5-19.

Mills, C. Wright 1943 "The Professional Ideology of Social Pathologists." *American Journal of Sociology* 49(2): 165-180.

Minturn, L. and W. W. Lambert 1964 *Mothers of Six Cultures—Antecedents of Child Rearing.* New York: Wiley.

Money, J. and A. A. Ehrhardt 1972 *Man and Woman, Boy and Girl: The Differentiation and Dimorphism of Gender Identity from Conception to Maturity.* Baltimore: Johns Hopkins University Press.

Monque, Alice 1898 "The Mistakes of Mothers." *Proceedings of the National Congress of Mothers Second Annual Convention.* Washington, D.C.

Morgan, Marabel 1975 *The Total Woman.* Old Tappan, N. J.: Revell.

Morland, J. Kenneth 1969 "Race Awareness Among American and Hong Kong Chinese Children." *American Journal of Sociology* (November): 360-374.

Morland, J. Kenneth 1972 "Racial Acceptance and Preference of Nursery School Children in a Southern City." Pp. 51-58 in John Brigham and Theodore Weissbach (eds.), *Racial Attitudes in America.* New York: Harper & Row.

Moynihan, Daniel P. 1965 *The Negro Family: The Case for National Action.* U.S. Department of Labor. Washington, D.C.: GPO.

Moynihan, Daniel P. (ed.) 1968 *On Understanding Poverty.* New York: Basic Books.

Myrdal, Gunnar (with the assistance of Richard Sterner and Arnold Rose) 1944 *An American Dilemma.* New York: Harper & Row.

Neill, A. S. 1960 *Summerhill: A Radical Approach to Child Rearing.* New York: Hart.

Nelson, Linden L. and Spencer Kagan 1972 "Competition: The Star-Spangled Scramble." *Psychology Today* (September): 53-56, 90-91.

Neugarten, Bernice 1970 "The Old and Young in Modern Societies." *American Behavioral Scientist* 14: 13-24.

Neugarten, B. L., and Associates 1964 *Personality in Middle and Late Life.* New York: Atherton Press.

Newton, Huey P. 1971 "In Defense of Self-Defense." Pp. 424–427 in Arthur C. Littleton and Mary W. Burger (eds.), *Black Viewpoints*. New York: Mentor.

Noel, Donald L. 1968 "A Theory of the Origin of Ethnic Stratification." *Social Problems* (Fall): 157–172.

Novak, Michael 1971 *The Rise of the Unmeltable Ethnics*. New York: Macmillan.

O'Hara, Robert C. 1961 *Media for the Millions*. New York: Random House.

Palmer, Stuart 1960 *The Psychology of Murder*. New York: Crowell.

Parker, Seymour and Robert J. Kleiner 1968 "Reference Group Behavior and Mental Disorder." Pp. 350–373 in Herbert H. Hyman and Eleanor Singer (eds.), *Readings in Reference Group Theory and Research*. New York: Free Press.

Parsons, Talcott and Kenneth B. Clark (eds.) 1966 *The Negro American*. Boston: Houghton Mifflin.

Patterson, Orlando 1977 *Ethnic Chauvinism: The Reactionary Impulse*. New York: Stein & Day.

Pearce, Diana M. 1979 "Gatekeepers and Homeseekers: Institutional Patterns in Racial Steering." *Social Problems* 26, No. 3 (February): 325–342.

Petroni, Frank A. 1972 "Adolescent Liberalism—The Myth of a Generation Gap." *Adolescence* (Summer): 221–232.

Pettigrew, Thomas F. 1964 *A Profile of the Negro American*. New York: Van Nostrand Reinhold.

Pettigrew, Thomas F. 1971 *Racially Separate or Together?* New York: McGraw-Hill.

Pettigrew, Thomas F., Robert T. Riley, and Reeve D. Vanneman 1972 "George Wallace's Constituents." *Psychology Today* (February): 47–49, 92.

Phillips, Bernard S. 1957 "A Role Theory Approach to Adjustment in Old Age." *American Sociological Review* 22: 212–217.

Phillips, Bernard S. 1969 *Sociology: Social Structure and Change*. New York: Macmillan.

Prosterman, Roy L. 1972 *Surviving to 3000*. Belmont, Calif.: Duxbury Press.

Quanty, Michael B., John A. Keats, and Stephen G. Harkins 1975 "Prejudice and Criteria for Identification of Ethnic Photographs." *Journal of Personality and Social Psychology* 32: 449–454.

Rainwater, Lee 1966 "Crucible of Identity: The Negro Lower-Case Family." Pp. 167–181 in Talcott Parsons and Kenneth B. Clark (eds.), *The Negro American*. Boston: Houghton Mifflin.

Redding, Saunders 1950 *They Came in Chains*. Philadelphia: Lippincott.

Reich, Charles A. 1970 *The Greening of America*. New York: Random House.

Reich, Michael 1972 "The Economics of Racism." Pp. 313–321 in Richard C. Edwards, Michael Reich, and Thomas E. Weisskopf (eds.), *The Capitalist System*. Englewood Cliffs, N.J.: Prentice-Hall.

Richman, J. 1977 "The Foolishness and Wisdom of Age: Attitudes Toward the Elderly as Reflected in Jokes." *Gerontologist* 17: 210–219.

Riley, Matilda W. 1971 "Social Gerontology and the Age Stratification of Society." *Gerontologist* 11(1, part 1): 79–87.

Riley, Matilda W., Marilyn Johnson, and Anne Foner 1972 *Aging and Society. Vol. 3. A Sociology of Age Stratification*. New York: Russell Sage Foundation.

Rogers, Carl R. 1969 "The Facilitation of Significant Learning." Pp. 172–182 in Richard C. Sprinthall and Norman A. Sprinthall (eds.), *Educational Psychology*. New York: Van Nostrand Reinhold.

Rogers, Harrell R. Jr. 1975 "On integrating the public schools: An empirical and legal assessment." Pp. 125–159 in Harrell R. Rogers Jr. (ed.), *Racism and Inequality: The Policy Alternatives*. San Francisco, Calif.: Freeman.

Rokeach, Milton 1952 "Attitude as a Determinant of Recall." *Journal of Abnormal and Social Psychology* 47: 482–488.

Rokeach, Milton 1960 *The Open and Closed Mind*. New York: Basic Books.

Rose, Arnold M. (ed.) 1951 *Race Prejudice and Discrimination*. New York: Knopf.

Rose, Arnold M. 1958 *The Roots of Prejudice*. New York: United Nations, UNESCO.

Rose, Arnold M. 1964 "A Current Issue in Social Gerontology." *Gerontologist* 4: 45–50.

Rose, Arnold M. 1965 "The Subculture of Aging: A Framework for Research in Social Gerontology." Pp. 201–209 in Arnold M. Rose and Warren A. Peterson (eds.), *Older People and Their Social World*. Philadelphia: Davis.

Rose, Peter I. (ed.) 1972 *Nation of Nations: The Ethnic Experience and the Racial Crisis*. New York: Random House.

Rose, Peter I. 1974 *They and We*. New York: Random House.

Rosnow, Ralph L. 1972 "Poultry and Prejudice." *Psychology Today* (March): 53–56.

Rosnow, Ralph L., Robert F. Holz, and Jack Levin 1966 "Differential Effects of Complementary and Competing Variables in Primacy-Recency." *Journal of Social Psychology* 69: 135–147.

Rosow, Irving 1974 *Socialization to Old Age*. Berkeley: University of California Press.

Rossi, Peter H. 1972 "Alienation in the White Community." Pp. 289–293 in Peter I. Rose (ed.), *Nation of Nations: The Ethnic Experience and the Racial Crisis*. New York: Random House.

Roszak, Betty, and Theodore Roszak (eds.) 1969 *Masculine/Feminine: Readings in Sexual Mythology and the Liberation of Women*. New York: Harper & Row.

Rubin, Irwin M. 1967 "Increased Self-Acceptance: A Means of Reducing Prejudice." *Journal of Personality and Social Psychology* 5: 233–238.

Rubin, Z., F. J. Provenzano, and Z. Luria 1974 "Social and Cultural Influences on Sex-Role Development. The Eye of the Beholder: Parents Views on Sex of Newborns." *American Journal of Orthopsychiatry* 44(4): 512–519.

Rule, Brendan G. and Elizabeth Percival 1971 "The Effects of Frustration and Attack on Physical Aggression." *Journal of Experimental Research on Personality* 5: 111–188.

Rustin, Bayard 1971 "'Black Power' and Coalition Politics." Pp. 193–200 in Gary T. Marx (ed.), *Racial Conflict*. Boston: Little, Brown.

Ryan, William 1971 *Blaming the Victim*. New York: Vintage.

Sagarin, Edward (ed.) 1971 *The Other Minorities*. Boston: Ginn.

Sartre, Jean-Paul 1965 *Anti-Semite and Jew*. New York: Schocken.

Schelling, Thomas C. 1972 *Discrimination Without Prejudice: Some Innocuous Models*. Discussion paper No. 8, (May). Cambridge, Mass.: JFK School of Government, Harvard University.

Schermerhorn, Richard A. 1970 *Comparative Ethnic Relations: A Framework for Theory and Research*. New York: Random House.

Schlossberg, Nancy K., and John J. Pietrofesa 1973 "Perspectives on Counseling Bias: Implications for Counselor Education." *The Counseling Psychologist* 4 (April): 44–54.

Schulz, James H. 1976 *The Economics of Aging*. Belmont, Calif.: Wadsworth.

Scodel, Alvin and Paul Mussen 1953 "Social Perceptions of Authoritarians and Nonauthoritarians." *Journal of Abnormal and Social Psychology* 48: 181–184.

Seefeldt, Carol, Richard K. Jantz, Alice Galper, and Kathy Serock

1977 "Using Pictures to Explore Children's Attitudes Toward the Elderly." *Gerontologist* 17: 506–512.

Segal, Bernard E. (ed.) 1966 *Racial and Ethnic Relations*. New York: T. Y. Crowell.

Selznick, Gertrude J. and Stephen Steinberg 1969 *The Tenacity of Prejudice*. New York: Harper & Row.

Sherif, Muzafer et al. 1961 *Intergroup Conflict and Cooperation: The Robbers Cave Experiment*. Norman: Institute of Intergroup Relations, University of Oklahoma.

Sherif, Muzafer and Carolyn W. Sherif 1956 *An Outline of Social Psychology*. New York: Harper & Row.

Sherman, Howard 1972 *Radical Political Economy*. New York: Basic Books.

Shuey, Audrey M. 1953 "Stereotyping of Negroes and Whites: An Analysis of Magazine Pictures." *Public Opinion Quarterly* 17: 281–292.

Silberman, Charles E. 1964 *Crisis in Black and White*. New York: Random House.

Simmel, Georg 1955 *Conflict*. New York: Free Press.

Simmen, Edward (ed.) 1972 *Pain and Promise: The Chicano Today*. New York: Mentor.

Simmons, Ozzie G. 1961 "The Mutual Images and Expectations of Anglo-Americans and Mexican-Americans." *Daedalus* (Spring): 286–299.

Simpson, George E. and J. Milton Yinger 1972 *Racial and Cultural Minorities: An Analysis of Prejudice and Discrimination*. New York: Harper & Row.

Sinha, Gopal Sharan and Ramesh Chandra Sinha 1967 "Explorations in Caste Stereotypes." *Social Forces* (September): 42–47.

Smelser, Neil J. and William T. Smelser (eds.) 1963 *Personality and Social Systems*. New York: Wiley.

Smythe, Dallas W. 1954 "Reality as Presented by Television." *Public Opinion Quarterly* 18: 143–156.

Sociobiology Study Group 1979 *Sociobiology: A New Biological Determinism*. Published by Science for the People, 16 Union Square, Somerville, Mass. 02143.

Sorkin, Alan L. 1969 "Education, Migration and Negro Unemployment." *Social Forces* (March): 265–274.

Spiegalman, M., C. Terwilliger, and F. Fearing 1953 "The Content of Comics: Goals and Means to Goals of Comic Strip Characters." *Journal of Social Psychology* 37: 189–203.

Sprinthall, Richard C. and Norman A. Sprinthall (eds.) 1969 *Educational Psychology.* New York: Van Nostrand Reinhold.

Srole, Leo 1956 "Social Integration and Certain Corollaries: An Exploratory Study." *American Sociological Review* (December): 709–716.

Stagner, R. and C. S. Congdon 1955 "Another Failure to Demonstrate Displacement of Aggression." *Journal of Abnormal and Social Psychology* 51: 696–697.

Stampp, Kenneth M. 1956 *The Peculiar Institution.* New York: Vintage.

Steiner, Ivan D. and Homer H. Johnson 1963 "Authoritarianism and Conformity." *Sociometry* (March): 21–34.

Stember, Charles Herbert 1961 *Education and Attitude Change: The Effect of Schooling on Prejudice Against Minority Groups.* Washington, D.C. Institute of Human Relations.

Strauss, Helen May 1968 "Reference Group and Social Comparison Processes Among the Totally Blind." Pp. 222–237 in Herbert H. Hyman and Eleanor Singer (eds.), *Readings in Reference Group Theory and Research.* New York: Free Press.

Sung, B. L. 1961 *The Mountain of Gold: The Story of the Chinese in America.* New York: Macmillan.

Sweeny, Arthur 1922 "Mental Tests for Immigrants." *North American Review* (May): 600–612.

TenHouten, Warren D. et al. 1971 "School Ethnic Composition, Social Contexts, and Educational Plans of Mexican-American and Anglo High School Students." *American Journal of Sociology* (July): 89–107.

Taves, M. J., and G. D. Hansen 1963 "Seventeen Hundred Elderly Citizens." Pp. 73–181 in Arnold M. Rose (ed.), *Aging in Minnesota.* Minneapolis: University of Minnesota Press.

Taylor, D. Garth, Paul B. Sheatsley, and Andrew M. Greeley 1978 "Attitudes Toward Racial Integration." *Scientific American* (June), Vol. 238: 42–49.

Tedesco, Nancy S. 1974 "Patterns in Prime Time." *Journal of Communication* 24: 119–124.

Thurow, Lester 1969 *Poverty and Discrimination.* Washington, D.C.: The Brookings Institution.

Toffler, Alvin 1970 *Future Shock.* New York: Bantam.

Torrence, W. and Paul Meadows 1958 "American Culture Themes." *Sociology and Social Research* 43: 3–7.

Triandis, Harry C. and Leigh M. Triandis 1972 "Some Studies of Social Distance." Pp. 97–105 in John Brigham and Theodore Weissbach (eds.), *Racial Attitudes in America*. New York: Harper & Row.

Tumin, Melvin 1965 "The Functionalist Approach to Social Problems." *Social Problems* (Spring): 379–388.

Turner, Ralph H. 1960 "Preoccupation with Competitiveness and Social Acceptance among American and English College Students." *Sociometry* 23: 307–325.

United States Commission on Civil Rights 1980 *Affirmative Action in the 1980's: Dismantling the Process of Discrimination*. Clearinghouse Publication 65, January.

U.S. Advisory Commission on Civil Disorders 1968 *Report*. New York: Bantam.

U.S. Department of Commerce 1979 *Statistical Abstract of the United States*. 100th ed. Bureau of the Census, Washington, D.C.

U.S. Department of Labor 1976 *The Earnings Gap Between Women and Men*. Employment Standards Administration, Women's Bureau, Washington, D.C.

van den Berghe, Pierre L. 1966 "Paternalistic Versus Competitive Race Relations: An Ideal-Type Approach." Pp. 53–69 in Bernard E. Segal (ed.), *Racial and Ethnic Relations*. New York: Crowell.

van den Haag, Ernest 1969 *The Jewish Mystique*. New York: Dell.

Vander Zanden, James W. 1960 "The Klan Revival." *American Journal of Sociology* (March): 456–462.

Vander Zanden, James W. 1972 *American Minority Relations*. New York: Ronald.

Vidmar, Neil and Milton Rokeach "Archie Bunker's Bigotry: A Study in Selective Perception and Exposure." *Journal of Communication* 24: 36–47.

Wahrhaftig, Albert L. and Robert K. Thomas 1969 "Renaissance and Repression: The Oklahoma Cherokee." *Transaction* (February): 42–48.

Watson, J. B. 1926 "Experimental Studies on the Growth of the Emotions." Pp. 77 in C. Murchison (ed.), *Psychologies of 1925*. Worcester, Mass.: Clark University Press.

Weber, Max 1947 *The Theory of Social and Economic Organization*. Trans., A. M. Henderson and Talcott Parsons (ed.), Talcott Parsons. New York: Oxford University Press.

References

Weitzman, Lenore J., Deborah Eifler, Elizabeth Hokada, and Catherine Ross   1972   "Sex Role Socialization in Picture Books for Pre-school Children.: *American Journal of Sociology* 77 (May): 1125–1150.

Westie, Frank R.   1964   "Race and Ethnic Relations." Pp. 576–618 in R. E. L. Faris (ed.), *Handbook of Modern Sociology*. Skokie, Ill.: Rand McNally.

White, Ralph K. and Ronald Lippitt   1960   *Autocracy and Democracy: An Experimental Inquiry*. New York: Harper & Row.

Wilhelm, Sidney M.   1970   *Who Needs the Negro?* Cambridge, Mass.: Schenkman.

Williams, Robin M., Jr.   1947   *The Reduction of Intergroup Tensions*. Bulletin No. 57. New York: Social Science Research Council.

Williams, Robin M., Jr.   1964   *Strangers Next Door*. Englewood Cliffs, N.J.: Prentice-Hall.

Williams, Robin M., Jr.   1965   *American Society*. New York: Knopf.

Willie, Charles V.   1978   "The Inclining Significance of Race." *Society* (July/August): 10–15.

Wilson, E. O.   1975   *Sociobiology: The New Synthesis*. Cambridge, Mass.: Harvard University Press.

Wilson, Stephen R. and Larry A. Benner   1971   "The Effects of Self-Esteem and Situation upon Comparison Choices During Ability Evaluation." *Sociometry* (September): 381–397.

Wilson, William J.   1978   *The Declining Significance of Race*. Chicago: University of Chicago Press.

Wirth, Louis   1945   "The Problem of Minority Groups." Pp. 347–372 in Ralph Linton (ed.), *The Science of Man in the World Crisis*. New York: Columbia University Press.

Woodward, C. Vann   1955   *The Strange Career of Jim Crow*. New York: Oxford University Press.

Wright, Nathan Jr.   1971   "The Economics of Race." Pp. 305–313 in Arthur C. Littleton and Mary W. Burger (eds.), *Black Viewpoints*. New York: Mentor.

Yancey, William L., Leo Rigsby, and John D. McCarthy   1972   "Social Position and Self-Evaluation: The Relative Importance of Race." *American Journal of Sociology* (September): 338–359.

Yinger, J. Milton   1961   "Social Forces Involved in Group Identification or Withdrawal." *Daedalus* (Spring): 247–262.

Index

Ability grouping, 180–181
Acquired inferiority, 28–38, 115
   age, 34–36
   race, 30–34
   sex, 36–38
   Supreme Court decisions, 29
Adorno, T. W., 137, 144–147, 154
Aged. *See* Elderly
Aggression
   displacement of, 134–140, 156
   frustration and, 134–139
   frustration-aggression hypothesis, 137
Allport, Gordon W., 66, 207, 218
Alston, John P., 96
Anderson, Henry, 180
Anomie, 152, 212
Anomie Scale, 152
Anti-Defamation League, 53
Anti-Semitism, 113–114, 184
Antonousky, Aaron, 51
Apitzka, E. A., 18
Armendariz, Albert, 43–44
Aronoff, Craig, 151
Aronson, Elliot, 217–218
Attitude, 65–81
Authoritarian personality, 144–149, 156

Bachrach, Peter, 58, 63
Banfield, Edward, 32–33, 39
Baran, Paul A., 170–171
Baratz, Morton S., 58, 63
Barcus, F. Earle, 75
Barker, Ernest, 37
Beck, E. M., 165
Becker, Gary S., 166
Bellisfield, Gwen, 92

Bem, Daryl, 85–86
Benner, Larry A., 141–142
Bennett, Rex, 95, 151
Berelson, Bernard, 68, 70, 75, 149
Berger, M., 47
Berkowitz, Leonard, 135, 137, 183
Berry, Brewton, 104, 173
Bettelheim, Bruno, 66, 67, 68, 139
Black Americans, 2–3, 4
   acquired inferiority, 30–34
   in advertising, 95
   aggression and frustration, 136
   antiblack norms, 78
   blaming the victim, 42
   culture of poverty, 32–34
   differential treatment, 4–5
   discrimination against, 57, 64, 84
   desegregation, 110–111
   earnings, 98–99, 162
   exceptionalist program, 46
   group identity, 5
   group solidarity, 195
   identifiability, 4
   mass media stereotypes, 149–150
   natural inferiority, 16–21, 26
   negative feelings against, 71
   playing the role of, 80–81
   prejudice against, 173–175, 220–221
   reduction of competition, 190–192
   slavery, 73, 78
   and the split labor market, 165–167
   stereotypes of, 93, 95
   unemployment of, 99

Black power, 195–196, 224
Blalock, Hubert M. Jr., 142
Blaming the victim, 14, 41–46, 49–50, 115
Blassingame, John W., 80
Blauner, Robert, 175
Block, J., 155
Block, Jeanne, 155
Bluestone, Barry, 170
Boadu, Samuel O., 151
Bogardus, Emory S., 74–75
Bonacich, Edna, 165, 173
Braly, Kenneth, 67, 92
Braun, John R., 211
Breen, Leonard Z., 21
Brigham, Carl C., 107
Brink, William, 93, 95
Broca, Paul, 25, 28, 106
Brody, Eugene, 75
Brody, Jane E., 211
Broverman, D. M., 11, 71
Broverman, I. K., 11, 71
Bugelski, Richard, 137, 139
Burgess, Ernest W., 59, 79
Burke, Peter J., 183
Burkey, Richard M., 78
Burnette, Robert, 173
Burnstein, Eugene, 137
Burt, Sir Cyril, 105
Butler, Robert, 70

Campbell, Angus, 92, 95
Carmichael, Stokely, 53, 195
Cassata, Mary B., 151
Caudill, William, 193
Champlin, John, 64
Chapko, M., 147
Children
  competition among, 204
  ethnic difference awareness, 76
Chinese Americans
  competitiveness and, 204
  labor role in California, 179–180
  stereotypes, 161
Christie, Richard, 149

Civil Rights Act, 60
Clark, Kenneth B., 76
Clark, Mamie, 76
Clarkson, T. E., 11, 71
Cloward, Richard A., 197
Coffman, Thomas L., 90, 92
Cognitive dissonance theory, 85–87
Cole, Stewart G., 70
Coleman, James S., 214
Colfax, J. David, 93
Comer, James P., 71, 76, 179
Comfort, Alex, 21
Commission on the Cities, 96
Competition
  among Anglo-American children, 204
  and antiblack prejudice, 173–175
  educational program and, 214
  prejudice and, 203–204
  reduction of, 213–214
Condran, John G., 92
Congdon, C. S., 137
Constantini, Arthur F., 211
Cooley, Charles, 30
Coser, Lewis A., 182, 183, 184
Couch, Arthur, 148
Cowen, Emory L., 139
Culley, James D., 95, 151
Culture of poverty, 31–33
Cumming, Elaine, 35, 175

D'Antonio, William V., 192
Darwin, Charles, 26
Davis, Jack, 211
Dawes General Allotment Act of 1887, 173
de Beauvoir, Simone, 13
Deckard, Barbara, 168, 170
Decline, 21–24
DeFleur, Lois B., 192
DeFleur, Melvin L., 192
Deloria, Vinc Jr., 151
Department of Health, Education and Welfare, 60

Depression
  economic, 161
Derbyshire, Robert L., 75
Desegregation, 110–111, 184
  white flight, 111
Deutsch, Morton, 216, 223
deVos, George, 193
Dimont, Max I., 176
Discrimination, 51–65
  advantages of, 56
  disadvantages of, 57
  dissonance and, 82–83
  in employment, 163–164
  functionalism of, 114–121
  individual, 54, 83
  institutional, 54–56, 83, 84
  mechanism of control, 63–65
  persistence of, 96
  severity of, 60–62
  and the split labor market theory, 165–168
Disengagement, 23, 35
Displaced aggression
  defined, 134
  experimental evidence for, 137, 139
  frustration-aggression hypothesis, 137–138
  minorities as scapegoats, 136–139
Dollard, John, 73, 134–135, 137, 142, 161, 173–174, 179
Doob, Leonard W., 134–135
Dorfman, D. D., 105
Douglas, Jack D., 205
Dunbar, Paul Lawrence, 80
Durkheim, Emile, 212

Economics
  acquiring and maintaining economic advantages, 160–162
  in contemporary American society, 179–181
  slavery, role in, 178–179
Education
  prejudice and, 214–218

Edwards, Richard C., 234
Ego-defensiveness
  self-esteem and, 141
Ehrenreich, Barbara, 25, 26, 27
Ehrlich, Howard J., 66, 153
Eifler, Deborah, 9
Eitzen, D. Stanley, 79
Elderly, 3, 5–9
  abuse of, 136
  acquired inferiority, 34–35
  age entitlement programs, 223–224
  blaming the victim, 42–43
  differential treatment, 7–8
  discrimination against, 57, 64
  disengagement, 23, 35
  exceptionalist program, 45–46, 47
  group identity, 8–9
  identifiability, 6–7
  mandatory retirement, 22, 62
  mass media stereotypes, 151
  natural inferiority, 21–24, 26
  negative stereotypes, 70, 72
  playing the role, 79
  role theory, 35
  self-fulfilling prophecy, 22–23
  as senior citizen, 8
  Social Security, 102–103
  subculture of, 35–36
Elshtain, Jean Bethke, 36, 37
English, Deirdre, 25, 26, 27
Erhardt, A. A., 9
Ethnocentrism Scale, 155
Exceptionalist programs, 44–47, 49, 89
Explanations of minority situations, 14–38
  acquired inferiority, 28–38
  natural inferiority, 15–28
Eysenck, Hans, 104

Faris, R. E. L., 234
Farm workers, 179–180
Feagin, Clairece B., 53, 88
Feagin, Joe R., 53, 88
Fearing, F., 70

Index

Featherstone, J., 184
Feelings, negative, 71–73
Festinger, Leon, 85–86
Figes, Eva, 26
Fischer, David Hackett, 6
Foner, Anne, 36
Foner, Philip S., 220
Francher, J. S., 151
Franklin, John Hope, 174
Frazier, E. Franklin, 190
Freeman, Jo, 12, 37, 58–59
Freud, Sigmund, 27, 28
Friedricks, Robert W., 104
Frieze, Irene H., 67
Frustration
   and aggression, 134–137
   and relative deprivation, 139–140
F-Scale, 145–146
Functionalism, 116–131
   system levels, 122–125
Future shock, 208–209

Gains theory, 173–174
Gallagher, James J., 217
Gans, Herbert J., 171, 220
Geen, Russell G., 135, 137
Genetics
   and intelligence, 103–107
   and sociobiology, 107–110
Genovese, Eugene D., 73, 179
Gerbner, George, 151
Gerth, H. H., 185
Gilbert, G. M., 92
Glazer, Nathan, 111
Glenn, Norval D., 165, 169, 180, 224–225
Gold, Byron, 222, 224
Goldberg, Marilyn Power, 13, 168
Golden, Harry, 194
Golden, Patricia, 148
Goldstein, Jeffrey, 135
Gordon, Milton M., 236
Gorer, Geoffrey, 203
Gould, Stephen, 18, 25, 26, 105–106
Grabb, Edward G., 92

Gray Panthers, 8, 222
Greeley, Andrew M., 111
Greenwald, Herbert J., 76
Gross, Larry, 151
Group therapy, 218

Haimowitz, Morris L., 218
Haimowitz, Natalie R., 218
Hakmiller, Karl L., 141
Haller, John S., Jr., 16, 17, 19–20, 73
Hamblin, Robert L., 214
Hamilton, Charles V., 53, 195
Hanaver, Joan, 151
Handlin, Oscar, 177
Hansen, G. D., 8
Harkins, Stephen G., 155
Harris, Louis, 8, 70
Harris, Marvin, 93, 95, 173
Havel, Joan, 149
Heer, David M., 237
Heiss, Jerold, 197
Henry, A. F., 133, 197
Henry, Jules, 135
Henry, William E., 35
Herrnstein, Richard J., 104, 107
Hofman, John E., 193
Hokada, Elizabeth, 9
Holmes, David S., 139
Holmes, Thomas H., 209
Holz, Robert F., 137
Horney, Karen, 203
Hovland, Carl I., 136
Howard, David H., 191–192
Howe, Florence, 181
Hoyenga, Katherine, 38
Hoyenga, Kermit, 38
Hughes, Langston, 153
Hyman, Hubert H., 92

Iervolino, Annette, 210
Immigrants, 176–180
   intelligence testing of, 107
   occupational role of, 177
   prejudice against, 161
Independent variable, 201
Indians, 76

Indians, American, 2
  acquired inferiority, 30
  land acquisition of, 172–173
  stereotype, 172
Intelligence Quotient, 103–106
Intervening variable, 201
Irish, 68
Italians
  prejudice against, 161
  stereotype, 68

Jacklin, C. N., 10
Jacobs, Paul, 172
Janowitz, Morris, 66, 67, 68, 139
Japanese Americans, 193
  labor role in California, 180
Jensen, Arthur R., 103–106
Jerdee, Thomas H., 153
Jews
  anti-Semitism, 113–114, 184
  internal cohesion, 193
  in Medieval Europe, 176
  playing the role, 81
  in seventeenth and eighteenth century Germany, 182
  stereotype, 68, 93
Johnson, Homer H., 154
Johnson, Marilyn, 36
Jones, James M., 54

Kagan, Spencer, 204
Kamin, Leon, 105, 106
Karlins, Marvin, 90, 92
Katz, Daniel, 133, 141, 152, 153
Katz, David, 67, 92
Katznelson, Ira, 52, 58, 87–88
Kaufman, Walter, 142, 148
Keats, John A., 155
Keniston, Kenneth, 148
Killian, Lewis M., 96
King, Larry L., 150
King, Wayne, 136, 154
Kleiner, Robert J., 197
Knapp, Melvin J., 96
Knowles, Louis L., 54
Koenig, Fredrick W., 154

Kogan, Nathan, 152
Kramer, Bernard M., 66
Kronenberger, Louis, 70
Kuhlen, Raymond G., 35
Ku Klux Klan, 54, 57, 136, 175
Kutza, Elizabeth, 222, 224

LaGumina, Salvatore J., 161
Lam, Margaret M., 77
Land, acquisition of
  from American Indians, 172–173
  from Mexican-Americans, 172
Landau, Saul, 172
Landes, Judith, 139
Lauter, Paul, 181
Lazarwitz, Bernard, 193
Leong, William J., 204
LePage, A., 135
Lerner, Janet W., 217
Lerner, Max, 177, 213
Levin, Jack, 5, 49, 75, 94, 137, 142–143, 204, 213, 214, 216
Levin, William C., 5, 49, 94, 215
Levine, Daniel U., 111
Levy, Sheldon G., 96
Lewis, M., 147
Lewis, Oscar, 31
Lindblom, Charles E., 63
Lippitt, Ronald, 137, 141, 184
Lippman, Walter, 66
Literature, 2
Logan, Rayford W., 179
London, Joan, 180
Lower class poverty. *See* Culture of poverty
Luria, Z., 10, 38
Lynch, Helen, 196

McCarthy, John D., 197
Maccoby, Eleanor, 10
MacDonald, Kenneth W., 195
McManus, J. T., 70
McWilliams, Carey, 184
Madsen, M. C., 204

Index

Majority group
  literature of, 2
  social power, 3
Malcolm X, 46
Mangum, Paul L., 209
Marmor, Theodore R., 222, 224
Martin, James, 154
Martinez, Thomas M., 69
Marx, Gary T., 241
Mass media
  anti-Mexican advertising, 69
  stereotypes in, 68–70
Mead, G. H., 30
Meadows, Paul, 203
Megargee, Edwin I., 241
Meier, August, 241
Merton, Robert K., 81–83, 117–118, 122, 126–128
Metzger, Paul L., 241
Mexican-Americans
  blaming the victim, 43–44
  land acquisition of, 172
  prejudice against, 88
  stereotype, 67
Meyer, Jeanie K., 111
Middleton, Russell, 148
Miller, L. Keith, 214
Miller, Neal E., 134–135, 137, 139
Miller, Walter, 31
Mills, C. Wright, 49–50, 185
Minority groups, 1–38
  American Indians, 2
  Black Americans, 2–3
  differential treatment, 4–5, 7–8
  elderly, 3
  ethnic groups, 3
  group identity, 5, 8–9, 12–14
  ideal type, 5
  identifiability, 4, 6–7, 9–10
  literature of, 2
  negative reference group, 140–141
  physically disabled, 3
  self-hatred, 77
  women as, 3, 9–14
  working and middle classes, 3

Minturn, L., 204
Money, J., 9
Monque, Alice, 27
Morgan, Lewis H., 16
Morgan, Marabel, 78
Morgan, Michael, 151
Morland, J. Kenneth, 76
Mowrer, O. H., 134–135
Moynihan, Daniel Patrick, 33, 46, 111
Mussen, Paul, 154
Myrdal, Gunnar, 13–14

National Association for the Advancement of Colored People, 53
National Organization of Women, 12, 53
Native Americans. *See* American Indians
Natural inferiority, 16–28, 114–115
  age, 21–24
  race, 16–21
  sex, 24–28
Neill, A. S., 217
Nelson, Linden L., 204
Neugarten, Bernice, 8, 35
Newton, Huey P., 221
Noel, Donald L., 178
Norms
  antiblack, 78
  for elderly, 79–81
  for women, 78–79
Novak, Michael, 111
Null environmental hypothesis, 12

O'Hara, Robert C., 149
Ohlin, Lloyd E., 197
Oppenheim, Don B., 76
Owens, Susan, 197

Palmer, Stuart, 135
Parker, Seymour, 197
Parsons, Jacquelynne E., 124
Parsons, Talcott, 243

Patterson, Orlando, 111–112
Pearce, Diana M., 84–85
Percival, Elizabeth, 135
Petroni, Frank A., 93
Pettigrew, Thomas F., 80, 140
Phillips, Bernard S., 23, 35, 205, 207
Pietrofesa, John J., 38
Polish-Americans, 68, 70
Prejudice, 65–89
   ambiguity, role in, 154–155
   anomie, role, 152
   as attitude, 66
   authoritarian personality, 144–149
   blaming the victim, 41–46, 49–50
   child awareness, 76
   competitiveness and, 203–205
   definition of, 65
   economic depression, role in, 161
   and education, 214–218
   ethnocentrism scale, 155
   functionalism of, 114–122
   and group therapy, 218–219
   as justification for discrimination, 85–89
   negative feelings, 71–73
   as normative, 78–81
   persistence of, 92–95
   reduction of, 213–214, 216–225
   relative deprivation and, 139–140
   social change and, 207
   stereotypes, 66–71
   and television, 222
   zero sum and, 204–206, 225–226
Prewitt, Kenneth, 54
Prosterman, Roy L., 196
Provenzano, F. J., 10, 38

Quanty, Michael B., 155

Rahe, Richard H., 209
Rainwater, Lee, 243–244
Redding, Saunders, 80
Reich, Charles A., 213
Reich, Michael, 164, 166–167
Relative deprivation
   defined, 139
   prejudice and, 139–140
   relative evaluator vs. self-evaluator, 144
Relative evaluators, 144
Renegade Christians, 182
Richman, J., 70
Rigsby, Leo, 197
Riley, Matilda W., 36, 140
Rogers, Carl R., 244
Rogers, Harrell R. Jr., 60
Rokeach, Milton, 147, 149, 155, 222
Roles, playing of, 79
Role takers, 154–155
Role theory, 35
Rose, Arnold M., 6–7, 23, 35, 39
Rose, Peter I., 190
Rose, S. D., 47
Rosen, Bernard, 153
Rosenkrantz, P. S., 11, 71
Rosnow, Ralph L., 65, 71–72, 137
Rosow, Irving, 79
Ross, Catherine, 9
Rossi, Peter H., 175
Roszak, Betty, 27, 28
Roszak, Theodore, 27, 28
Rubin, Irwin M., 218–219
Rubin, Z., 10, 37–38
Rule, Brendan G., 135
Rule enforcement, 59–60
Rustin, Bayard, 224
Ryan, William, 14–15, 33–34, 41–43, 44–46

Sagarin, Edward, 4
Salter, Patricia, 68, 70, 75, 149
Sartre, Jean-Paul, 72, 132
Scapegoat
   hypothesis of, 137
   minority groups as, 136–137
   safety valve functions of, 183, 186

Index

Schaet, Donald E., 139
Schelling, Thomas C., 163
Schermerhorn, Richard A., 88
Schlossberg, Nancy K., 38
Schulz, James H., 103
Scodel, Alvin, 154
Sears, Robert R., 134–135
Seefeldt, Carol, 6
Segal, Bernard E., 246
Seidenberg, Bernard, 149
Self-esteem
    relative evaluator vs. self-evaluator, 143–144
    social comparison and, 141–144, 215
Self-evaluators, 144
Self-fulfilling prophecy, 22–23
Selznick, Gertrude J., 93, 214
Senior citizens, 8
Sheatsley, Paul B., 92
Sherif, Muzafer, 160
Sherman, Howard, 168, 170
Short, J. F. Jr., 134, 197
Shuey, Audrey M., 70, 93
Signorielli, Nancy, 151
Silberman, Charles E., 80, 196
Simmel, Georg, 192
Simmen, Edward, 246
Simmons, Ozzie G., 88
Simpson, George E., 70, 75, 83, 161
Sinha, Gopal Sharan, 76
Sinha, Ramesh Chandra, 76
Skill, Thomas D., 151
Slavery, 73
    economic role of, 178–179
    norms of, 78
    role playing, 80
Smelser, Neil J., 246
Smythe, Dallas W., 70
Social change
    future shock, 208–209
    and prejudice, 207–212
    reduction of prejudice, 213–214, 216–225
Social distance, 74–76

Social Distance Scale, 74–75
Socialization, 30
Social power, 3
Social Readjustment Rating Scale, 209
Social Security, 102–103
Sociobiology, 107–110
Sorkin, Alan L., 246
Spates, James L., 213
Spiegelman, M., 70
Sprinthall, Richard C., 247
Srole, Leo, 148, 152
Stagner, R., 137
Stampp, Kenneth M., 173, 178
Starr, Isidore, 174
Steinberg, Stephen, 93, 214
Steiner, Ivan D., 154
Stember, Charles Herbert, 214
Stereotypes
    Black American, 93, 95
    elderly, 94
    Irish, 68
    Italian, 68
    Jews, 68, 93
    in mass media, 93, 149–155
    Mexican-American, 67
    negative, 66–71
    Polish-Americans, 68, 70
    women, 94–95
Sternberg, Susan Frankel, 93
Strauss, Helen May, 216
Subculture of the aged, 35–36
Sung, B. L., 161
Supreme Court decisions, 29, 59
Sweeny, Arthur, 107
Sweezy, Paul M., 170–172

Taves, M. J., 8
Taylor, D. Garth, 91
Tedesco, Nancy S., 151
TenHouten, Warren D., 247
Terwilliger, C., 70
Thomas, Robert K., 179
Thurow, Lester, 162
Tischler, Henry L., 104
Toffler, Alvin, 208–209, 212, 219

Torrence, W., 203
Treaty of Guadalupe-Hidalgo, 172
Triandis, Harry C., 154
Triandis, Leigh M., 154
Tumin, Melvin, 220
Turner, Ralph H., 124, 214
Tylor, E. B., 16

Uncertainty
  coping with, 211–212
  reduction of, 196–197
U.S. Advisory Commission on Civil Disorders, 96
U.S. Commission on Civil Rights, 55–56
U.S. Department of Commerce, 102
U.S. Department of Labor, 11
Universalistic programs, 44, 46, 47, 48–50

van den Berghe, Pierre L., 161
van den Haag, Ernest, 193
Vander Zanden, James W., 4, 71, 73, 164, 175, 222
Vanneman, Reeve D., 141
Vidmar, Neil, 222
Vogel, R. S., 11, 71
Vogt, Carl, 26

Wahrhaftig, Albert L., 179
Walters, Gary, 91, 92
Watson, J. B., 29
Weber, Max, 5, 185
Weitzman, Lenore J., 9
Westie, Frank R., 76, 154
White, Ralph K., 137, 141, 184
Wiese, Mildred, 70

Wilhelm, Sidney M., 178
Williams, Robin M. Jr., 137, 142, 203
Willie, Charles V., 97
Wilson, Edward O., 107–108
Wilson, Stephen R., 141–142
Wilson, William J., 97
Wirth, Louis, 4, 7
Women, 9–14
  acquired inferiority, 36–38
  in advertising, 95
  anti-women norms, 78–79
  blaming the victim, 42–43
  differential treatment, 10–12
  earnings, 99, 101
  Equal Rights Amendment, 12
  exceptionalist program, 46, 47, 89
  group identity, 12–14
  identifiability, 9–10
  mass media stereotypes, 151
  mechanism control, 64
  National Organization of Women, 12, 53
  natural inferiority, 24–28
  negative feelings against, 72
  null environmental hypothesis, 12
  playing the role, 79
  sexual harrassment, 57
  and the split labor market, 168
  Suffragists, 37
Woodward, C. Vann, 173
Worchel, Philip, 137
Wright, Nathan Jr., 221

Yancey, William L., 197
Yinger, J. Milton, 70, 75, 83, 161, 195